Oxford AQA History

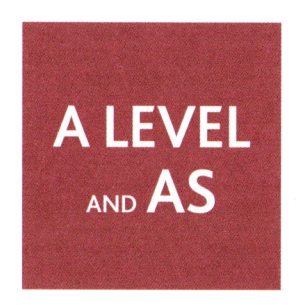

A LEVEL AND AS

The Tudors: England 1485–1603

REVISION GUIDE

 RECAP APPLY REVIEW SUCCEED

David Brown
Margaret Haynes

OXFORD

OXFORD
UNIVERSITY PRESS

Great Clarendon Street, Oxford, OX2 6DP, United Kingdom

Oxford University Press is a department of the University of Oxford. It furthers the University's objective of excellence in research, scholarship, and education by publishing worldwide. Oxford is a registered trade mark of Oxford University Press in the UK and in certain other countries

© Oxford University Press 2017

The moral rights of the authors have been asserted.

First published in 2017

All rights reserved. No part of this publication may be reproduced, stored in a retrieval system, or transmitted, in any form or by any means, without the prior permission in writing of Oxford University Press, or as expressly permitted by law, by licence or under terms agreed with the appropriate reprographics rights organization. Enquiries concerning reproduction outside the scope of the above should be sent to the Rights Department, Oxford University Press, at the address above.

You must not circulate this work in any other form and you must impose this same condition on any acquirer.

British Library Cataloguing in Publication Data
Data available

978-0-19-842140-5

11

Digital edition: 978-019-842141-2

Paper used in the production of this book is a natural, recyclable product made from wood grown in sustainable forests. The manufacturing process conforms to the environmental regulations of the country of origin.

Printed in India by Multivista Global Pvt. Ltd

Acknowledgements

The publisher would like to thank Michael Tilbrook and Sally Waller for their work on the Student Book on which this Revision Guide is based.

From the author, David Brown: I would like to thank the editorial staff at OUP, especially Janice Chan and Becky DeLozier, for their help and suggestions. I would also like to acknowledge the support of my parents, Gilbert and Evelyn, my late brother, Michael, my wife and children, Janet, Daniel and Ceri Brown, my work colleague, David Storey, Sally Waller and my friend, Dr. Rebecca Carpenter.

The publishers would like to thank the following for permissions to use copyright material:

T. Breverton: *Henry VII: The Maligned Tudor King*, (Amberley Publishing, 2016). Reproduced with permission from Amberley Publishing.

S. Doran: *Elizabeth I*, The Historian, 54, (Historical Association, 1997). Reproduced with permission from The Historical Association.

E. Duffy: *The Stripping of the Altars*, (Yale University Press, 1997). Reproduced with permission from Yale University Press.

G.R. Elton: *England Under the Tudors*, (Methuen, 1974). Reproduced with permission from Taylor & Francis Group.

J. Guy: *The Reign of Elizabeth I: Court and Culture in the Last Decade*, (Cambridge University Press, 1991). Reproduced with permission from Cambridge University Press.

C. Haigh: *Elizabeth I*, (Pearson, 1988). Reproduced with permission from Taylor & Francis Group.

R. Hutton: *The Local Impact of the Tudor Reformations*, from The English Reformation Revised edited by C. Haigh, (Cambridge University Press, 1987). Reproduced with permission from Cambridge University Press.

D. Loades: *The Six Wives of Henry VIII*, (Amberley Publishing, 2009). Reproduced with permission from Amberley Publishing.

J. McGurk: *The Tudor Monarchies 1485-1603*, (Cambridge University Press, 2010). Reproduced with permission from Cambridge University Press.

W. Palmer: *The Problem of Ireland in Tudor Foreign Policy, 1485-1603*, (Boydell Press, 2005). Reproduced with permission from Boydell Press.

J. Pound: *Poverty and Vagrancy in Tudor England*, (Pearson, 1971). Reproduced with permission from Taylor & Francis Group.

C. Rogers and R. Turvey: *Henry VII*, (Hodder, 2005). Reproduced with permission from Hodder & Stoughton Ltd, an Hachette UK company.

J. Scarisbrick: *Henry VIII*, (Eyre & Spottiswoode, 1969). Reproduced with permission from Yale University Press.

Although we have made every effort to trace and contact all copyright holders before publication this has not been possible in all cases. If notified, the publisher will rectify any errors or omissions at the earliest opportunity.

Cover illustration: Shutterstock.com

Artwork: Aptara

Links to third party websites are provided by Oxford in good faith and for information only. Oxford disclaims any responsibility for the materials contained in any third party website referenced in this work.

Contents

Introduction to this Revision Guide 5
How to master the AQA extracts question 6
How to master the AQA essay question 7
AQA AS and A Level History mark schemes 8
The Tudors: England 1485–1603 timeline 9

PART ONE AS AND A LEVEL

Consolidation of the Tudor dynasty: England, 1485–1547

SECTION 1 Henry VII, 1485–1509

1 The consolidation of power 10
2 Henry VII's government 16
3 England's relations with Scotland and other foreign powers, 1485–1509 21
4 English society at the end of the 15th century 26
5 Economic development: trade, exploration, prosperity and depression 31
6 Religion, humanism, arts and learning 36

Exam Practice: AS Level essay sample answer 41

SECTION 2 Henry VIII, 1509–1547

7 The character and aims of Henry VIII 43
8 Henry VIII, government and Parliament 46
9 Foreign relations and securing the succession 51
10 English society in the reign of Henry VIII 56
11 Economic development in the reign of Henry VIII 62
12 Religion, ideas and reform 64

Exam Practice: AS Level extracts sample answer 71

RECAP   APPLY   REVIEW

Contents *continued*

PART TWO A LEVEL
England: turmoil and triumph, 1547–1603

SECTION 3 Instability and consolidation: 'the Mid-Tudor Crisis', 1547–1563

- 13 Edward VI, Somerset and Northumberland 74
- 14 The social impact of religious and economic change under Edward VI 78
- 15 Mary I and her ministers 82
- 16 The social impact of religious and economic changes under Mary I 86
- 17 Elizabeth I: character and aims 90
- 18 The impact of economic, social and religious developments in the early years of Elizabeth's rule 94

Exam Practice: A Level essay sample answer 98

SECTION 4 The triumph of Elizabeth, 1563–1603

- 19 Elizabethan government, 1563–1603 100
- 20 Foreign affairs 104
- 21 Society in Elizabethan England 108
- 22 Economic development in Elizabethan England 112
- 23 Religious developments and the 'Golden Age' of Elizabethan culture 116
- 24 The last years of Elizabeth 121

Exam Practice: A Level extracts sample answer 125

Activities: Suggested answers 128
Glossary 139
Top revision tips for A Level History 140

Introduction

The **Oxford AQA History for A Level** textbook series has been developed by a team of expert teachers and examiners led by Sally Waller. This matching Revision Guide offers well-researched, targeted revision and exam practice advice on the new AQA exams.

This guide offers you step-by-step strategies to master your AQA History exam skills, and the structured revision approach of **Recap**, **Apply and Review** to prepare you for exam success. Use the progress checklists on pages 3–4 as you work through the guide to keep track of your revision, and use the traffic light feature  on each page to monitor your confidence level on each topic. Other exam practice and revision features include the **'How to…' guides** for each AQA question type on pages 6–7 and a **Timeline** of key events to help you see the themes.

RECAP

Each chapter recaps key events and developments through a variety of concise points and visual diagrams. **Key terms** appear in bold and red; they are defined in the glossary. indicates the relevant Oxford AQA History Student Book pages so you can easily cross-reference for further revision.

SUMMARY highlights the most important points at the end of each chapter.

Key Chronology provides a short list of dates to help you remember key events.

APPLY

Carefully designed revision activities help drill your grasp of knowledge and understanding, and enable you to apply your knowledge towards exam-style questions.

 Apply Your Knowledge activity tests your basic comprehension, then helps apply what you know to exam questions.

 Plan Your Essay activity prepares you for essay exam questions with practical essay plans and techniques.

 Improve an Answer activity shows you one or more sample student answers, and helps you to evaluate how the answers could be improved.

 A Level essay activities (for example, **To What Extent** or **Assess the Validity of This View**) are extension activities that help you practise the A Level essay question.

 Revision Skills provides different revision techniques. Research shows that using a variety of revision styles can help cement your knowledge and understanding.

 Examiner Tip highlights key parts of an exam question, and gives you hints on how to avoid common mistakes in exams.

 Extract Analysis activity helps you practise evaluating extracts and prepares you for the extracts question in your exam.

 Key Question covers the six thematic questions, which are strongly linked to the essay questions you might find in your exams. This activity helps to drill your understanding of the key themes for The Tudors: England 1485–1603:

- How effectively did the Tudors restore and develop the powers of the monarchy?
- In what ways and how effectively was England governed during this period?
- How did relations with foreign powers change and how was the succession secured?
- How did English society and economy change and with what effects?
- How far did intellectual and religious ideas change and develop and with what effects?
- How important was the role of key individuals and groups and how were they affected by developments?

REVIEW

Throughout each chapter, there will be opportunities to reflect on the work you have done, and support on where to go for further revision to refresh your knowledge. You can tick off the Review column from the progress checklist once you've completed this. **Activities: Suggested answers** and the **Exam Practice** sections with full sample student answers also help you review your own work. Also, don't forget to refer to the **Top Revision Tips for A Level History** on page 140 to help you organise your revision successfully.

The topic The Tudors: England 1485–1603 is a **Component 1: Breadth Study**, which means you should be familiar with the Key Questions relating to the topic and the skill of evaluating differing historical interpretations.

The AS exam lasts 1.5 hours (90 minutes), and you have to answer two questions.

The A LEVEL exam lasts 2.5 hours (150 minutes), and you have to answer three questions.

On these pages, you will find guidance on how to tackle each type of question in your exam.

How to master the AQA extracts question

In **Section A** of your Tudors exam, you will encounter one extracts question that you must answer. Here are the steps to consider when tackling the extracts question:

1 Look at the question posed
Note (underline or highlight) the topic in relation to which the extracts need to be evaluated.

> **EXAMINER TIP**
>
> **AS** You have to answer one extracts question on two interpretations (worth 25 marks). Try to spend about 50 minutes on this question.
>
> **A LEVEL** You have to answer one extracts question on three interpretations (worth 30 marks). Try to spend about 60 minutes on this question.

2 Read the first extract carefully
Keep the topic in mind. Underline or highlight the parts of the extract that provide an argument in relation to this topic (remember this will not always be in the first sentence). These parts should give you the 'overall' argument.

> **EXAMINER TIP**
>
> Look again at the extract: see if there are any sub-arguments or interpretations. Underline or highlight these in a different colour.

3 Begin your evaluation
Identify the overall argument of the extract, then evaluate the argument. Refer to your own knowledge. You should cite material which both supports and challenges the view the extract puts forward.

> **EXAMINER TIP**
>
> To provide a fully convincing answer, repeat step **3** for any sub-arguments.

4 Make a judgement
Provide some supporting comment on how convincing the argument in the extract is in relation to the topic of the question.

5 Repeat steps 2–4 for the next extract or extracts.
At **AS** you will need a further paragraph in which you **compare** the two extracts directly and give a judgement on which is the more convincing.

At **A LEVEL** you **don't** need to make any comparative judgements and there is no need for an overall conclusion.

> **REVIEW**
>
> Take a look at the Exam Practice sections starting on pages 71 and 125 of this guide to reflect on sample answers to the extracts question.

How to master the AQA essay question

In **Section B** of your Tudors exam, you will encounter a choice of essay questions. Here are the steps to consider when tackling an essay question:

1 Read the question carefully
Note (underline or highlight) key words and dates.

> **EXAMINER TIP**
>
> You have to answer one essay question (worth 25 marks) from a choice of two questions. Try to spend about 40 minutes on this question.
>
> You have to answer two essay questions (each worth 25 marks) from a choice of three questions. Try to spend about 45 minutes on each answer.

2 Plan your essay and form a judgement
Decide which approach will best enable you to answer the question – this may be chronological or thematic.

> **EXAMINER TIP**
>
> Plans can be in the form of columns, spider diagrams, mind-maps, flow charts and other styles, but should help you to both form a judgement and to devise a coherent structure for your answer.

3 Introduce your argument
State your judgement (view) in the introduction. The introduction should also be used to show your understanding of the question, particularly key terms and dates, and to acknowledge alternative views and factors.

4 Develop your argument
The essay should proceed logically, supporting your balanced argument through the opening statements of the paragraphs. Remember: comment first, then provide specific and precise supporting information.

> **EXAMINER TIP**
>
> Don't forget to write analytically. Your job is to argue a case and evaluate events, developments and ideas, rather than simply describing what happened in a story-telling (narrative) fashion.

> **EXAMINER TIP**
>
> A good essay will have a balanced argument. You should examine alternative ideas and factors, and explain why they are less convincing than those you are supporting.

5 Conclude your argument
Your conclusion should repeat the judgement given in the introduction and summarise your argument. A good conclusion will not include any new information and will flow naturally from what has gone before.

> **REVIEW**
>
> In the Exam Practice sections starting on pages 41 and 98, you will find sample answers and helpful examiner tips to the essay exam question.

AQA AS and A Level History mark schemes

Below are simplified versions of the AQA mark schemes, to help you understand the marking criteria for your **Component 1: Breadth Study** History exam paper.

AS Level	Section A: Extracts	Section B: Essay
5	Good understanding of interpretations. Very good knowledge. Comparison contains a substantiated judgment. [21–25 marks]	Good understanding of the question. Range of knowledge, with specific supporting information. Analytical, well-argued answer. Structured effectively. Substantiated judgement. [21–25 marks]
4	Good understanding of interpretations. Good knowledge. Partly substantiated comparison. [16–20 marks]	Good understanding of the question. Range of knowledge. Analytical, balanced answer. Structured effectively. Some judgement. [16–20 marks]
3	Reasonable understanding of interpretations. Adequate own knowledge. Partial comparison. [11–15 marks]	Reasonable understanding of the question. Some knowledge, with limited scope. Answer contains some balance. Structured adequately. Partial judgement. [11–15 marks]
2	Partial understanding of interpretations. Some knowledge. Undeveloped comparison. [6–10 marks]	Partial understanding of the question. Some knowledge, with very limited scope. Answer contains limited balance, or is descriptive. There is some structure. Undeveloped judgement. [6–10 marks]
1	Little understanding of interpretations. Limited knowledge. Vague or too general comparison. [1–5 marks]	Limited understanding of the question. Limited knowledge. Answer is vague or too general. Structure is weak. Unsupported judgement. [1–5 marks]

A Level	Section A: Extracts	Section B: Essays
5	Very good understanding of interpretations. Strong and well-supported evaluation of arguments. Very good knowledge, used convincingly. [25–30 marks]	Very good understanding of the question and of the issues/concepts. Range of knowledge, with specific and precise supporting information. Full analytical, balanced answer. Good organisation, structured effectively. Well-substantiated judgement. [21–25 marks]
4	Good understanding of interpretations. Good and mostly well-supported evaluation of arguments. Good knowledge, used convincingly. [19–24 marks]	Good understanding of the question and of the issues/concepts. Range of knowledge, with specific and precise supporting information. Analytical, balanced answer. Good organisation, structured effectively. Some judgement. [16–20 marks]
3	Reasonable understanding of interpretations. Some evaluation of arguments, may contain some imbalance or lack of depth. Knowledge is present, used accurately. [13–18 marks]	Reasonable understanding of the question, with some awareness of the issues/concepts. Range of knowledge, may contain imprecise supporting information. Answer links to the question and contains some balance. Structured effectively. Partial judgement. [11–15 marks]
2	Partial understanding of interpretations (accurate for at least two extracts). Little evaluation of arguments, may contain some generalisations. Some knowledge is present. [7–12 marks]	Partial understanding of the question, with some awareness of the issues/concepts (may contain generalisations). Some knowledge, with limited scope. Answer contains limited balance, or is descriptive. There is some structure. Undeveloped judgement. [6–10 marks]
1	Partial understanding of interpretations (accurate for one extract, or limited accuracy for two to three extracts). Evaluation of arguments is too general and inaccurate/irrelevant. Limited knowledge is present. [1–6 marks]	Limited understanding of the question, with inaccurate or irrelevant understanding of issues/concepts. Limited knowledge. Answer is vague or too general. Structure is weak. Unsupported judgement. [1–5 marks]

Timeline

The colours represent different types of event as follows:
- **Red**: political events
- **Blue**: economic events
- **Yellow**: social and cultural events
- **Green**: religious events
- **Black**: international events

1485	Battle of Bosworth; Henry VII becomes king
1486	Lovell rebellion
1487	Lambert Simnel conspiracy; defeated at Battle of Stoke Field
1487	French invasion of Brittany
1492	Treaty of Etaples following invasion of France
1495	Perkin Warbeck lands in Kent; defeated, takes refuge in Scotland
1496	Intercursus Magnus
1497	Cornish Rebellion
	Truce of Ayton between England and Scotland
1506	Treaty of Windsor
	Intercursus Malus
1509	Death of Henry VII; Henry VIII succeeds
1512	First invasion of France
1513	Second invasion of France (Battle of the Spurs)
	War against Scotland; Battle of Flodden
1514–29	Wolsey as chief minister
1518	Treaty of London
1520	Field of the Cloth of Gold
1532–40	Cromwell as chief minister
1534	Royal supremacy established
1535–40	Dissolution of the monasteries
1536	Ten Articles issued
	Pilgrimage of Grace
1539	Six Articles Act
1542	Battle of Solway Moss
1546	Peace with France
1547	Death of Henry VIII; Edward VI succeeds
1547	Battle of Pinkie against Scotland
1549	First Book of Common Prayer introduced
	Fall of Somerset
1550	Warwick becomes Lord Protector and Duke of Northumberland
1552	Second Book of Common Prayer introduced
1553	Forty-Two Articles of Religion published
	Death of Edward VI; Lady Jane Grey proclaimed queen; Mary I succeeds
1553	Edwardian religious laws repealed
1554	Mary marries Philip of Spain
	Wyatt's rebellion
1555–56	Harvest failures
1558	England loses Calais
	Death of Mary I; Elizabeth succeeds
1559	Elizabethan religious settlement
	Treaty of Câteau-Cambrésis ends war with France
1562	English intervention in France on the side of the Huguenots
1563	Thirty-Nine Articles of Religion published
	Statute of Artificers
1564	Peace with France (Treaty of Troyes)
1566	Vestiarian Controversy
1569–70	Northern Rebellion
1570	Pope Pius V excommunicates Elizabeth
1585	Start of war between England and Spain
1588	Spanish Armada
1594–97	Harvest failures
1601	Poor Law
	Essex Rebellion
1603	Death of Elizabeth

PART ONE CONSOLIDATION OF THE TUDOR DYNASTY: ENGLAND, 1485–1547

Henry VII, 1485–1509

REVISION PROGRESS

1 The consolidation of power

RECAP

England had experienced political instability in the 15th century. The unsuccessful reign of Henry VI had culminated in 1455 in the outbreak of the Wars of the Roses between the royal houses of Lancaster and York. Between 1455 and 1485, England had suffered from 30 years of intermittent civil war and five violent changes of monarch.

The unpopularity of the Yorkist King Richard III allowed Henry Tudor to successfully seize the throne at the Battle of Bosworth in August 1485, beginning the reign of the Tudors. However his claim to the throne was weak:

- He was descended through the female line, through his mother Lady Margaret Beaufort.
- The Beaufort line came from John of Gaunt's third wife; their son had been born before their marriage and many considered him illegitimate.
- Henry was the Lancastrian claimant only because there was no other suitable candidate.

As a result, the early years of Henry VII's reign were characterised by insecurity, and by fears of a potential Yorkist challenge.

Proclaimed king on the battlefield by the hesitant Lord Stanley (later Earl of Derby), who finally declared for Henry, the new king was cheered on his arrival in London, where the unpopularity of Richard III was enough for the public to accept him.

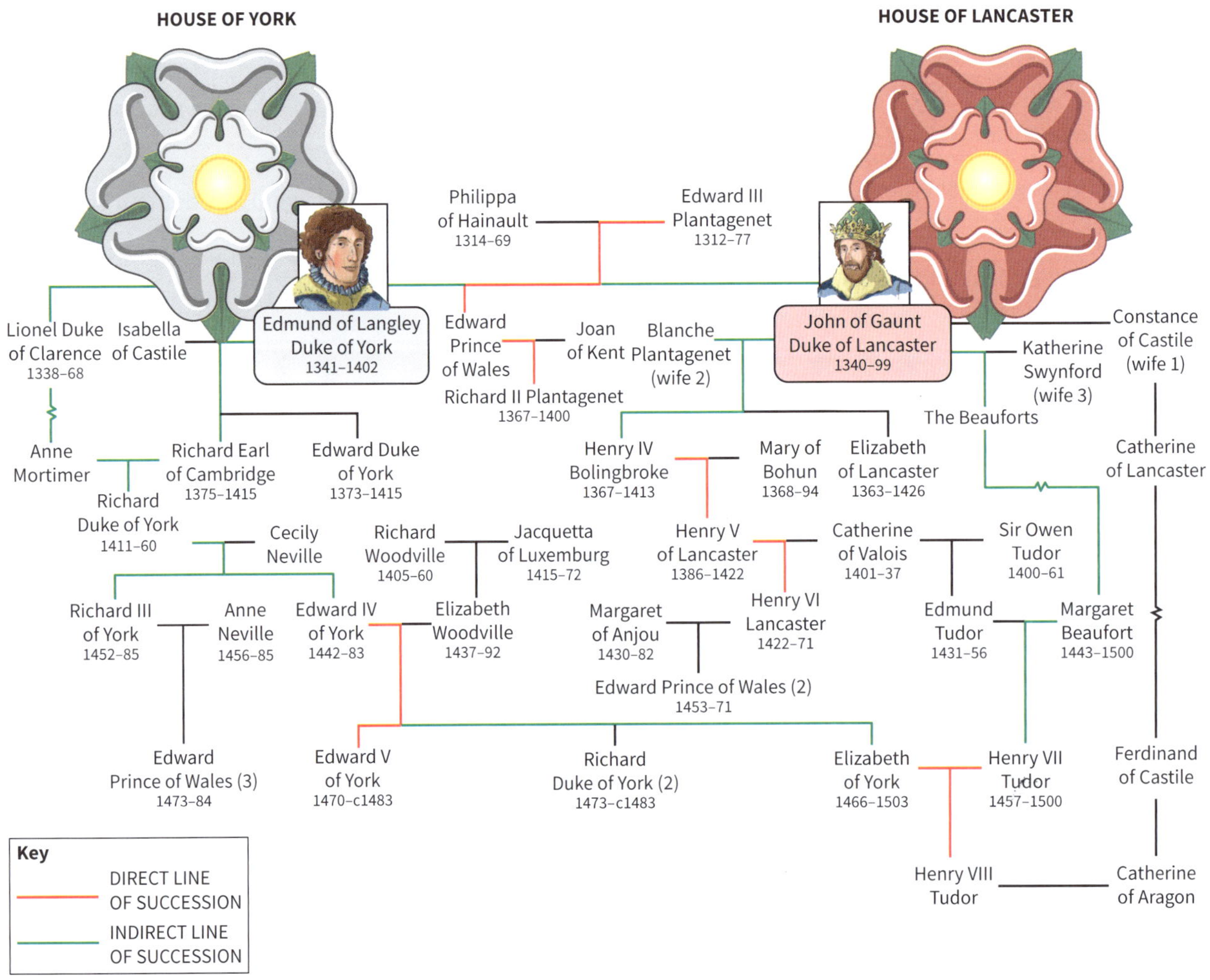

The houses of Lancaster and York

Henry VII's character and aims

Henry VII had not been brought up to rule. He had lived in exile in Brittany since the age of 14, following the Yorkist victory at the Battle of Tewkesbury, in which many of his relations, the Lancastrians, died or were executed. Henry fled to France, where he lived for most of the time as a fugitive in the Duchy of Brittany. Many of his personality traits (he was shrewd, calculating and self-restrained) were probably shaped by his life as a fugitive.

From 1485, Henry's main aim was to consolidate his power in order to keep his throne. He accomplished this through both political actions and military success.

Henry had to work to retain his throne and establish his dynasty. Above all, he had to reduce the power of nobles who had used the previous period of instability to enhance their own authority. He also had to improve the Crown's financial position and secure the recognition of foreign powers.

KEY CHRONOLOGY

Henry VII's steps to secure the throne

1485 Aug
- He dated his reign from 21 August, the day before the Battle of Bosworth; thus anyone who had fought on the Yorkist side could be accused as a traitor
- He publicly rewarded many key supporters (e.g. by conferring 11 knighthoods)
- He detained the Earl of Warwick (Edward IV's nephew), whose claim to the throne could be seen to be much greater than his own

Oct
- He arranged his coronation for a week before the meeting of his first parliament in November, to show that his right to the throne was hereditary, and not just based on **parliamentary sanction**
- He made key appointments to his council and household (e.g. Sir Reginald Bray as Chancellor of the Duchy of Lancaster and Sir William Stanley as Chamberlain of the Household)
- He issued parliamentary **Acts of Attainder** against Yorkists who had fought at Bosworth; their property became forfeit to the Crown
- He further increased his income by demanding the customs revenues of **tonnage and poundage** for life at his first parliament

1486 Jan
- Having consolidated power in his own right, Henry married Elizabeth of York. This enabled royal propaganda to exploit the union of the houses of Lancaster and York

Sept
- An heir, Prince Arthur, was born

Establishing the Tudor dynasty

Henry's position was extremely insecure at first. There were several threats:

Yorkist claimants:

- **John de la Pole, Earl of Lincoln**
  - Nephew of Edward IV and Richard III
  - Designated successor of Richard III
  - Regarded as the Yorkist leader after Bosworth

- **Edward, Earl of Warwick**
  - Nephew of Edward IV and Richard III
  - Imprisoned in Tower of London, 1485, aged 10
  - Beheaded for alleged conspiracy with Perkin Warbeck, 1499

Yorkist supporters (e.g. Lovell and the Staffords)

Margaret of Burgundy
- Sister of Edward IV and Richard III
- Able and willing to fund Yorkist ambitions

Pretenders:
- Lambert Simnel
- Perkin Warbeck

1486 — Viscount Lovell and the Staffords

Minor rising, focused on traditional Yorkist heartlands of Yorkshire and the Midlands:

- Led by Viscount Lovell (Yorkshire) and Humphrey Stafford, with his brother Thomas (Midlands)
- Attracted little support and was easily suppressed
- Lovell escaped to Burgundy; Humphrey Stafford was captured and executed (though Thomas was pardoned)

Significance
Showed that there was little support for a Yorkist rising at this point

↓

Yorkists realised the need for a figurehead and funds

↓

1487 — Lambert Simnel and the rebellion of the Earl of Lincoln

Yorkist conspiracy arranged by the Earl of Lincoln, using Lambert Simnel as a figurehead:

- Simnel impersonated the imprisoned Earl of Warwick, and was crowned as King Edward in Ireland in May 1487
- Henry exhibited the real Earl of Warwick in London
- Lincoln fled to the court of Margaret of Burgundy and joined Lord Lovell; they persuaded Margaret to support Simnel and to pay for a force of mercenaries to invade England
- Henry neutralised Yorkist support in the north by reinstating the Earl of Northumberland, a traditional Yorkist supporter, to power in the north as his supporter (a calculated gamble)
- The rebels landed on the north-west coast of England in Cumberland, and tried to muster support in the Yorkist heartland of the North Riding of Yorkshire; however they failed to attract followers
- Henry's army defeated the mercenary army at the Battle of Stoke Field, June 1487; the Earl of Lincoln was killed

Reasons for Henry's victory:

- His own shrewdness and hard work
- Organisational skills and military leadership of his key supporters
- Willingness of landowners in many parts of the country to support his cause

Significance
This battle effectively ended the Wars of the Roses and Henry's position became safe, though not completely secure

Henry's lenient treatment of the rebels won over some Yorkists who had previously opposed him

He also began to develop the policy of using bonds of good behaviour, providing lump sums of money to landowners that they did not have to repay if they behaved well

The Perkin Warbeck imposture

Imposture of a cloth trader from Flanders, who claimed to be Richard, Duke of York (one of Edward IV's sons, and one of the two murdered 'princes in the Tower'):

1491: Warbeck began to impersonate Richard, Duke of York, in Ireland

1492: He fled to the court of Margaret of Burgundy, was trained as a potential Yorkist prince, and began to draw English courtiers into his conspiracies

1495: He attempted to land in England in 1495, but was quickly defeated; he fled to the court of James IV of Scotland

1491–99

1496: He tried to invade England with a small Scottish force; this soon retreated, and James IV agreed to marry Henry's daughter, Margaret

1497: He tried to claim the throne by exploiting the Cornish Rebellion; his forces were crushed; Warbeck surrendered; he was treated leniently at first but tried to escape

1499: He was tried and executed along with the Earl of Warwick

Significance

Patronage from foreign rulers made Warbeck a potentially serious threat and demonstrated how fragile Henry's position was considered to be by other rulers

The involvement (in 1495) in the conspiracy of Sir William Stanley (Henry's step-uncle and Lord Chamberlain, the head of the royal household) showed how vulnerable Henry was even within his own household

Edmund de la Pole, Earl of Suffolk and Richard de la Pole, 'The White Rose'

Younger brothers of the Earl of Lincoln:

1506

- Edmund (Suffolk) largely lived in exile from 1498 to 1506, under the protection of Margaret of Burgundy; returned in 1506 and was imprisoned in Tower of London; executed in 1513 by Henry VIII
- Richard de la Pole was exiled until his death fighting for France at the Battle of Pavia, 1525

Significance

The imprisonment of Suffolk effectively eliminated the remaining threats, leaving only Richard de la Pole at large in exile

SUMMARY

- Having successfully seized the throne at the Battle of Bosworth in 1485, Henry's immediate aim was to consolidate his power.
- His shrewdness and skill at planning allowed him to achieve this to a great extent in the first years of his reign, through a series of astute political moves.
- However his position remained insecure and the years 1486–99 saw a succession of threats to his rule, including rebellions and claims by Yorkist rivals and pretenders; almost all of which he had successfully defeated by 1506.

REVISION PROGRESS

APPLY

APPLY YOUR KNOWLEDGE

Complete the chart below. In the 1st column, list the problems that Henry Tudor faced in terms of consolidating his power, following his victory at the Battle of Bosworth in 1485. In the second, record how he addressed each problem.

Problem	Actions

EXAMINER TIP

This activity will help you in any essay question requiring you to analyse Henry's success in consolidating his power and establishing the Tudor dynasty.

ASSESS THE VALIDITY OF THIS VIEW

A LEVEL 'In the years 1485 to 1509, Henry VII's claim to the throne of England was never secure.' Assess the validity of this view.

To help you answer this question, complete the diagram below.

- Factors to show that Henry's claim was insecure
- Changes that occurred during Henry's reign
- Factors to show that Henry's claim became secure

EXAMINER TIP

In answering this essay question, you would need to think carefully about what 'secure' would actually mean in practice.

HENRY VII, 1485–1509

IMPROVE AN ANSWER

Here are 2 example paragraphs from different students answering an essay question asking:

> 'By 1509, Henry VII had successfully secured his power.' Explain why you agree or disagree with this view of the years 1485 to 1509.

Answer 1

Henry VII became king in 1485 when he won the Battle of Bosworth. After this he marched to London, where he was cheered, because the people didn't like Richard III and were pleased to welcome a new king. Then, Henry dated his reign to the day before the battle and married Elizabeth of York to bring the two houses of York and Lancaster together. However, he still had to put down various rebellions and pretenders such as the Lovell and Stafford rebellion, Lambert Simnel and Perkin Warbeck. He dealt with all of these successfully and executed the Earl of Warwick. His last threat, Richard de la Pole, was in exile abroad. This shows that, by 1509, Henry was secure in his power.

Answer 2

By 1506, Henry VII's power was far more secure than at any earlier point in his reign. In 1485, despite his victory at Bosworth, the weakness of Henry VII's claim to the throne (through the female and, in some people's eyes, illegitimate line) made his position precarious. Although his actions in 1485–86, such as dating his reign to the day before the battle and marrying Elizabeth of York, enabled him to consolidate his power quickly, he faced various rebellions and impostures in 1486–99, so his position was still seriously threatened. For example, Henry was subject to the behaviour of foreign rulers such as Margaret of Burgundy and even disloyalty in his own household, as Sir William Stanley was involved. Henry's execution of the Earl of Warwick and Perkin Warbeck in 1499, followed by the imprisonment of Edmund de la Pole in 1506, meant that by 1506 almost all rival claimants had been eliminated. Since Richard de la Pole was in exile abroad, it can be said that by 1509 Henry VII had successfully secured his power.

Which is the better answer and why?

REVISION SKILLS

Prepare a set of 6 cards – 1 for each of the Key Questions for this component. As you revise each chapter, consider what Key Questions it addresses. Write no more than 3 bullet points per chapter on each of the relevant cards, so that you can see how the material you have studied links to these Key Questions.

EXAMINER TIP

Take care to distinguish between description and analysis. The first sentence of every paragraph in an essay is crucial. This is what moves an argument forward. It is not enough to have 'this shows …' at the end.

EXAMINER TIP

This revision exercise will enable you to address the key themes that you will be asked about in the examination questions. Many chapters focus on 1 specific Key Question, but some address more than 1. For example, a chapter that primarily discusses intellectual and religious ideas may also contain information relevant to the Key Question on the role of individuals and groups.

2 Henry VII's government

RECAP

Councils and the court

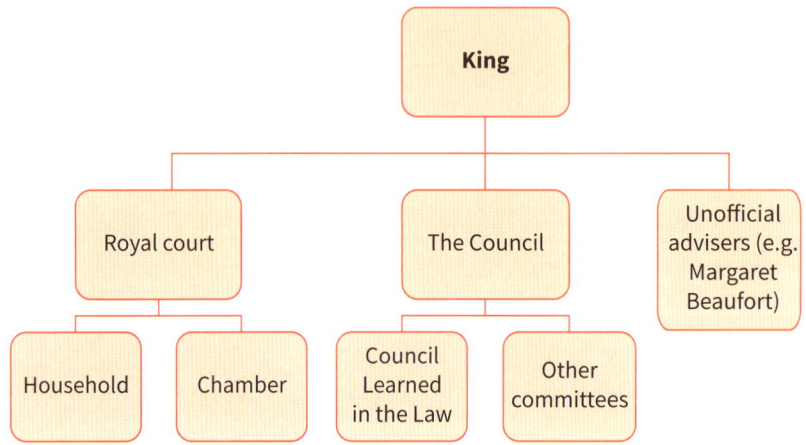

Central government

The Council

The king ruled with a 'council' of advisers who supported him in making key decisions. The working Council contained around six or seven members. Its functions were:

- to advise the king
- to administer the realm on the king's behalf
- to make legal judgements.

There were three main types of councillor:

1. Nobles, such as Lord Daubeney, though the working Council only rarely included the great **magnates**.
2. Churchmen such as John Morton and Richard Fox, who often had legal training and were excellent administrators.
3. Laymen, either gentry or lawyers, who were skilled administrators, such as Sir Reginald Bray and Edmund Dudley.

Under Henry VII the Council was a permanent body with a core membership, though with no established procedures. Sometimes members also met separately to discuss legal or administrative issues.

Non-councillors could also advise the king – for example, Henry's mother, Lady Margaret Beaufort, acted as an unofficial adviser.

The Council Learned (or Council Learned in the Law)

An offshoot of the Council, this body developed during the second half of Henry's reign, initially under Bray. Its function was to maintain the king's revenue and to exploit his **prerogative rights**. It made the system of **bonds** and **recognisances** work effectively, thus helping to ensure loyalty and raise finance. It was not a recognised court of law and there was no right of appeal against it. This council was important in maintaining Henry's authority as well in raising finance.

Bray's associate in the Council Learned was Sir Richard Empson – a fiercely ambitious lawyer and bureaucrat. After Bray's death in 1503, Empson was joined by Edmund Dudley. Empson and Dudley were able and conscientious bureaucrats, whose ruthless extraction of money from the king's subjects made them feared and unpopular, and created enemies out of some of the king's other advisers. They were removed and executed after Henry's death.

Court and household

The royal court was the centre of government. It was a focus for personal monarchy – a system in which a person's power was determined by his relationship with the monarch. Rewards and status were distributed through the court; courtiers enjoyed paid positions or the right to receive free food, and it was there that the support of the king or other influential persons could be obtained.

In 1485, the court comprised:

- the household proper, responsible for looking after the king, courtiers and guests, supervised by the Lord Steward
- the **Chamber**, presided over by the Lord Chamberlain, a powerful and influential courtier who was also a member of the king's Council and often spoke for the monarch – this was the politically important part of the system.

In 1495, after the involvement of Sir William Stanley, the Lord Chamberlain, in the Perkin Warbeck conspiracy, Henry remodelled the Chamber as the Privy Chamber. He could retreat into this, protected by his most intimate servants; this made it more difficult for anyone to gain or regain the king's favour, and also cut Henry off from many of the king's traditional contacts at court.

Parliament

Parliament met infrequently and so was not central to government. It comprised the House of Commons and the House of Lords. Of these, the House of Lords was more important.

Only the king could call Parliament, and Henry demonstrated his right to rule by calling his first parliament in November 1485. Henry called seven parliaments in his reign. Five of these met in the first ten years and only two in the remaining 14 years; this shows that power centred on the Crown and when Henry felt more secure, Parliament could be dispensed with.

Henry's early parliaments were largely concerned with the following:

- **National security:** For example, his first two parliaments passed numerous Acts of Attainder (by which individuals could be declared guilty without trial if alive; if dead, their property would be forfeit to the Crown).
- **Raising revenue:** For example:
  - His first parliament granted tonnage and poundage (customs revenues) for life.
  - Other parliaments granted **extraordinary revenue** (taxation granted as a one-off payment, for example to enable the king to wage war).

Parliament appears in general to have operated effectively under Henry VII, with the king accepting its decisions.

Domestic policy: justice and the maintenance of order

It was essential for the king to maintain law and order to prevent uprisings or rebellions, and so that potential enemies had no excuse to challenge his authority.

Regional government (in the hands of the nobility)

Following losses of land and power during the Wars of the Roses, the great magnates (the wealthiest nobles) were powerful only in the north of England. The Stanleys controlled the north-west. The Earl of Northumberland ruled the north-east until 1489, when the Yorkist Earl of Surrey was released from prison and sent to the north; this risk paid off, and Surrey served loyally for ten years.

The Earl of Surrey ruled this area through the Council of the North. There were other regional councils in Wales and the Marches, and in Ireland.

Henry preferred to rely on the lesser magnates, but he trusted few and employed a spying network to ensure all the nobility remained loyal.

Local government (justices of the peace)

At a local level, Henry gradually increased the powers of justices of the peace (JPs) who, together with the sheriff (the man responsible for elections to Parliament and peace-keeping), were appointed to each county.

- JPs were unpaid and mostly local gentry (of lower social status than the nobles); a few were royal officials.
- They met four times a year to deliver judgements on disputes at the quarter sessions.
- They were responsible for routine administration, e.g. tax assessments, complaints against local officials and maintenance of law and order.

More serious cases were heard at the courts of assize by judges appointed by the Crown. The Court of King's Bench dealt with appeals from the quarter sessions and courts of assize and could overturn the decisions of the lesser courts. There was also a wide range of other courts, e.g. Church courts, manor and borough courts, and king's courts.

Domestic policy: improving royal finances

Royal income could come from various sources:

Profits from feudal dues and exercise of the royal prerogative
Revenue increased by reviving/extending medieval feudal dues, e.g.:
- Profits from wardship (when property was held by a minor) increased
- Feudal aid (the Crown's right to impose taxes for certain services) granted in 1504
- Dues paid by landowners on death of a feudal tenant-in-chief

Crown lands (income from rents)
- Large proportion of ordinary revenue
- Around £12,000 per year at beginning of reign, collected by inefficient Court of Exchequer
- From c1492, administered through the Chamber (as under Edward IV)
- By end of reign, had risen to around £42,000 per year

Sources of income

Other sources
- Customs revenue (tonnage and poundage)
- Legal system and profits of justice (including fines and income from bonds)
- Bonds and recognisances
- Clerical taxes and grants
- Loans and benevolences
- Parliamentary grants
- Pensions from other powers (£5000 per year from France from 1492 under Treaty of Etaples)

Purple: ordinary revenue (ie. regular income)

Red: extraordinary revenue (ie. irregular income)

Note: Over £400,000 was raised from extraordinary revenue. But this helped provoke rebellions in 1489 and 1497. In 1504, Henry had to promise not to raise any more money by this method

Henry and his officials focused heavily on increasing Crown revenues from all the sources above. However, many of his policies were politically risky, in that those most affected were the landowners, on whose support Henry relied.

SUMMARY

- Henry VII largely maintained the traditional structures of government; however there were developments, such as the establishment of the Privy Chamber in 1495 and the creation of the Council Learned in the Law.
- He kept law and order through the nobility (helped at a local level by justices of the peace), while his system of bonds and recognisances enforced obedience; a network of spies ensured the performance of both.
- A key focus was the improvement of royal finances, in which he achieved considerable success, though at the cost of rising unpopularity and at the risk of alienating the group on whom his throne most depended.

APPLY

APPLY YOUR KNOWLEDGE

a   Look at the text and define or briefly explain the following terms (in relation to government between 1485 and 1509).

courtier	
magnate	
bonds and recognisances	
prerogative rights	
personal monarchy	
Chamber	
Privy Chamber	
Act of Attainder	
tonnage and poundage	
extraordinary revenue	
feudalism / feudal aid	

b   How might these terms contribute to an understanding of the government in England under Henry VII?

EXAMINER TIP

This activity will help you in any essay requiring you to analyse change and continuity in government during the reign of Henry VII. Use of terms such as these will show your depth of knowledge.

PLAN YOUR ESSAY

AS LEVEL 'Henry VII's efforts to increase the royal finances were very successful.' Explain why you agree or disagree with this view of the years 1485 to 1509.

a   Draw a balance diagram like the one below. Label one side 'Successes of financial policies' and the other side 'Failures of financial policies'. Write a list of factors on each side. When you have finished, decide for yourself: is the balance tilted towards 'successes' or towards 'failures' – and by how much? List what issues seem to be raised by this 'weighing up'.

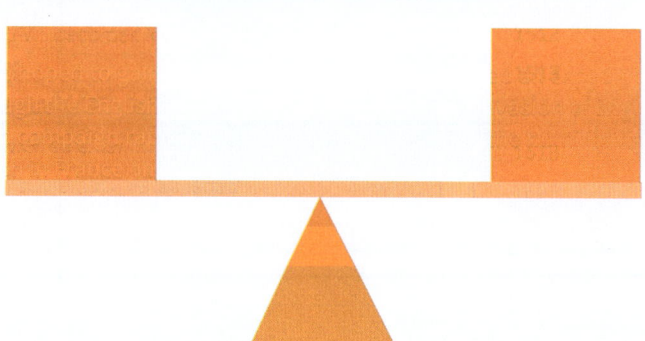

b   Now plan your answer to the question and write the first sentence of each paragraph. Ensure your argument makes clear whether you agree or disagree with the quotation.

REVISION SKILLS

Planning your exam essay is essential, so you should practise writing essay plans as much as you practise writing full answers.

EXAMINER TIP

Before you start to write an essay, you should always decide on what judgement you will come to, and state it clearly in your introduction. Also, remember that successes or failures may be political as well as financial.

REVISION PROGRESS

KEY QUESTION

One of the Key Questions asks:

How important was the role of key individuals and groups and how were they affected by developments?

Key individuals mentioned in this chapter include John Morton, Sir Reginald Bray, Sir Richard Empson, Edmund Dudley and Lady Margaret Beaufort. Compile a set of flashcards, 1 for each individual mentioned. For each, note 1–3 bullet points about their role and influence and how they were affected by developments.

REVIEW

You can add to your flashcards as you find out more about these individuals in Chapter 4.

ASSESS THE VALIDITY OF THIS VIEW

 'Henry VII was an expert financial manager who should be praised for increasing the royal income.' Assess the validity of this view of the years 1485 to 1509.

This question illustrates a difference between AS and A Level in terms of complexity. The AS question in this chapter requires you simply to weigh up 1 issue. Here, there are 2 debates: 'Was he an expert financial manager?' and 'Should he be praised for increasing the royal income?' In planning, you will need to separate the 2 parts of the question and identify the factors that are relevant to each.

a   Copy the diagram below and fill in the gaps. Sort out the factors which would determine whether the king was an 'expert financial manager' and list them as either supporting (yes) or opposing (no) this view.

b   Do the same with respect to 'increasing the royal income'. Reflect also on whether this deserves praise or criticism.

c   Review what you have written and fill in your conclusion on both aspects.

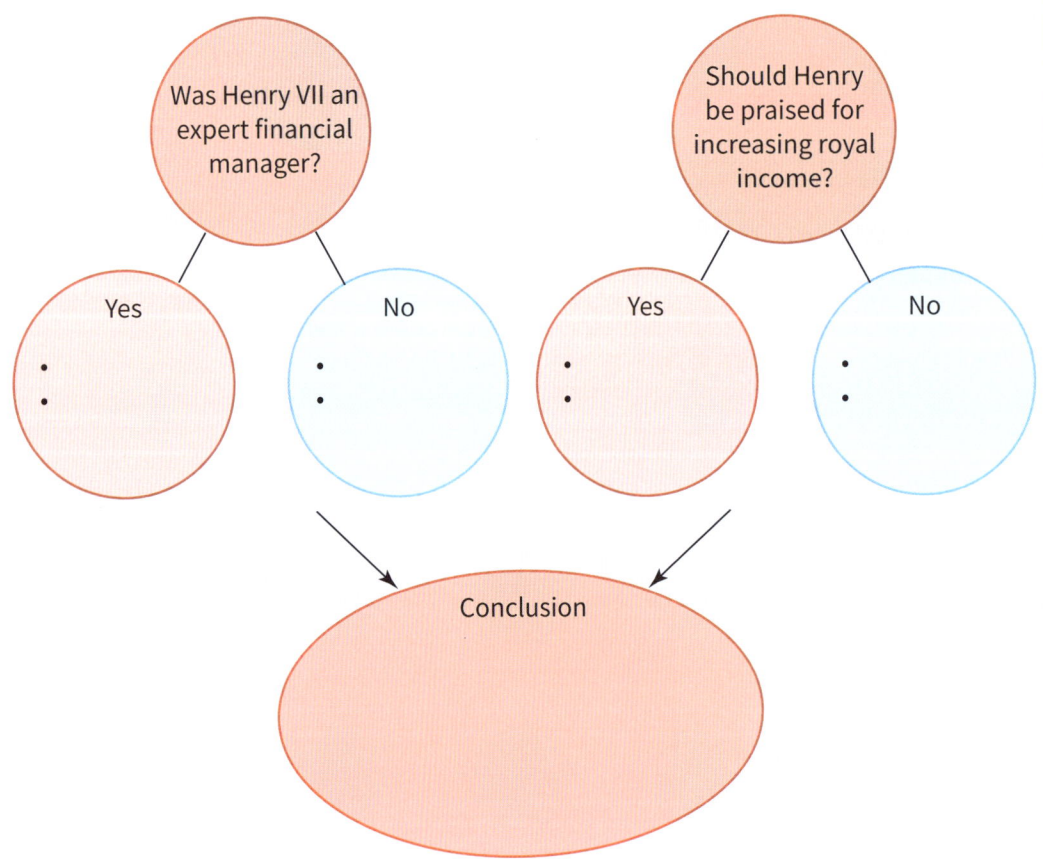

3 England's relations with Scotland and other foreign powers, 1485–1509

RECAP

Henry VII's relations with foreign powers

Henry's foreign policy aims were straightforward:

- to maintain good relations with European powers (thus allowing him to consolidate his power at home)
- to gain international recognition for the Tudor dynasty
- to maintain national security
- to defend English trading interests.

Brittany and France

KEY CHRONOLOGY

Relations with Brittany and France

1487	The French invaded the Duchy of Brittany, the last independent area within France
	The death of Duke Francis II of Brittany, without a male heir, provided the excuse
1489	Treaty of Redon – Henry agreed to support the claim of Duke Francis' young daughter, Duchess Anne, although he was anxious not to antagonise the French
1491	6000 English 'volunteers' were sent to Brittany but Anne surrendered to the French; it was arranged that she should marry Charles VIII of France, ending Breton independence
1492	Based on intelligence that Charles was more interested in invading Italy than fighting the English, Henry raised two parliamentary subsidies and invaded France with 26,000 men. The French rapidly sought peace
	November – Treaty of Etaples; Charles agreed that he would no longer assist any pretenders to the English throne. Henry was also to receive 745,000 crowns, paid in annual instalments of 50,000 crowns a year. This was around 5% of Henry's total annual income

European powers during the reign of Henry VII

Burgundy, the Netherlands and the Holy Roman Empire

The ports of the Netherlands were important for English trade, particularly in cloth. However:

- The Netherlands had been under the control of Burgundy: Margaret of Burgundy (Edward IV's sister) had married the ruler, Charles the Bold, who died in 1477. Thereafter she ruled as protector, while the duke's title passed to Maximilian, who became Holy Roman Emperor in 1493 and, in turn, placed his son, Philip, in control of the area as Duke Philip IV.
- Margaret, Maximilian and Philip supported the pretenders to Henry's throne, Lambert Simnel and Perkin Warbeck.

Henry's strategy had proved successful. He had defended national and dynastic interests, improved his financial position and ensured a period of relative friendliness in Anglo-French relations.

KEY CHRONOLOGY

Relations with Burgundy, the Netherlands and the Holy Roman Empire

1493	Following Margaret's support for Perkin Warbeck, Henry broke trade relations with Burgundy. (He was more concerned with securing his dynasty than protecting the commercial interests of London and east-coast merchants, but the embargo harmed both the English and Flemish economies)
1496	Henry VII and Philip IV agreed the **Intercursus Magnus** ('Great Intercourse') which ended the trade embargo, and Margaret recognised Henry's position as king
1503	Death of Margaret of Burgundy
1506	Philip and his wife, Juana, daughter of Isabella of Castile (in Spain) were blown into the English coast as they set out for Spain following Isabella's death in 1504. Henry VII entertained them for three months and negotiated two treaties:

- By the Treaty of Windsor, he recognised Philip's claim to Castile, and they each promised to assist one another against rebels
- A trade treaty was agreed, but became known as the Intercursus Malus ('Evil Intercourse') by the Flemish because it was over-generous to England

Further agreements meant that:

- Philip handed over the Yorkist Earl of Suffolk, who had been sheltering in Burgundy, to Henry
- A marriage was arranged between Henry (widowed in 1503) and Philip's sister, Margaret, Dowager Duchess of Savoy. (This came to nothing)

Philip died in September, and the trade treaty, of which Margaret (who became the new Burgundian governor) disapproved, was never implemented

1507	A third treaty reverted to the terms of the first Intercursus Magnus
1508	Henry VII was diplomatically isolated by not being a signatory to the League of Cambrai, which was formed by the Holy Roman Empire, Spain, France and the Papacy

Spain

Spain (ruled by Ferdinand of Aragon and Isabella of Castile) was a powerful state, with which Henry hoped to develop good relations.

KEY CHRONOLOGY

Relations with Spain

1489	The Treaty of Medina del Campo agreed a marriage alliance between Catherine of Aragon (Ferdinand and Isabella's youngest daughter) and Prince Arthur (Henry's eldest son)
1501	Marriage between Arthur and Catherine took place
1502	Arthur died; Henry (anxious to retain Catherine's dowry) proposed a new marriage between Catherine and Arthur's younger brother, Henry; a treaty was signed in 1503 and a marriage planned for 1506, Henry's 15th birthday
1504	Isabella died; Henry supported the claims of Juana (married to Philip IV) to succeed in Castile. (This was confirmed during their stay in England in 1506)
1506	Philip's death led Ferdinand to deprive his daughter Juana of her inheritance. The marriage between Catherine and Henry was jeopardised and did not take place until June 1509, after Henry VII's death

Scotland

Scotland was the only country which shared a border with England. It often supported France against England.

Ireland

In Ireland, Henry VII ruled only the 'Pale', the land around Dublin. The rest of Ireland was ruled by independent chieftains.

The Earl of Kildare (Lord Deputy of Ireland since 1477) was a threat to Henry because of his Yorkist sympathies. Kildare crowned Lambert Simnel King of Ireland in 1486 and supported Perkin Warbeck in 1491.

Consequently, Henry replaced him with Sir Edward Poynings who passed 'Poynings' Law' of 1495 which declared that the Irish Parliament needed the approval of the English monarch before it could pass laws. Poynings also tried to subdue the Irish by force. However, Kildare was persuaded to abandon the Yorkist cause and was reinstated in 1495. Thereafter, he served Henry loyally and secured the submission of various Irish chieftains. By 1500, Henry had established a reasonable level of control.

Securing the succession and marriage alliances

Henry VII had four children who survived childhood: Arthur, Henry, Margaret and Mary.

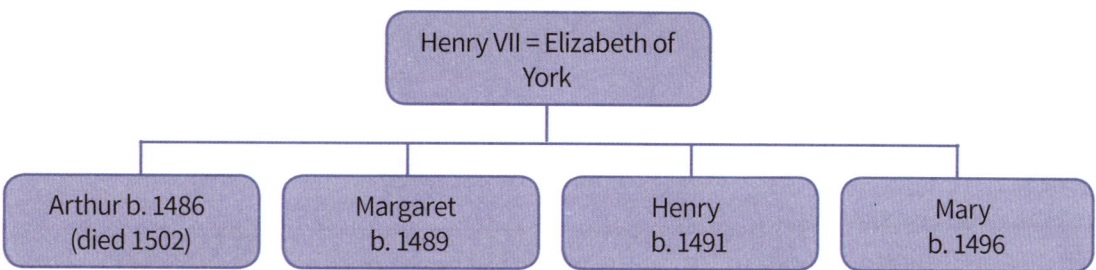

Despite Henry's efforts at arranging suitable marriage alliances for Arthur (with Catherine of Aragon) and Margaret (with James IV of Scotland), Arthur's unexpected death in April 1502 increased the insecurity of the dynasty.

- The new heir, Prince Henry, was still a child.
- The Yorkists had a powerful claimant in the Earl of Suffolk.
- Henry VII's health was deteriorating.

The death of Henry's wife, Elizabeth of York, in 1503, meant that no more children would be forthcoming. Despite the imprisonment of the Earl of Suffolk in 1506, the succession remained insecure as it rested on the survival and acceptance by ministers of Prince Henry.

Henry VII died in April 1509. One faction, led by Bishop Fox and supported by Lady Margaret Beaufort, declared for Henry; Empson and Dudley were arrested.

> **SUMMARY**
> - Henry VII's foreign policy aims were broadly to maintain good relationships with Europe, with a view to strengthening the Tudor dynasty.
> - In this, he was largely successful, overcoming various setbacks to reach agreements with France, Burgundy, Spain and Scotland and achieving a certain level of security in Ireland.
> - Agreements with Spain and Scotland were cemented with marriage alliances, ensuring that by the end of his reign the Tudor dynasty seemed to have been accepted internationally.

REVISION PROGRESS

APPLY

APPLY YOUR KNOWLEDGE

Complete the graph below. Read the material on changing relationships with Scotland, and plot each key event on the graph.

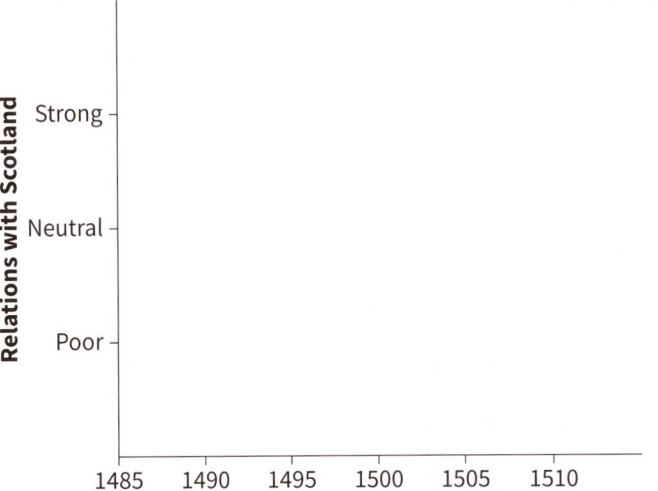

EXAMINER TIP

This activity will help you visualise the ups and downs of foreign relations, which will help you with an essay question that asks you to examine change and continuity, or to assess the success or failure of Henry's foreign policies. You could go further, and plot all the major European powers in different colours; this would help you form an overall view of Henry's relationships with foreign powers at different points during his reign.

ASSESS THE VALIDITY OF THIS VIEW

> **A LEVEL** 'Henry VII's foreign policy was driven by the need to preserve the Tudor dynasty.' Assess the validity of this view of the years 1485 to 1509.

a Create a mind-map to help you answer this question.
  - Put 'Henry's foreign policy' in the centre.
  - Around this add other countries: Burgundy/Netherlands/HRE; Spain; Brittany/France; Ireland; Scotland.
  - You might like to start by adding Henry VII's key involvement with each of the countries.
  - Then you can extend the mind-map further with the key motives behind that involvement.
  - Use 1 colour for those that were concerned with the need to preserve the dynasty.
  - Use a different colour for other motives.
b Now use your mind-map to reach a judgement in relation to the question.

EXAMINER TIP

Use a diagram such as a mind-map to help you formulate your answer by clarifying the facts that support and challenge a statement visually.

IMPROVE AN ANSWER

Here is an example paragraph from a student answering an essay question asking:

> **AS LEVEL** 'Henry VII's foreign policy failed to achieve its key aims in the years 1485 to 1509.' Explain why you agree or disagree with this view.

a Read the following paragraph from a mediocre essay. This comes immediately after the introduction:

Answer

The king's only aim in foreign policy was to secure the succession. This was so important that he married all of his children to foreign rulers – in one case twice! Henry built up alliances with Spain and Scotland through marriage to secure the succession of his son, the future Henry VIII, by being connected to all of the leading powers in Europe. He also made treaties which stopped other countries from supporting pretenders. This is why Henry VIII was able to succeed to the throne and this shows that Henry had achieved his only goal in foreign policy – to support his own weak claim and that of his son after the long conflict called the Wars of the Roses.

b Consider this paragraph both as a whole and 1 sentence at a time, and assess its strengths and weaknesses. Think about the style and the content, and comment on whether the question is being addressed properly. Could you produce a better paragraph?

EXAMINER TIP

A good paragraph will begin with a comment, linked to the question, which is then supported by precise and specific information. Dates and detail help to convince and enable high examination marks.

REVIEW

Paragraph construction is very important in essays. What have you learned about paragraph construction from this exercise? Look at any essay you have written and see if your paragraphs follow the formula suggested above. If not, could you rearrange your text to make them more analytical?

KEY QUESTION

One of the Key Questions asks:

How did relations with foreign powers change and how was the succession secured?

On a large A3 sheet of paper, copy out the chart below. Fill the chart in with a list of the key ways in which relations changed between England and the country concerned during the years 1485–1509. You can complete the remaining columns as you read the next 3 sections.

Foreign power	1485–1509	1509–47	1547–63	1563–1603
Brittany				
Burgundy/Netherlands/HRE				
France				
Spain				
Scotland				
Ireland				

REVISION SKILLS

A3 charts can be a useful way of consolidating key points of information. They can also help you to see a broad sweep of events and consider change and continuity 'at a glance'. Note, if you are studying for AS, you will only need to fill in the columns marked 1485–1509 and 1509–47.

4 English society at the end of the 15th century

RECAP

The structure of society

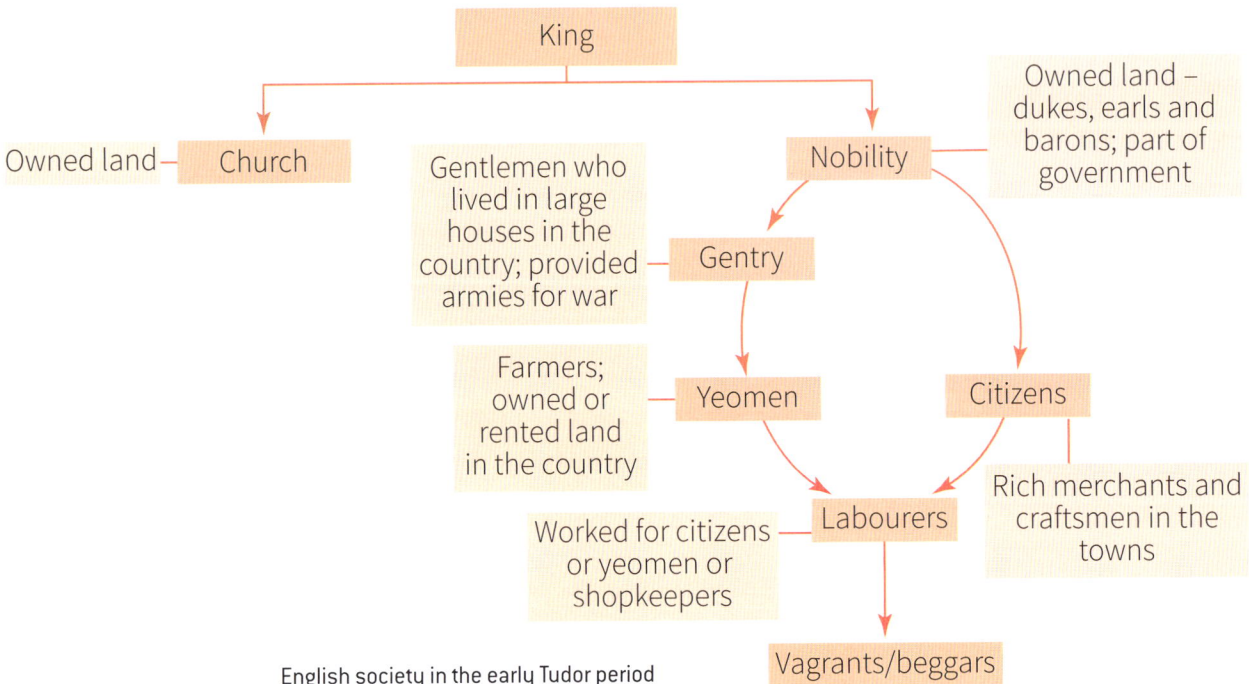

English society in the early Tudor period

In some ways, society was still structured in a **feudal** arrangement, with the monarch at the top, the great noble landowners and senior churchmen, closely followed by 'gentry', below the monarch, and the labouring classes – of both peasants and craftsmen – at the base. However, there was a growing professional and mercantile group in London and the major cities, and there was some (and growing) social mobility.

Nobility

The nobility dominated landownership. They comprised around 50–60 peers (nobles), who were entitled to sit in the House of Lords. As noble families died out they were replaced by others who had acquired the king's favour. However, Henry VII distrusted the nobility as a class, and was reluctant to create new peers.

Henry controlled the nobility through bonds and recognisances. He also sought, in a law of 1487, to limit their power; this restricted the practice by which wealthy magnates recruited knights and gentlemen, known as 'retainers', to serve them as administrators or for military purposes.

Churchmen

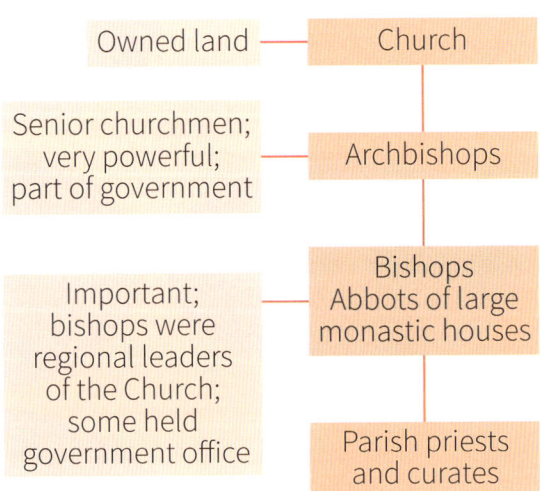

The hierarchy of the Church in England

The Church was important both for its spiritual role and as a great landowner. England was a Catholic country and Churchmen had a dual allegiance – to both the Pope and the king. The Pope was elected by cardinals, under whom came the archbishops; in England, there were two archbishops, Canterbury and York. Archbishops, bishops and the abbots of larger religious houses were such important figures that the king intervened in their appointments. They sat in the House of Lords and often undertook political roles.

Henry VII ensured that he had men of administrative ability as archbishops and bishops, and preferred men with legal training (e.g. the royal councillors, Morton and Fox).

At the parish level, curates and priests dealt with the spiritual needs of ordinary people, living modestly. However, Church influence was all-pervasive and the Church even had its own courts. All clergy were tried in these, as were those convicted of 'religious crimes' such as adultery.

Gentry

The gentry (around 500 knights, 800 esquires and 5000 gentlemen in 1500) comprised:

- The greater gentry – often great landowners in their own right, some sought knighthoods to confirm their social status.
- Esquires and 'mere gentry' – these were far more numerous and had far less social prestige than the greater gentry. They too were landowners and both groups might be office-holders.

The nobility and gentry combined made up around 1% of the total population of the time.

Commoners

Beneath the nobility and gentry were a little more than two million commoners.

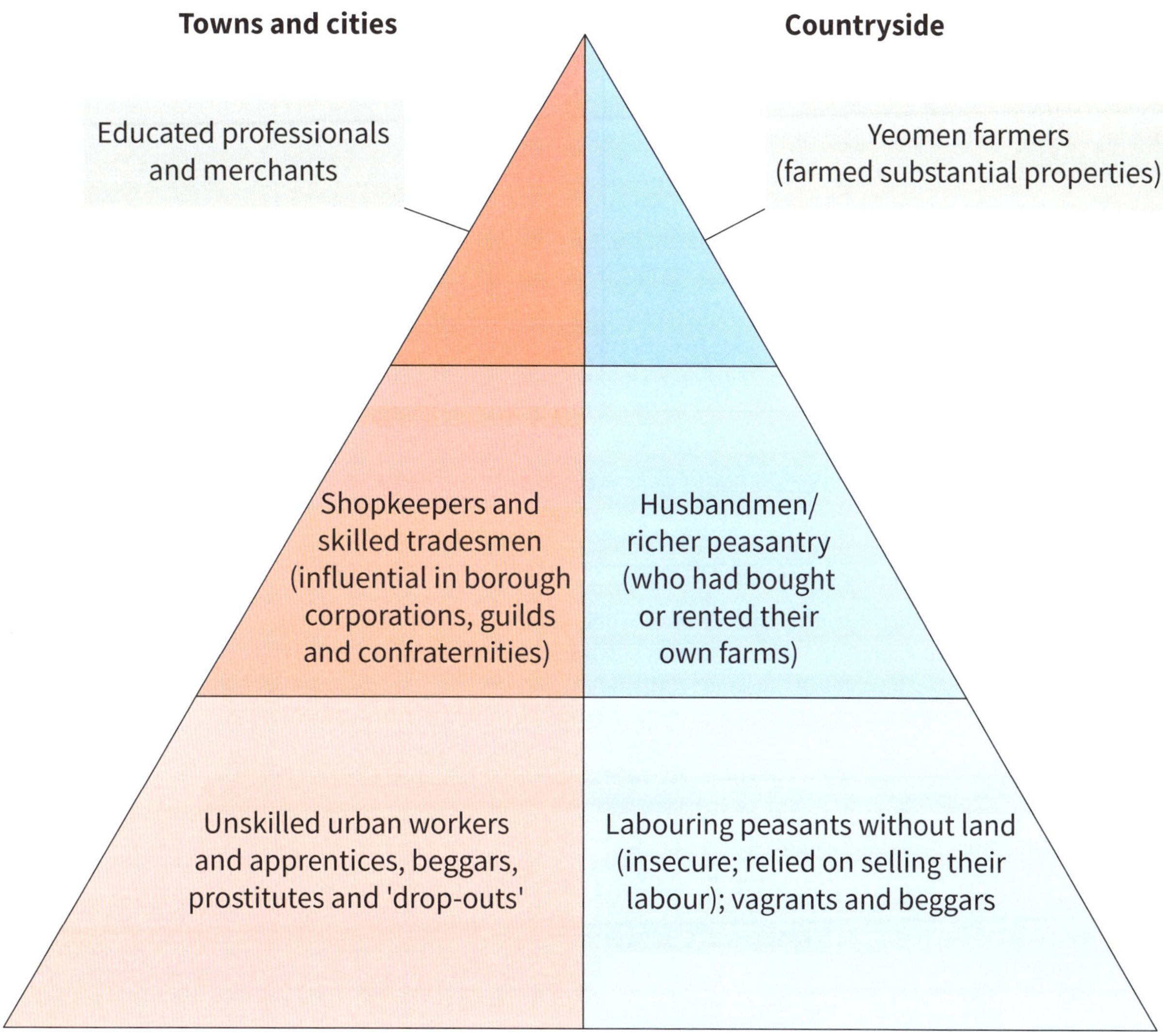

Towns and cities

- Educated professionals and merchants
- Shopkeepers and skilled tradesmen (influential in borough corporations, guilds and confraternities)
- Unskilled urban workers and apprentices, beggars, prostitutes and 'drop-outs'

Countryside

- Yeomen farmers (farmed substantial properties)
- Husbandmen/richer peasantry (who had bought or rented their own farms)
- Labouring peasants without land (insecure; relied on selling their labour); vagrants and beggars

Regional divisions

There were some regional social variations, arising from:

- Demographic differences. The sparsely populated rural areas to the north/west of an imaginary line from the Tees estuary to Weymouth contained a quarter of the population, while three quarters lived in more densely populated counties to the south/east of that line (see Chapter 5 for a map and further detail).
- Differences in agriculture between the two areas either side of this line (see Chapter 5).
- Social attitudes (Londoners might see northerners as less refined; northerners might envy southern wealth).
- Government structures. There were separate councils for the north of England, Wales, Ireland and the Welsh Marches; nobles also had considerable influence across county boundaries. Some areas, such as the County Palatines of Chester and Durham, enjoyed considerable independence.
- Church influence. This varied by area and equally cut across other boundaries.
- Linguistic and cultural differences within the kingdom, most particularly in Wales, Cornwall and Ireland.

In an age of limited travel, regional loyalties were strong and officials appointed by or sent from London could be resented as 'outsiders'. However the sense of a single English identity would seem to have been relatively strong at this time.

Social discontent and rebellions

In the late 15th century, there was relatively little explicit sign of discontent, probably because living conditions for the poor were improving. However, there were two rebellions, in 1489 and 1497, both triggered by taxation.

The Yorkshire Rebellion of 1489 was sparked by resentment of the taxation granted by Parliament in 1489 in order to finance an army for the Brittany campaign. The Earl of Northumberland was murdered by his tenants when his retainers deserted him (punishing him because he himself had deserted Richard III at Bosworth).

The Cornish Rebellion of 1497 arose from the need to finance the campaign against Scotland. A mob protested against the taxation, blaming the king and ministers such as Morton (Archbishop of Canterbury) and Bray. This uprising was a more serious threat to Henry's rule than the Yorkshire Rebellion, because:

- Large numbers were involved (15,000 according to some estimates).
- Perkin Warbeck attempted to exploit the rebellion.
- A march on London reached Blackheath, raising questions as to the effectiveness of Henry's system of maintaining order in the countryside.

In the short term, the revolt forced Henry to withdraw Lord Daubeney and his troops from the Scottish border in order to crush the rebellion. This was easily done, and the leaders were executed (although most of the rebels were leniently treated). In the longer term, it had the effect of making Henry ensure that Anglo-Scottish tensions were eased, and it made him cautious about entering into further foreign conflicts.

> **SUMMARY**
> - Socially, England remained broadly stable in this period.
> - Under Henry VII, internal peace was generally maintained, and the various pretenders and claimants were unable to attract much support.
> - The two rebellions of the reign, the Yorkshire Rebellion (1489) and the Cornish Rebellion (1497), were exceptional, and easily suppressed.

APPLY

APPLY YOUR KNOWLEDGE

AS LEVEL — 'Henry VII's policies weakened the nobility in the years 1485 to 1509.' Explain why you agree or disagree with this view.

a Complete the diagram of the measures taken by Henry VII in his dealings with the nobility and show how each action would affect the nobility.

b Colour code your diagram with 1 colour for maintaining noble powers and another colour for reducing noble powers.

c Use this diagram to help you plan an answer to the question.

Measure — **Group(s) affected**

- Did not create many new peers
- Used bonds and recognisances
- Limited the numbers of retainers
- Used lesser magnates to govern
- Used spying network on noblemen
- Used great magnates in the regional councils
- Dated his reign from the day before Bosworth
- Used Acts of Attainder to take estates

EXAMINER TIP

Using the information in the diagram, consider how the policies might be considered to have weakened the nobility. You would, of course, need to consider if any of his actions did not weaken the nobility also, in order to produce a balanced answer.

REVIEW

You will need to look back at previous chapters for contextual material on Henry's actions towards the nobility in this period.

REVISION SKILLS

When considering 2 sides of an argument it can be helpful to draw up a chart to arrange your points. This should help you decide which side of the argument is better supported by the evidence.

REVISION PROGRESS

HOW IMPORTANT?

In the table below, indicate the ways in which each group was important to late 15th-century society.

Examples of the Church's importance to society	Examples of the nobility's importance to society

REVIEW

You will find it useful to read part of Chapter 6 for your list. Once you have completed the table, compare your list with the one in the answers section on page 129. Were there points you missed out?

EXAMINER TIP

The detail in this chart should help you in answering any examination question about society and social developments.

PLAN YOUR ESSAY

 'The Church was more influential than the nobility in the years 1485 to 1509.' Assess the validity of this view.

Consider this question by looking back at your answers to the Apply Your Knowledge and How Important? activities, and write an introduction advancing your view and summarising the key points of your comparison.

EXAMINER TIP

Although the introduction is the place to give your views and breakdown, you should avoid using the first person or statements such as, 'First I will do this and then I will do that …'. Introduce your argument directly and incorporate the necessary detail in your statements. The rest of the essay should uphold the view put forward here.

5 Economic development: trade, exploration, prosperity and depression

RECAP

Most of England's 2.2 million population made a living from agriculture. Only around 10% lived in towns or cities, and while London probably contained more than 50,000 people, only 20 towns at most (including Norwich, Bristol, York and Coventry) had a population of 3000 or more.

The agrarian economy

As the population began to increase in the 1480s and 1490s, there was a move towards more sheep farming at the expense of arable (cereal crops) because of the increasing demand for wool as trade developed.

This development was most acute in the 'lowland zone' to the south and east of an imaginary line running from the Tees estuary to Weymouth. Traditionally, peasant farmers had practised open-field husbandry (farming strips of land in open fields, and enjoying **common rights**, e.g. keeping animals on shared land). The growth of sheep farming could mean the loss of common land and changes to the strip system (enclosure), although this did not become common until the first half of the 16th century. In general, English agriculture changed little in the late 15th and early 16th centuries.

Trade and industry

At the end of the 15th century, cloth amounted to about 90% of English exports, and farm labourers were able to supplement their farming incomes by spinning, weaving, **fulling** (wool-cleaning) and dyeing. Some towns, such Lavenham in Suffolk, flourished from the cloth trade. The finished cloth was increasingly exported from London to the commercial centre of Antwerp, from where it was sent all over Europe. Other industries included:

- mining – tin, lead, coal and iron ore (which required capital investment, but was still fairly small scale)
- metal working
- leatherwork
- shipbuilding
- papermaking
- brewing (in small-scale craft operations).

Trade

Henry was keen to develop English trade in order to boost wealth through customs duties and taxes, as well as to enhance his own position by securing positive relationships with foreign powers. His actions included:

- Navigation Acts of 1485 and 1489; these ruled that only English ships could carry certain products to and from English ports; they were designed to boost the English shipbuilding industry and challenge the Hanseatic League which had a monopoly over trade in the Baltic
- support for the Merchant Adventurers – an English company which controlled the cloth trade
- the Intercursus Magnus of 1496 (confirmed 1499) between Henry and Philip IV; this ended Henry's 1493 embargo on trade with the Netherlands and stated that:
  - English merchants could export to any part of Burgundy except Flanders
  - merchants would be granted swift and fair justice
  - disputes would be resolved swiftly and fairly
- other trade treaties, sometimes made as subsidiary clauses in diplomatic treaties with foreign powers.

Despite the relaxation of restrictions there was no major breakthrough in Mediterranean trade. Moreover the Hanseatic League was largely successful in limiting the development of English trading interests in the Baltic.

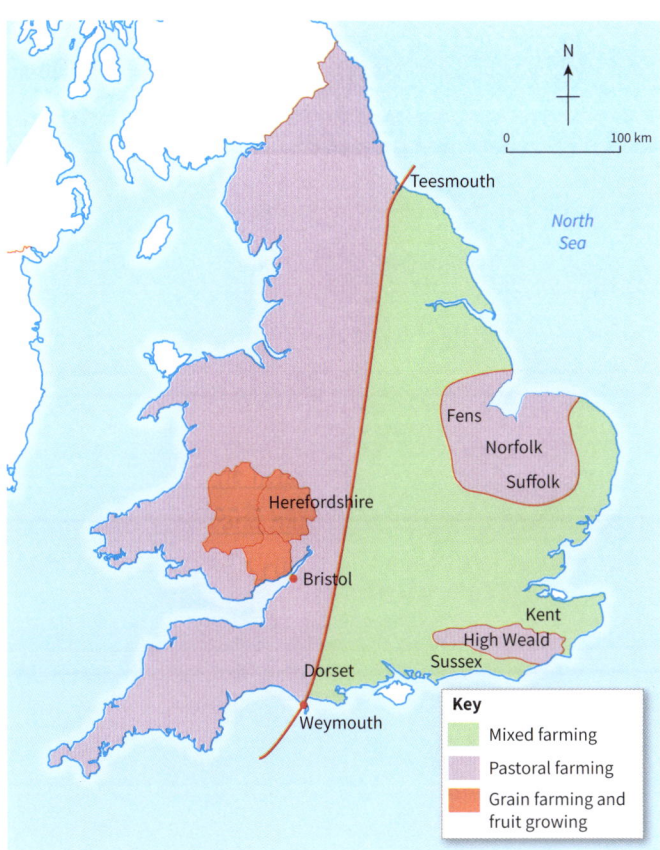

Farming regions of England

Early English exploration

English sailors were slower at making new discoveries than 15th-century Spanish or Portuguese seamen. However Bristol merchants and seamen were interested in transatlantic exploration and voyages of exploration were underway by the end of the 15th century.

- In 1497, John Cabot set sail from Bristol in search of new fishing grounds, with authorisation from Henry VII to search out any unknown parts of the world. Cabot found what became known as Newfoundland and reported the existence of extensive fishing grounds (but failed to return from a second voyage the following year).
- William Weston, a Bristol merchant, led an expedition to the New World, and may have landed there in 1499 or 1500.

John Cabot's son, Sebastian, also received sponsorship from Henry VII and led an unsuccessful attempt to find the 'north-west passage' to Asia in 1508. However, Henry VIII had little interest in supporting exploration, and in his reign the new fishing grounds were left to seamen from Portugal and Spain.

Prosperity and depression

On the whole, the late 15th century was a time of relative economic stability with signs of growing prosperity, particularly in the more developed areas. The population was growing and trade was expanding, with the cloth trade leading the way in stimulating the economy. However, depressions could and did occur, whenever events disrupted normal economic development; a bad harvest at home or an embargo abroad, such as that of 1493, are examples. Such depressions were usually quite localised but between 1493 and 1496 the depression in the cloth industry had quite a wide effect.

> **SUMMARY**
> - The reign of Henry VII was a period of relative economic stability.
> - The economy remained firmly based on agriculture, with some small-scale industrial enterprises.
> - The king made some attempts to encourage English trade; this was partly from a desire to increase wealth and partly out of a concern for dynastic security.

APPLY

APPLY YOUR KNOWLEDGE

Here is a list of trading and economic developments:

- Intercursus Magna
- Sebastian Cabot's journey to find a 'north-west passage' to Asia
- the embargo on trade with the Netherlands
- John Cabot's discovery of Newfoundland
- Weston's expedition to the New World
- the depression in the cloth industry
- Navigation Acts.

a Place them in the correct chronological order, and add relevant dates next to each event.

_____

_____

_____

_____

_____

_____

_____

b Give a one-sentence explanation of each. Try to include the intended impact of the change on the economy.

EXAMINER TIP

Precise information on economic developments will enable you to support answers to questions on the economy fully.

REVIEW

Reflect on the impact of these measures. Try to produce 1 or 2 generic reasons as well as a specific reason for either the failure or the success of each. When considering the Netherlands trade embargo, you could refer to Perkin Warbeck, who is discussed in Chapter 1, on pages 12–13.

TO WHAT EXTENT?

A LEVEL **To what extent was the growth of the economy between 1485 and 1509 due to the development of agriculture?**

Draw a mind-map showing the various factors which influenced the growth of the economy, and show the connections between these. For example, while there was some change in agriculture due to the opening up of markets for English cloth, this was only in the 'lowland zone' and generally agriculture changed little.

REVIEW

Look back at Chapters 3 and 4 to identify other possible reasons for the growth of the economy.

REVISION PROGRESS

EXTRACT ANALYSIS

In the AS and A Level exam questions, you will be given 2 or 3 extracts to study. You will need to identify the arguments put forward in each extract and evaluate these, with reference to your own knowledge. This task helps you analyse 2 or 3 related interpretations.

> **REVIEW**
> All these extracts refer to foreign policy issues which are often connected with trade. In order to answer this question fully, you should first read Chapter 4, which covers Henry VII's foreign policy.

EXTRACT A

In assessing the success of Henry's commercial policy, it is not possible to reach a simple conclusion. He did increase outlets for English trade and he deserves credit for the forward-looking treaty with Spain and the openings he forged with Venice and Scandinavia. However his achievements did not, as he hoped, greatly benefit his financial position. Although the customs revenue rose, this was probably as a result of the more efficient collection of customs duties as of any expansion of trade. However English shipping did expand under his patronage and by 1509 English merchants were shipping more cloth abroad than the combined exports of all other merchants. Nevertheless, English trade was on a small scale compared to that of Venice or Spain. Dynastic considerations were always his first priority; for example, Henry stopped trading with the Netherlands because of its ruler's support for Warbeck. Henry had begun the development of English trade but it was left to his successors to build on the very limited start he had made.

Adapted from C. Rogers and R. Turvey, *Henry VII*, 2005

EXTRACT B

Henry came to a throne with little income compared to Edward IV's rule. Henry's Navigation Acts of 1485 and 1489 tried to concentrate trade in English hands by forbidding certain imports from foreign ships. His overseas trade, essential for the economy, was concentrated on the Netherlands, but its Habsburg rulers made a habit of supporting opponents and from 1494 to 1496 he embargoed trade to stop this assistance. Even with the Magnus Intercursus in 1496 he could not achieve the English right to trade widely at fixed traditional rates. This forced him to use trade alliances as with Spain in 1489 to secure trade. His investment in the alum trade, vital to the cloth industry, complemented his support for shipbuilding and the Company of Merchant Venturers which controlled wool and cloth exports. About 60,000 woollen cloths were exported in the 1480s, rising to over 90,000 by 1500. They were the largest single source of royal revenue. Henry demonstrated an economic wisdom that enabled the continued resurgence of the kingdom.

Adapted from Terry Breverton, *Henry VII: The Maligned Tudor King*, 2016

EXTRACT C

Henry's chief activity in foreign trade was to encourage the export of cloth, so he attempted to promote and protect the industry at home. Numerous acts were passed to accomplish this, including the Navigation Acts, which amounted to a policy of protection. However, it is doubtful whether they really represent a consistent policy of economic nationalism. The king did not interfere with the privileges of the Hanseatic League in England and overlooked English interests when he used the cloth trade to put pressure on the Netherlands. The only thing he did not like about foreign merchants was the exemptions from customs payments they had extorted, and these he revoked; it did not concern him that they might deprive English merchants of some trade. Nevertheless, his measures greatly assisted commercial revival while their effect on customs revenue was small – in the five years after 1485 customs revenue averaged £33,000; twenty years later it was no more than £38,000.

Adapted from G. R. Elton, *England under the Tudors*, 1974

EXTRACT ANALYSIS

> **A LEVEL** Using your understanding of the historical context, assess how convincing the arguments in these three extracts are, in relation to Henry VII's contribution to economic growth in England between 1485 and 1509.

a Read each extract in turn. For each:
- Summarise the argument it puts forward in your own words.
- Using your own knowledge, make a short list of bullet points to support or challenge the argument.

b Using your answers to the above, plan your answer to the question.

> **AS LEVEL** With reference to Extracts A and B and your understanding of the historical context, which of these two extracts provides the more convincing interpretation of the role of Henry VII in economic growth in the years 1485 to 1509?

a Read Extracts A and B in turn. For each:
- Summarise the interpretation in your own words.
- Using your own knowledge, make a short list of bullet points to support or challenge the argument.

b Using your answers to the above, plan your answer to the question.

EXAMINER TIP

As you read each extract, try to decide what the overall argument is. You should always present this first in your answer, before looking more closely at any sub-arguments or specific detail.

EXAMINER TIP

After evaluating the views in each extract, you should provide a full paragraph of comparison. You will need to show which of the arguments you find the more convincing by using your own knowledge to support or criticise what is written.

6 Religion, humanism, arts and learning

RECAP

Religion in the reign of Henry VII

The function of the Church and churchmen

All English people belonged to the Catholic Church, under the spiritual leadership of the Pope in Rome.

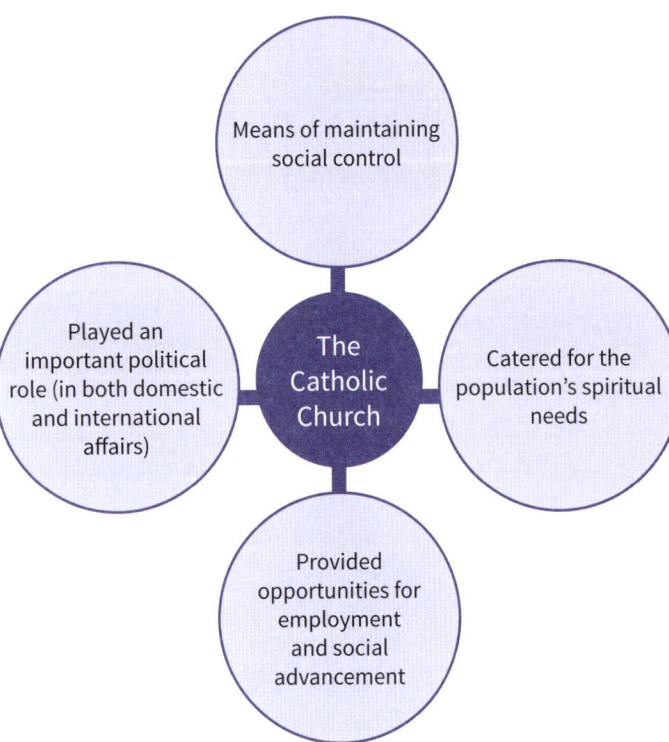

In England the Church was administered through the archbishops of Canterbury and York. There were also 17 dioceses, each under a bishop. The Pope was not expected to interfere in the running of the Church, and senior churchmen enjoyed positions of great political power and influence.

Religious community, belief and services

Religious experience was an essential part of daily life and the parish and its church was central both to personal religious experience and to community life. Lives were governed by religious festivals and the rituals of baptism, marriage and death. The threat of hell and **purgatory** (the limbo state when a soul had to be cleansed of sins before entering heaven) acted as a major influence on behaviour.

- The Church provided a framework for controlling thinking and behaviour; it reinforced allegiance to authority and particularly the monarch.
- It spread and upheld Catholic Christian teaching.
- It offered ways by which a person could acquire **grace** in order to reach heaven and minimise the time a soul would spend in purgatory (e.g. by observing the seven sacraments or going on pilgrimage).

The central religious experience came with the Mass, during which the priest would perform the sacrament of Holy Communion (**Eucharist**). Catholics believed that at the point where the priest consecrated the bread and the wine (i.e. declared them to be sacred), the bread and the wine were transformed literally into the body and blood of Christ, a process known as **transubstantiation**.

The Church's social role

The Church played an important role in the community. Lay people (non-clergy) might do the following:

- Donate towards rebuilding parish church buildings or pay for church objects.
- Leave money to the parish church in their wills (to enhance worship, perpetuate their memory and reduce their time in purgatory).
- Leave money for the foundation of **chantries** (chapels where Masses for the souls of the dead were said).
- Gather together in a **confraternity** (religious guild or lay brotherhood) to provide collectively for Masses or funeral costs of members, to help maintain church fabric, to make charitable donations, and to socialise.
- Take part in the practice of 'beating the bounds' on Rogation Sunday, walking around the parish boundaries and praying for protection for the parish.

Individual religious experience became increasingly important throughout the 15th century. This was emphasised in the writing of mystics, who believed in the personal communication of the individual with God.

Religious orders

These included the following.

Monastic orders:

- Around 1% of adult males were monks, living in some 900 monasteries.
- The Benedictine Order often had large houses; some operated cathedrals and their members often came from wealthier parts of society.
- Cistercian and Carthusian monasteries were frequently situated in more remote rural areas.

Friars:

- There were three main orders (Dominicans, Franciscans and Augustinians).
- They worked among lay people and were largely supported by charitable donations.
- They were recruited from lower down the social scale than the larger monasteries.
- They were declining in importance by the late 15th century.

Nunneries:
- They usually enjoyed less prestige than monasteries (they were often populated by women considered unsuitable for marriage).
- They were often relatively poor.

The Lollards, heresy and anticlericalism

A small minority was critical of the beliefs and practices of the Church. Lollardy, which had first emerged in the late 14th century, following the teachings of John Wycliffe, continued in pockets around Britain. Lollards emphasised the importance of understanding the Bible and wanted it to be translated into English. They were sceptical about transubstantiation and the principles of the Eucharist, and viewed the Catholic Church as corrupt.

The burning of heretics had been introduced into English law in 1401, but few had died this way and by the late 15th century Lollardy was in decline, while other forms of **heresy** were rare. Criticism of the Church did exist, but **anticlericalism** was not widespread.

Humanism, arts and learning

Humanism and humanists

'Humanism' was a development of the 14th and 15th century **Renaissance**. It was concerned with establishing the reliability of Latin and Greek translations by going back to the original texts. It was an intellectual movement which affected religious teaching, politics and economics, but the impact was largely restricted to a minority of the educated nobility and gentry, and it made only a limited impression on England in Henry VII's reign.

English humanism was influenced by the visit of the Dutch scholar Desiderius Erasmus to England in 1499. Erasmus criticised Church abuses, and sought to regenerate Christianity through emphasis on education and rejection of some of the Church's traditional ceremonies. He associated with English humanists such Colet and More.

Key English humanists included:

William Grocyn
(c1449–1519)
Had discovered humanism in Florence
Lectured on Plato and Aristotle at Oxford

Thomas Linacre
(c1460–1524)
Had also discovered humanism in Florence
Influenced by scientific thinking; took medical degree in Padua

John Colet
(1467–1519)
Dean of St Paul's Cathedral
Refounded St Paul's School in 1512
Saw humanist scholarly approaches as a way to reform the Church from within

Thomas More
(1478–1535)
Distinguished lawyer and humanist scholar
His friendship with the Dutch scholar Desiderius Erasmus boosted humanist ideas under Henry VIII

Humanists patronised education and thus educational opportunities increased with the spread of grammar schools for the wealthy and the founding of new university colleges at Cambridge, e.g. by Lady Margaret Beaufort.

William Caxton brought printing to England in 1476, and printed everything from traditional medieval works such as Chaucer's *Canterbury Tales* to 'modern' versions of Erasmus. Printing meant that more texts became available, the language became more standardised, and literacy increased (while Henry also used the press for propagandist purposes). Although initially there was little direct connection between printing and humanism, printing allowed new ideas (e.g. the writings of Erasmus) to be more widely circulated, and by 1509 the works of humanist scholars had become more fashionable.

Other arts

Drama was popular with church-ale festivals, and troupes of players toured the country. The guilds of certain towns and cities performed mystery plays at the feasts of Corpus Christi, setting out simple moral and religious messages.

Music ranged from local wind groups that entertained the crowds on saints' days (sometimes with bawdy drinking songs) to the great choral performances in the country's cathedrals. Composers benefited from the patronage of important nobles and even the king.

Much building and rebuilding of parish churches occurred at this time. These included the major wool churches of East Anglia, such as Lavenham. These were built in the **Gothic perpendicular style**, which Henry VII approved in 1502 for the Lady Chapel at Westminster Abbey.

SUMMARY

- During Henry VII's reign the English Church was in a generally healthy state, with little dissent and generally cordial relationships between king and Pope.
- Humanism had begun to take root, but its major influence would not be felt until the reign of Henry VIII.

KEY CHRONOLOGY

Political events		International events and foreign relations	
1485	Henry VII becomes king after Battle of Bosworth	1487	French invasion of Brittany
1486	Lovell rebellion fails	1489	Treaty of Redon between England and Brittany
1487	Lambert Simnel conspiracy; defeated at Battle of Stoke Field		Treaty of Medina del Campo between England and Spain
1495	Perkin Warbeck lands in Kent; defeated, takes refuge in Scotland	1492	England invades France
			Treaty of Etaples between England and France
1497	Cornish Rebellion		
1499	Warbeck and Duke of Warwick executed	1496	Magnus Intercursus
1502	Death of Prince Arthur		Scotland invades England
1509	Death of Henry VII; accession of Henry VIII	1497	Truce of Ayton between England and Scotland
		1501	Marriage of Prince Arthur and Catherine of Aragon
		1502	Death of Prince Arthur
		1503	Marriage of Princess Margaret and James IV of Scotland
		1506	Treaty of Windsor
			Malus Intercursus
			Death of Philip of Burgundy (September)

APPLY

APPLY YOUR KNOWLEDGE

Look back at the sections on humanists and religious orders. Create a balance diagram, like the one below, to show which had the greater impact on society based on their numbers, the classes they were drawn from, and their influence on people.

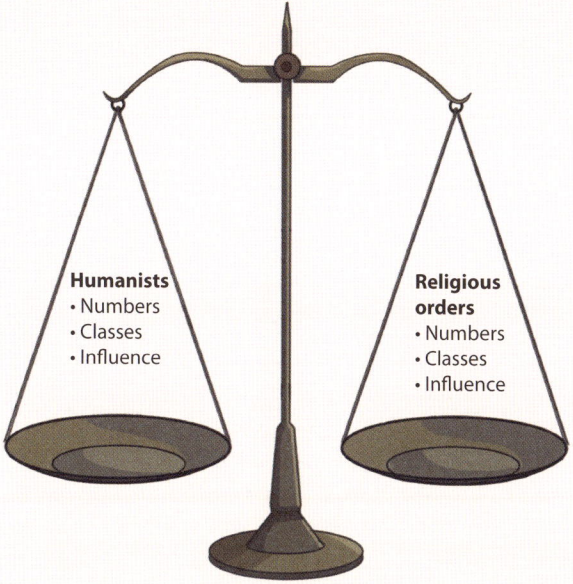

Humanists
- Numbers
- Classes
- Influence

Religious orders
- Numbers
- Classes
- Influence

> **EXAMINER TIP**
> When comparing the significance of 2 or more groups, always try to find criteria like this against which to compare them.

> **REVIEW**
> You might like to reflect on the weighting of each side. Should the scales remain perfectly balanced or tip in one direction? You may wish to review this balance when you deal with religion in the reign of Henry VIII.

ASSESS THE VALIDITY OF THIS VIEW

A LEVEL 'The years 1485 to 1509 were a time of stability for the Church in England.' Assess the validity of this view.

a To answer this question you will need to think about 'stable' in a variety of senses. Use the chart below to help organise your arguments.

Examples of the Church being stable	Judgement	Examples of the Church not being stable
•	•	•
•	•	•
•	•	•

b Now decide the argument you will adopt and write a suitable introduction to this question.

> **EXAMINER TIP**
> Remember, an introduction should make your view clear. In order to do this, you will also need to explain what you understand by 'stable'; perhaps discuss whether this means that there was no threat to the Church's position, or whether the threats were not really serious enough to threaten its stability.

> **REVIEW**
> You could follow up your work above by writing a plan for the whole essay.

REVISION PROGRESS

KEY QUESTION

One of the Key Questions asks:

How far did intellectual and religious ideas change and develop and with what effects?

a Read the chapter and identify 2 examples of change and 2 examples of continuity.

b Explain:

Change	Continuity
• the impact of the changes	• whether the changes outweighed the continuities.

EXAMINER TIP

Understanding 'how far' something changed is different from identifying changes. You need to think carefully when responding to any essay that asks 'how far' or 'to what extent' and try to be as precise as you can with your answer.

REVISION SKILLS

Change and continuity

Having studied Section 1, make a large revision chart on a sheet of A3 paper. For each chapter you should select and record no more than 6 key facts. These should be the most important in the chapter. When you have filled in the first row, try to identify the main points of change and continuity in the 2 rows below.

Topics	The consolidation of power	Henry VII's government	England's relations with foreign powers	English society at the end of the 15th century	Economic developments under Henry VII	Religion, humanism, arts and learning
Key facts to remember						
Change						
Continuity						

EXAM PRACTICE

AS Level essay sample answer

REVISION PROGRESS

REVIEW

On these Exam Practice pages, you will find a sample student answer for an AS Level essay question. What are the strengths and weaknesses of the answer? Read the answer and the corresponding Examiner Tips carefully. Think about how you could apply this advice in order to improve your own answers to questions like this one.

> **AS LEVEL** 'Henry VII was very successful in establishing his dynasty between 1485 and 1509.' Explain why you agree or disagree with this view.
>
> 25 marks

REVISION SKILLS

In the AS exam you will have to answer one essay question from a choice of two, from within the period 1485–47. The essays will each draw on material over at least 10 years, as this is a breadth paper. Read page 7 for details on how to master the essay question.

Sample student answer

Henry VII became king in 1485 by his victory at Bosworth against Richard III who had a far better claim to the throne. The claim of Henry and his family, the Tudors, largely relied on conquest. However, by 1509, Henry had passed on a secure crown to his only surviving son, Henry VIII, and so had established his family as the Tudor dynasty. This suggests the dynasty had been established; but to what extent was this due to Henry or due to other factors?

There were many challenges to the Tudor succession during Henry VII's reign. They came from men with a legitimate claim to the throne, such as the Duke of Buckingham, and imposters who pretended to have a right. Henry dealt with the legitimate claim of the Duke of Buckingham who had taken refuge in Burgundy. When the Duke of Burgundy had to land in England due to a storm, Henry persuaded that duke to return Buckingham to England. He defeated the impostor who pretended to be the Earl of Warwick in 1487 and also one who pretended to be Richard, Duke of York, one of the two princes in the Tower. He made two landings in Britain but was captured and executed. Henry therefore dealt with challenges effectively.

Henry also used marriage to establish his dynasty. By the leading member of the York family, Elizabeth, he had two male heirs. He married his children well, one to the King of Scotland and one to the King of Spain's daughter. He combined the white rose of York and the red rose of Lancaster to form the Tudor Rose, which represented his family. This helped reinforce the Tudor dynasty and meant that Henry had again dealt with the issue of establishing his dynasty successfully.

EXAMINER TIP

This introduction has a good focus on the question, gives a reasonable argument to support the view and shows an understanding of the key term 'dynasty'. The use of the rhetorical question should be avoided, though, and it would have been better to end the introduction with a clear statement of agreement/disagreement about Henry's own responsibility and some indication of the other factors to be considered.

EXAMINER TIP

This paragraph tends to be over-descriptive and yet lacks specific and clarifying detail, such as the names of the impostors. Nevertheless, the candidate shows understanding of the dynastic challenges faced by Henry and the final sentence links the material to the question.

EXAMINER TIP

This paragraph shows good understanding and some detailed knowledge. Although it would have been better to have made the concluding comment first – and then supported it – the material is linked to the question well.

41

Henry also established his dynasty by crushing potential opposition. He dated his reign from before the Battle of Bosworth. He used bonds and recognisances to blackmail the nobles into submission and to raise money, and did not allow Parliament to challenge him. However, it could be argued that Henry was lucky. It was Richard III's mistakes which led to Henry's victory at Bosworth and the failure of the Yorkists to organise proper opposition made it easier for Henry. Also, Henry was lucky that Henry VIII survived as, once his first son, Arthur, died, the king did not remarry and produce more heirs. So, the survival of the dynasty depended on one life and there were problems with the succession.

Overall, Henry Tudor was very successful in establishing the dynasty. Although he had luck – like the Duke of Burgundy's landing in England or the mistakes of the Yorkists – most of the reasons why Henry VIII and his children in turn succeeded were due to Henry VII's marriages, his control over the nobility and his military success in dealing with pretenders.

> **EXAMINER TIP**
> This paragraph provides some useful balance but, while it has focus, it covers the material in an undeveloped, list-like way.

> **EXAMINER TIP**
> The conclusion offers some judgement and provides a good summary of the essay. However, it, like the answer itself, is rather one-sided.

> **OVERALL COMMENT**
> The answer is generally well organised and shows understanding and awareness of relevant evidence. However, it is not always precise and points are not all clearly developed and explained. The balancing (disagree) factors are also extremely limited, so it is primarily a one-sided response. For this reason, this answer would reach no higher than the top of Level 3.

> **OVER TO YOU**
> Give yourself 45 minutes to answer this question on your own – take at least 5 minutes to sort out your ideas first. Then check to see if your answer avoids the mistakes of the sample student answer as shown in the purple Examiner Tips. Have you:
> - ❏ Provided a sentence linking to the question and advancing an argument at the beginning of each paragraph?
> - ❏ Supplied sufficient precise detail to support the comments you make?
> - ❏ Developed several 'balancing factors' and explained and argued the importance of these?
> - ❏ Made your view clear in a well-balanced conclusion?
>
> Now check Chapter 1 and Chapter 3. Are the details in your essay factually accurate? Have you missed any issues or details you should have included?

Henry VIII, 1509–1547

7 The character and aims of Henry VIII

RECAP

The character of Henry VIII

Henry VIII succeeded to the throne in April 1509, two months before his 18th birthday. In the seven years since the death of his elder brother, Arthur, he had been well educated for this role as king. He was well read and had been introduced to humanist ideas. He was charming and agreeable and produced a positive first impression.

The manner of Henry VIII's succession displays astuteness and ruthlessness on the part of the new king. The death of Henry VII was concealed for two days, while Prince Henry and some of the old king's councillors secured his position. Richard Fox, Thomas Lovell and Richard Weston established themselves in power and arranged the imprisonment of Dudley and Empson on the first day of the new reign. This was a popular move, which seemed to symbolise an end to the old ways of ruling.

Henry VIII's way of ruling was very different from his father's:

- He lacked a strong work ethic, enjoying courtly activities such as pageants, revelry, sports, hunting and tournaments.
- While he had little interest in the daily business of government, he could act decisively when he chose.
- He relied heavily on others – members of his Council and, at times, a chief minister (Wolsey or Cromwell).

Henry also exhibited certain character traits:

- ruthlessness and cynicism (for example in his execution of Empson and Dudley)
- insecurity (as demonstrated by his willingness to resort to execution for treason, often on flimsy excuses)
- impulsiveness (examples include the speed with which he married Catherine of Aragon, his later marriages to Anne of Cleves and Catherine Howard, and his decision to execute Thomas Cromwell – all of which he later regretted).

Henry believed in his own 'divine right' to rule and conformed to the practices of the Catholic Church.

The legacy of Henry VII

Henry VII's main legacy to his son was a full Crown coffer (around £300,000), but he also bequeathed a peaceful kingdom in which the nobility had been checked and the Tudor dynasty secured. Although some of his methods of raising revenue had been unpopular, his peaceful foreign policy and efficient government had helped to provide stability and a welcome respite after the Wars of the Roses.

The aims of Henry VIII's government

Henry's early aims related to establishing himself and preserving the best of what his father had left him, while marking out a new course as king.

Once his position was consolidated, his aims became less clear. Although always eager to pursue glory and secure the succession to the throne, he showed little interest in policy-making, except when it affected him personally.

The lasting effects of his reign, such as the growing importance of Parliament, the destruction of much traditional religion and the plundering of Church wealth, arose from circumstances and were not the results of a clear set of policy aims.

REVISION PROGRESS

Aim	Actions
Dismantle unpopular aspects of his father's legacy, while maintaining stability	Empson and Dudley executed; Council Learned abolished (Jan 1510); many bonds cancelled
Establish his status among European monarchs through marriage and preserve the dynasty (through expectation of an heir)	Married Catherine of Aragon (June 1509)
Support the nobility while preserving strong government	Nobles' sons became Henry's personal companions in sport, leisure and war – but their political influence was limited (e.g. Wolsey dominated as chief minister)
Establish himself as a warrior king through success in battle	Pursued military glory through war with France

SUMMARY

- Henry's accession in 1509 brought general rejoicing, as a new young, educated and charming ruler swept away the unpopular mechanisms of Henry VII's government.
- Henry had little interest in daily government but could act decisively and ruthlessly when he chose.
- In the early years, Henry's main aims involved establishing himself as king.
- For the rest of his reign, his aims changed according to circumstances, though his determination to achieve military glory and to secure the succession were recurrent themes.

APPLY

APPLY YOUR KNOWLEDGE

The following are 8 descriptions of either Henry VII or Henry VIII. Using your knowledge from this chapter, sort the statements to match the description of each king.

| Jousted with the nobility | Used a chief minister to help him govern | Oppressed the nobility | Fought hard to get rid of pretenders |

| Was prudent with money | Spent heavily on war and entertainment | Used councillors but never had a chief minister | Fought for glory and enjoyment |

REVIEW

Look back at Chapters 1 and 2 on Henry VII to help you make the comparison. This activity will help you answer an exam question on a comparison between the first Tudor kings by pointing out key differences in their approaches and political aims.

ASSESS THE VALIDITY OF THIS VIEW

A LEVEL — 'Despite their differences in approach, Henry VII and Henry VIII shared the same political aims.' Assess the validity of this view.

a Plan out your answer to this question. Write out the aims of each monarch, then identify any shared aims.

REVISION SKILLS

You might find it helpful to create a Venn diagram showing each monarch's aims and those which were shared. Use a second diagram, with 2 columns, to compare differences in approach.

b Now try to answer the question. Remember that in a complete answer, you would need to address differences in approach too.

8 Henry VIII, government and Parliament

RECAP

Government under Henry VIII

Henry had inherited a strong and efficient central and local government structure, staffed by able administrators. Some of these continued in office and Henry's early years saw a good deal of continuity. However, there were some changes after 1514.

- **1509–c1514: Government by the Council**
  - Conciliar government had broken down by 1514. This was because of disagreements between Henry and his councillors, e.g. over war with France, or Henry's preference to surround himself with younger courtiers.

- **c1514–29: Thomas Wolsey as chief minister**
  - From c1514, Henry relied on Wolsey to manage government effectively. Wolsey's influence was derived more from his close relationship with the king than from formal positions.

- **1529–32: Conciliar government restored**
  - Wolsey's downfall brought a return to conciliar government.

- **1532–40: Thomas Cromwell as chief minister**
  - Cromwell rose to power as chief minister by 1532 and dominated royal government for the rest of the 1530s.

- **c1540–47: Conciliar government restored in a new form**
  - Following Cromwell's fall, a new Privy Council emerged with fixed membership and recorded proceedings. In the Privy Council power lay with the conservatives.

Parliament grew in importance, particularly from 1529, when the so-called 'Reformation Parliament' (1529–36) dealt with Henry's divorce from Catherine of Aragon and reformed the Church. Henry also used Parliament to grant extraordinary revenue to finance his wars.

The role of the Privy Chamber was also extended in the early years of Henry VIII's reign when the king's 'minions' (young courtiers who enjoyed Henry's favour) became Gentlemen of the Privy Chamber.

Domestic policies under Wolsey (1515–29)

Thomas Wolsey was a churchman of humble origins. His organisational abilities (especially in the French campaign) impressed Henry and he rose to become Archbishop of York in 1514, a cardinal in 1515 and papal legate (the Pope's personal representative) in 1518. He was appointed Lord Chancellor by Henry in 1515; this put him in control of royal government and gave him immense power because all other courtiers had to go through him to speak to the king.

During the years of Wolsey's chancellorship (1515–29), domestic policy centred on strengthening royal authority and raising finance, particularly to support Henry's wars with France and Scotland.

As Lord Chancellor Wolsey was responsible for overseeing the legal system, promoting royal authority by enforcing law and order.

- He presided over the court of **chancery**, which he used to uphold 'fair' justice in problems relating to enclosure of open fields for sheep farming, contracts, and land left to others in wills.
- From 1516 he extended the use of the court of Star Chamber, which had been established as an offshoot of the king's Council during Henry VII's reign, making it the centre of both government and the legal system. It was used to increase cheap and fair justice and heard cases of alleged misconduct and private lawsuits.
- Local law officers were appointed to enforce royal law.
- The authority of the Crown over regional councils was extended.

Wolsey also oversaw the raising of finance for the king.

- Instead of using local commissioners to assess taxpayers' wealth for the raising of **subsidies** (parliamentary taxation/extraordinary revenue), he set up a network of royal commissioners appointed by himself.
- In 1525, when the amount of extraordinary revenue raised still proved insufficient to finance Henry's war in France, he tried to raise the so-called **Amicable Grant** of 1525. This was, in theory, a voluntary gift to the king from his subjects; in reality it was a heavy tax, levied without Parliament's approval. It led to widespread resistance and had to be abandoned.
- In 1526, he introduced the Eltham Ordinances. These ostensibly aimed to reduce royal household expenditure by reforming the Privy Chamber's finances, but through them Wolsey also succeeded in reducing the influence of the Privy Chamber.

The establishment of royal supremacy

The 'King's Great Matter'

The 'King's Great Matter' concerned the annulment of Henry's marriage to Catherine of Aragon; something which could only be granted by the Pope, Clement VII. By the mid 1520s Henry had no male heir (and only one surviving daughter, Princess Mary), and his wife Catherine was past childbearing age. Henry feared for the kingdom should he die without a male heir; he was also in love with Anne Boleyn, the niece of Thomas Howard, the Duke of Norfolk.

HENRY VIII, 1509–1547

KEY CHRONOLOGY

1525 Henry asked Wolsey to secure a papal dispensation for the annulment of his marriage to Catherine, providing biblical justification that his marriage to his brother's widow had been illegal in the sight of God

1527 Wolsey, as the Pope's representative, called a special court to 'try' Henry for living in sin with his supposed wife – to which Henry agreed. Catherine appealed to Pope Clement VII. However, the Pope was reluctant to cooperate, partly because Catherine's nephew, Charles V, Holy Roman Emperor and King of Spain, fiercely opposed such an annulment, and in May 1527, Charles' troops (who were fighting the papal-backed French in Italy) entered Rome, sacked the city and took the Pope prisoner

Two years of fruitless diplomacy followed, during which the Pope deliberately procrastinated

1529 The Pope finally sent an envoy, Cardinal Campeggio, to hear the case along with Wolsey in a legatine court. The hearing opened in June but Campeggio adjourned it in July, without agreeing to the annulment. In October, Wolsey was charged with **praemunire** (using papal authority against the Crown) and retired to Yorkshire, surrendering his possessions to the king

1530 In November Wolsey was arrested, but died before he could be tried and executed. Henry was determined to press ahead with his 'Great Matter'. He used scholars such as Thomas Cranmer (who was rewarded with the Archbishopric of Canterbury in 1532) to put the theological case for annulment

1531 The English clergy were collectively accused of *praemunire* and ordered to pay a £100,000 fine

1532 Thomas Cromwell had emerged as the king's chief minister, and he took matters in hand, passing a series of measures, and laws through Parliament, to release the king from papal control, and thus enable him to remarry with a clear conscience

- An act was passed withholding the payment of **annates** (taxes on first fruits and tenths – a tax paid to the papacy by clergy on taking up their appointments)
- The **Supplication against the Ordinaries** accused bishops of over-stating their power
- Cromwell organised the surrender of the Church's law-making function to the king (known as the **Submission of the Clergy**)

1533 By January, Anne was pregnant, so Cranmer conducted a secret marriage ceremony. In May, Cranmer annulled Henry's previous marriage, allowing Anne to be crowned queen. However, the birth of a daughter, Princess Elizabeth, on 7 September did not solve the problem of the succession

Acts of Parliament (1533–41)

From 1533, Cromwell passed a series of Acts of Parliament to establish royal supremacy.

Date	Act	Significance
1533 (April)	**Act in Restraint of Appeals** No appeals could be made to Rome against decisions of Church courts in England	Catherine could not appeal to Rome against her marriage annulment
1534 (April)	**Act of Succession** Annulled Henry's marriage to Catherine; vested the succession in Anne's children; to deny Henry's new marriage was declared treason	Princess Mary became illegitimate; hopes for male heir rested with Anne
1534 (Nov)	**Act of Supremacy** King declared Supreme Head of the Church in England	Pope's authority no longer recognised in England: the 'break from Rome'
1534 (Nov)	**Treason Act** Became treasonable to call Henry a heretic	Used against opponents of royal supremacy and brought down Thomas More, scholar, courtier and Lord Chancellor 1530–32 (executed 1535)
1534 (Nov)	**Act in Restraint of Annates** Allowed the annates (which had been withheld from the papacy by the 1532 Act) to be transferred from Pope to king	Strengthened the king's position; a special court was set up to administer this
1536 and 1541	**First and Second Suppression Acts** Dissolved the monasteries	Confiscation of Church land to the Crown vastly increased wealth and power of the Crown

Domestic policies under Cromwell (1532–40)

Thomas Cromwell was a lawyer, who had come to the king's notice while working under Wolsey. His skills, which engineered the break with Rome, became invaluable to Henry. It has been suggested that Cromwell's policies revolutionised government as he achieved the royal supremacy through Acts of Parliament, so enhancing its status. Furthermore, he helped give parliamentary law (statute law), precedence over Church law (canon law).

Cromwell developed a more 'modern' form of government, replacing the 'personal' approach of earlier kings with a more bureaucratic approach that involved creating departments, controlled by rules and procedures, for different areas. For example, the Court of Augmentations and the Court of First Fruits and Tenths, which were established to look after Henry's income from the Church, were subject to scrutiny and the careful auditing of all accounts.

Cromwell changed the composition of the Privy Council, reducing it to 20 men who took responsibility for the business of government. This increased efficiency and a higher value was placed on talent as opposed to reward for personal service or status within government.

Cromwell also negotiated further marriages for Henry. When Henry's relationship with Anne Boleyn broke down, Cromwell made the case for Anne's adultery. Her execution in May 1536 followed the death, in January, of Catherine of Aragon. Henry's third marriage was to Jane Seymour. Jane finally produced a male heir, Prince Edward in 1537, but died in childbirth.

Cromwell's fall followed the failure of Henry's fourth marriage, to the Protestant German Princess Anne of Cleves: a marriage the minister had arranged to suit his foreign policy. Cromwell was tried for treason and heresy and executed in July 1540, on the same day that Henry married Catherine Howard, niece of the Duke of Norfolk.

Government in Henry VIII's last years (1540–47)

Under a revived system of conciliar government, Henry's final years were dominated by conservatives anxious to halt further religious change, such as Stephen Gardiner and Thomas Wriothesley. Norfolk's influence was threatened following Catherine Howard's execution for treason in 1542 and the king's sixth marriage to Katherine Parr. As the king's health began to deteriorate, factional rivalries between those of differing political and religious views intensified in a bid to be able to control his successor. Norfolk escaped execution by the timely death of the king in January 1547. The leading contender for power was Norfolk's rival Edward Seymour, the new king's uncle.

> **SUMMARY**
> - Henry VIII largely left the day-to-day running of the government to others, intervening when it suited him.
> - Periods of conciliar government were interspersed by government through a chief minister (Wolsey, c1514–29 and Cromwell, 1532–40).
> - The need to secure the succession gave rise to the 'King's Great Matter' – the annulment of Henry's marriage to Catherine of Aragon; this led to the breaking of the Church in England from the Church in Rome and the establishment of the royal supremacy.

APPLY

APPLY YOUR KNOWLEDGE

a. Create a timeline of the key events of the years 1525–34. Include the actions of the Pope in green and other events in black. Decide when you think the following key turning points may have occurred and plot these in red:

- Henry decided that Catherine would not have more children
- Henry decided that Wolsey would not get the divorce
- Henry decided to pressurise the Pope by increasingly hostile measures
- Henry decided that he must break with Rome to ensure the succession

b. Use the information in your timeline to address the question: To what extent was the break with Rome due to the Pope's opposition?

REVIEW

To remind yourself of the Pope's position in the Church, look back at Chapter 4.

EXAMINER TIP

A full answer would need reference to 20 years and require consideration of a range of factors. However, specific reference to the key turning points would be expected for high examination marks.

PLAN YOUR ESSAY

A LEVEL — How successful was Wolsey as the king's chief minister in the years 1515 to 1529?

In order to answer the question, it is important that you make clear the criteria against which you will assess 'success'. One way of doing this would be to identify the key aims of Wolsey as the king's chief minister. These aims might be referred to in the opening sentences of the paragraphs of your essay – so providing constant reference to the question and building up an argument.

a. Consider the following key aims and his successes and failures:
   - enforcing law and order
   - increasing royal authority
   - raising finance for the king
   - resolving the 'King's Great Matter'.

b. Plan an answer to this essay by comparing Wolsey's successes and failures in each aim.

c. Write the first sentence of each paragraph (excluding the introduction and conclusion) in full. These first sentences should show the direction of your argument.

REVIEW

This question does not address the 20 years that you would encounter in an A Level exam but practises important skills. Look forward to Chapter 11 to see how effectively Wolsey pursued his aims of making the law on enclosure fairer for the poor.

EXAMINER TIP

Remember that it is impossible to talk of 'success' without defining what success might look like. There are various ways of doing this, and in some essays it might be more appropriate to assess success in a different way, for example, in relation to the strength of the country or the well being of its people.

REVISION PROGRESS

EXTRACT ANALYSIS

Consider the following extract.

EXTRACT A

The changes in government under Cromwell were revolutionary, if that term may be applied to any changes which profoundly affect the constitution and government of a state even when no systematic and entire destruction was involved. The essential ingredient of the Tudor revolution was the concept of national sovereignty which Cromwell summarised in the Act of Appeals of 1533 by using the phrase 'this realm of England is an empire'. Previous kings like Edward I had claimed to rule an empire but the meaning here is different. Instead of a claim based on ruling a large extent of land, the Act said that Henry was the 'one supreme Head and King'. The royal supremacy over the Church virtually replaced the Pope in England by the king but the Reformation statutes demonstrate that the political sovereignty created in the 1530s was a parliamentary one. Cromwell's administrative reforms – like the Privy Council – provided the machinery for the new state he had started to construct.

Adapted from Geoffrey Elton, *England under the Tudors*, 1974

a Underline the key words of the extract that will help you to identify the overall argument which the extract puts forward in relation to Henry VIII's government.

b Underline (in a different colour) any references that it might be useful to quote in an answer, to illustrate this argument.

c Using the information you have identified above, write a paragraph in response to the question: 'Assess how convincing the argument in this extract is in relation to the existence of a Tudor revolution in government in the time of Thomas Cromwell.' In this paragraph, you should show your understanding of the argument with reference to the extract only.

EXAMINER TIP

This activity provides practice in the first step towards answering a full AS or A Level question. The next step would involve applying your own knowledge of the historical context to the arguments in the extract in order to respond to the instruction, 'how convincing …'. You will get an opportunity to practise this skill in Chapter 12.

REVISION SKILLS

Make a large chart to reflect the state of the government in 1547, as follows:

Area	Strengths	Weaknesses
Position of king		
Position of Parliament		
Government		
Succession		
Legal system		
Control of Church		

REVIEW

You can add more to your chart as you study Chapters 9, 10, 11 and 12.

9 Foreign relations and securing the succession

RECAP

Foreign relations

Foreign policy, 1509–14

Henry's early foreign policy demonstrated his enthusiasm to win military glory and make England a major player in international affairs. He was personally ambitious and believed he had a right to the French Crown.

KEY CHRONOLOGY

Foreign policy, 1509–14

1510	Henry entered an alliance (the Holy League), with Spain, the Holy Roman Empire and the papacy, against France
1512	Henry sent 10,000 soldiers to south-west France but Ferdinand of Spain failed to support the English who suffered defeat in Gascony
1513	Henry himself led a force to north-eastern France. He won the 'Battle of the Spurs' and captured Thérouanne and Tournai
	James IV of Scotland (allied to France) invaded England. He was defeated and killed at the Battle of Flodden, along with many of the Scottish nobility. This left the Scottish throne in the hands of the infant James V, with Henry VIII's sister, Queen Margaret, as regent

The results of the military campaigns of 1512/13 were:

- a huge drain on English finance
- trouble in Yorkshire, where resentment against taxation nearly led to another rebellion
- the loss of the French pension which Henry VII had won
- insignificant gains in France; Tournai was sold back to France in 1519
- peace with Scotland (which lasted until 1542).

A possible further campaign of 1514 was abandoned when Ferdinand and Maximilian made peace with France.

Foreign policy, 1514–26

Between late 1514 and 1526 Henry's foreign policy was inconsistent. Although Henry's younger sister, Mary, married Louis XII of France in 1514, the French king died in 1515 and was succeeded by Francis I, whom Henry regarded as a personal as well as political rival. The death of Ferdinand of Spain in 1516 and the accession of Charles V as Holy Roman Emperor and Spanish king also changed the balance of power in Europe; this affected Henry's actions.

KEY CHRONOLOGY

Foreign policy, 1514–26

1517	Charles V and HRE Maximilian agreed the Treaty of Cambrai with the French, leaving England isolated
1518	The Treaty of London was a personal achievement by Wolsey; England, France, Spain, the Holy Roman Empire and other smaller states signed a non-aggression pact
1520	Henry and Francis met at the 'Field of the Cloth of Gold'. This reinforced positive relations between England and France
1521	The Treaty of Bruges was negotiated by Wolsey with Charles V
1522	English armies invaded northern France but gained little; Parliament was reluctant to grant the extraordinary revenue to support the campaign
1525	Charles V defeated the French at the Battle of Pavia (Italy), but refused a joint invasion of northern France with Henry. Henry changed tactics and supported the League of Cognac, with France and the Pope, to counterbalance Charles's power in northern Italy

Foreign policy, 1527–40

From 1527 it was clear that Charles V was the dominant player in Europe. This made Henry's attempts to annul his marriage with Charles' nephew Catherine difficult, and domestic issues affected his foreign moves.

KEY CHRONOLOGY

Foreign policy, 1527–40

1527	Henry allied with the French in the Treaty of Amiens
1532	Henry formed a further alliance with France, in an attempt to pressurise Charles into supporting Henry's marriage annulment – but the tactic failed
1538	Henry's position was weakened: • Charles and Francis signed the Treaty of Nice, followed by the 1539 Pact of Toledo when they each agreed to sever connections with England • Pope Paul III deposed Henry and absolved English Catholics from obedience to their ruler
1539	Paul III sent Cardinal Beaton to Scotland and Cardinal Pole to France to rouse support for a Catholic crusade against Henry
	Henry responded by marrying the German Protestant Princess Anne of Cleves, seeking an alliance with the Protestant League of Schmalkalden
	However this became unnecessary when relations between Charles and Francis broke down, making Henry's position more secure

Ireland

The Earl of Kildare had governed Ireland on Henry's behalf. However, a rebellion in 1534 proved difficult to suppress. The subsequent attempt to bring Irish government more directly under English control failed, and Ireland became an increasing expense to the Crown.

An invasion of the Pale by two Irish nobles in 1539 was eventually controlled, and in 1541 the government tried to pacify Ireland by:

- establishing it as a separate kingdom, under English law
- creating counties out of the Gaelic lordships
- granting the Irish nobles peerage titles and the same legal protection as their English counterparts.

However, the government lacked the resources to follow through with the reforms, there was no residual Irish loyalty to the English Crown, and after 1534 the emerging religious differences between England and Ireland complicated the situation.

Foreign policy, 1540–47

The 1540s saw Henry's return to an aggressive foreign policy.

> **KEY CHRONOLOGY**
>
> **Foreign policy, 1540–47**
>
> **1542** An invasion of Scotland brought heavy defeat for the Scots at the Battle of Solway Moss. The death of James V weakened the Scots, but Henry failed to mount a full-scale invasion
>
> **1543** By the Treaty of Greenwich, Henry's son, Edward, was betrothed to Mary, Queen of Scots. However, since the Scots refused to ratify the treaty, the Earl of Hertford was sent to raid Edinburgh, Leith and St Andrews; this achieved little
>
> **1544** Henry, in alliance with Charles V, invaded France in 1544 at the head of a large army. He captured Boulogne, but Charles made a separate peace with Francis I
>
> **1545** Francis I sent troops to Scotland to support an invasion of England. The English were defeated at the Battle of Ancrum Moor, Scotland, but the Scots failed to invade
>
> Another French force landed in the Isle of Wight; Henry's flagship, the *Mary Rose*, sank in the Solent
>
> The French failed to recapture Boulogne
>
> **1546** Peace was agreed between England and France, as neither side could afford to continue the conflict

Henry had paid a high price for his final pursuit of glory. Unable to fund the war from extraordinary revenue, he sold much of the Crown estate, borrowed large sums and debased the coinage, thereby significantly increasing the rate of inflation.

Securing the succession

The need to secure the succession led to a number of Acts of Parliament, each of which repealed its predecessor. Even the birth of Prince Edward in 1537 did not solve the succession problem, as by 1543 the king's failing health made it likely that Edward would still be a minor when he succeeded to the throne.

1534 Succession Act
- Declared Mary (daughter of Henry and Catherine of Aragon) illegitimate
- Stated that the succession would rest with Anne's children

1536 Succession Act
- Followed Anne's execution for treason
- Declared Elizabeth (daughter of Henry and Anne) illegitimate
- Stated that in the absence of a legitimate heir, the king could determine the succession by will or letters patent; this would have allowed Henry to legitimise his illegitimate son, the Duke of Richmond, but Richmond died in 1536

1544 Succession Act
- Re-legitimated Mary and Elizabeth
- Affirmed Henry's right to determine the succession by will or letters patent

December 1546 Henry's will
- Confirmed the succession arrangements
- Stated that if Edward, Mary and Elizabeth died without children the heirs of Henry's sister Mary, Duchess of Suffolk, should succeed
- Set up a Regency Council to act on Edward's behalf

> **SUMMARY**
>
> - Henry's early policy, while inconsistent and largely unsuccessful, was primarily driven by a desire to pursue military glory in France.
> - In the 1530s, the dominance of Charles V and the emergence of the 'King's Great Matter' changed the focus of foreign policy.
> - In the 1540s, Henry returned to an aggressive foreign policy, launching attacks on both Scotland and France.

APPLY

APPLY YOUR KNOWLEDGE

Below are listed 9 aims of Henry VIII in foreign policy, in no particular order. Look at these then complete the following tasks:

a In the diagram below, put the aims in the rank order of their importance from top to bottom and on each row left to right. Number them accordingly.

b Explain why you have chosen your most important aim in the 'why' box at the top.

c Explain why you have chosen your least important aim in the 'why' box at the bottom.

Henry's aims in foreign policy

- Military glory
- Land in France
- Trade
- Annulment
- Alliance with Protestants
- Attempting to outdo Francis I
- Conquest of Scotland
- Control of Ireland
- Succession

EXAMINER TIP

This exercise should provide useful supporting material for an essay on the success of Henry's foreign policy between 1509 and 1547.

REVIEW

To remind yourself of Henry VIII's aims, ideas and ideology, look back at Chapter 7.

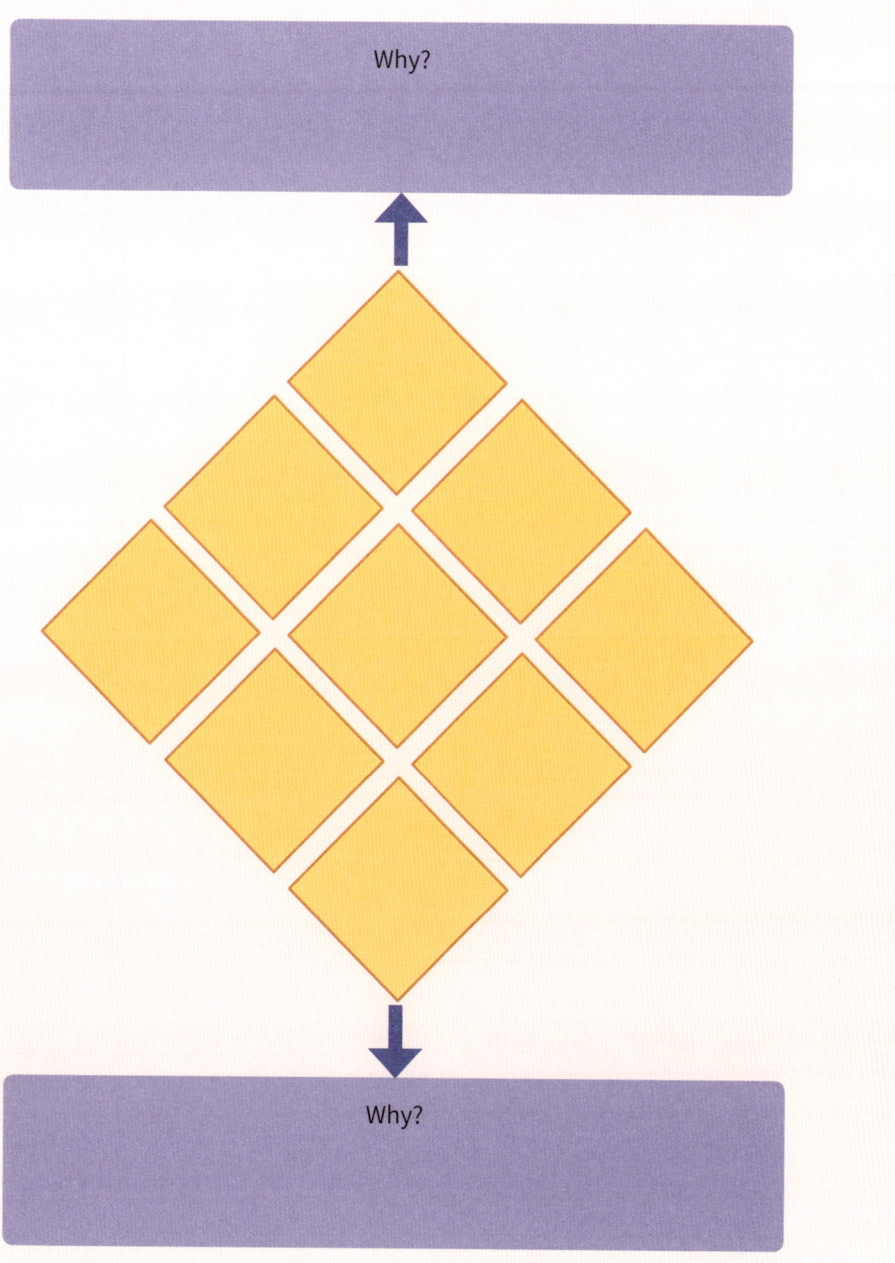

REVISION PROGRESS

ASSESS THE VALIDITY OF THIS VIEW

> **A LEVEL** 'Parliamentary legislation was more important than other factors in ensuring the succession of Edward VI in 1547.' Assess the validity of this view with reference to the years 1525 to 1547.

a This question requires an assessment of different factors, such as the actions of individuals, Henry VIII's will, securing peace at the end of Henry VIII's reign, and noble support, about which you are required to make a judgement on relative importance. Breaking the question down will help you to consider the evidence and formulate an opinion. Fill in the table below.

Parliamentary legislation		Other factors	
Acts of Parliament which determined the succession		Actions of individuals	
Other Acts which prevented challenges to the succession		Henry VIII's will	
Acts relating to religion which would make a Catholic succession difficult		Securing peace at the end of the reign	
		Gaining noble support for the Tudors	

b Study your chart carefully and choose 1 of the following judgements:
- Parliamentary legislation was more important than other factors in ensuring the succession of Edward VI in 1547.
- Other factors were more important than parliamentary legislation in ensuring the succession of Edward VI in 1547.
- Parliamentary legislation was of equal importance to other factors in ensuring the succession of Edward VI in 1547.

c Write an introduction to this question in which you convey your judgement.

> **EXAMINER TIP**
> Always take a little time before making a judgement. Diagrams that help you to separate factors often help you to formulate a view by showing the balance of evidence.

> **REVIEW**
> Look back to Chapter 8 for more information on relevant parliamentary legislation. For more on how Edward's succession was secured after Henry's death, look ahead to Chapter 13.

HENRY VIII, 1509–1547

EXTRACT ANALYSIS

Consider the following extract.

EXTRACT A

By the end of the 1520s, domestic politics replaced foreign policy as Henry VIII's top priority. It is not known when precisely he determined that he must sacrifice Catherine of Aragon to the cause of acquiring a male heir but, by 1529, Henry was devoting the bulk of his energies and those of his ministers towards obtaining a papal annulment of his marriage. The 'King's Great Matter' became the pivot around which foreign policy turned. Clement was still paralysed by the sack of Rome. Wolsey suggested war with Spain in 1528 but the nation lacked the means to wage it. Having failed utterly to secure the annulment by diplomatic means, Wolsey was dismissed as chancellor by Henry in October 1529 and replaced by Sir Thomas More. However, when Charles made peace with France and England in 1529, England was reduced to its previous and futile policy of trying to promote French hostility toward the Emperor as a means of pressuring Charles on the divorce issue.

Adapted from William Palmer, *The Problem of Ireland in Tudor Foreign Policy, 1485–1603*, 1994

a Use a highlighter to identify opinion (and potential bias) in this extract.

b Summarise the argument in this extract in 2 short sentences. (Try to avoid repeating the words used in the extract as you do this.)

c How might the argument in this extract be challenged?

PLAN YOUR ESSAY

AS LEVEL 'Henry VIII's government was strengthened by its international position in the years 1534 to 1547.' Explain why you agree or disagree with this view.

This question is asking you to account for the strength of Henry VIII's government from the break with Rome in 1534 to his death in 1547. It would be helpful here to produce a three- (rather than the more usual two-) column plan, so that you can consider not only the strengths of Henry VIII's international position, but also its weaknesses, as well as the part played by other factors. This plan should enable you to decide what view you will adopt.

a Complete the following table:

Strengths of Henry's international position 1534–47	Weaknesses of Henry's international position 1534–47	Other factors, e.g. the failures of domestic opposition

b You may want to address Henry's international position thematically or chronologically. Decide which approach you will adopt before you begin writing.

c Write a paragraph plan for this essay, showing how your argument will develop.

EXAMINER TIP

Ensure you are familiar with the chronology and make good use of dates in your answer. This is essential in breadth questions.

REVIEW

To remind yourself of the failures of domestic opposition and other possible factors, look back at Chapter 8. The failure of the main rebellion against Henry is covered in Chapter 11.

REVISION PROGRESS

10 English society in the reign of Henry VIII

RECAP

Elites and commoners

There was significant social change in Henry VIII's reign. This was partly the result of a growth in the numbers of those engaged in professional and commercial activities and partly because of greater social mobility. However, the actual structure of society remained much the same, with the nobles and greater gentry wielding political and considerable economic influence, while the rural majority experienced little change.

Henry relied on the landed elites (both nobles and gentry):

- He gave property and/or titles to nobles so that they could exert royal authority in particular areas (e.g. Suffolk was given property in Lincolnshire after the rebellion there in 1536).
- He ensured full support by executing nobles (such as the Duke of Buckingham in 1521) when there was any doubt of loyalty.
- He conferred knighthoods as a sign of royal favour.

The gentry provided Henry's justices of the peace (JPs) and often undertook unpaid administration for the Crown. This group grew considerably in the course of Henry's reign as more land became available, following the changes to the Church and dissolution of the monasteries. This offered opportunities to increase the size of landed estates and lease out farming land. The increased complexity of government also gave the gentry more opportunities to make their mark. Legal training became more highly valued and local administration was increasingly performed by lawyers rather than clergymen.

There was also a growth in the urban elites as towns and cities grew and the numbers of merchants and skilled artisans living by trade increased. The wealthy burgesses had a political voice in Parliament, to which they could be elected. For the semi-skilled and unskilled town workers, however, life could be tough, as food prices were subject to wild variations.

Most Englishmen continued to live in rural communities where they mostly worked as free self-sufficient peasant smallholders (husbandmen). Their standard of living changed little during the first half of the reign, but this varied by area, and distress (e.g. following a bad harvest or a change in agricultural practices) was never far away. Such problems became more acute in the later part of the reign.

With the royal supremacy and the greater availability of land (formerly belonging to the Church and monasteries), there was change. Some peasants acquired copyholds to land (paying a rent to members of the gentry who increasingly bought up landed estates in order to lease them out and make a profit). The more prosperous peasants bought land outright and increased the size of their holdings. Such entered the ranks of the yeomen, farming for profit rather than mere subsistence. These changes in the countryside were accompanied by an increased movement away from rural to urban communities as new opportunities opened up there.

Regional issues

Maintaining order in the regions on the borders of the kingdom was a continual problem for Tudor monarchs, and Henry VIII sought to impose royal control in Wales, Ireland and the North of England.

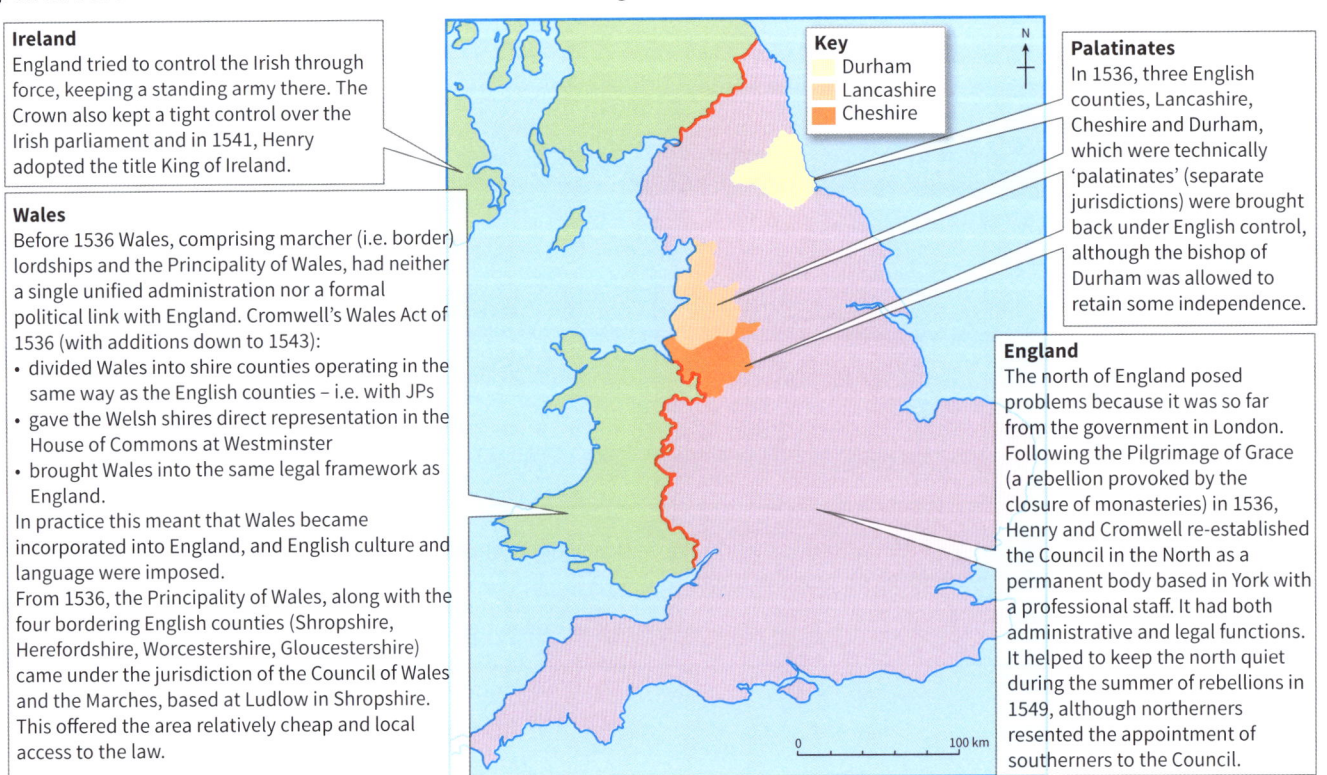

Ireland
England tried to control the Irish through force, keeping a standing army there. The Crown also kept a tight control over the Irish parliament and in 1541, Henry adopted the title King of Ireland.

Wales
Before 1536 Wales, comprising marcher (i.e. border) lordships and the Principality of Wales, had neither a single unified administration nor a formal political link with England. Cromwell's Wales Act of 1536 (with additions down to 1543):
- divided Wales into shire counties operating in the same way as the English counties – i.e. with JPs
- gave the Welsh shires direct representation in the House of Commons at Westminster
- brought Wales into the same legal framework as England.

In practice this meant that Wales became incorporated into England, and English culture and language were imposed.
From 1536, the Principality of Wales, along with the four bordering English counties (Shropshire, Herefordshire, Worcestershire, Gloucestershire) came under the jurisdiction of the Council of Wales and the Marches, based at Ludlow in Shropshire. This offered the area relatively cheap and local access to the law.

Palatinates
In 1536, three English counties, Lancashire, Cheshire and Durham, which were technically 'palatinates' (separate jurisdictions) were brought back under English control, although the bishop of Durham was allowed to retain some independence.

England
The north of England posed problems because it was so far from the government in London. Following the Pilgrimage of Grace (a rebellion provoked by the closure of monasteries) in 1536, Henry and Cromwell re-established the Council in the North as a permanent body based in York with a professional staff. It had both administrative and legal functions. It helped to keep the north quiet during the summer of rebellions in 1549, although northerners resented the appointment of southerners to the Council.

The social impact of religious upheaval

The religious upheaval of the 1530s had huge social consequences.

- In the short term, resentment at the dissolution of the monasteries and attacks on traditional Catholic practices was exacerbated by fears of an attack on parish churches. This led to a major rebellion, the Pilgrimage of Grace, in 1536.
- A huge amount of land was transferred from the Church to the Crown. This temporarily increased the Crown's wealth. However by 1547 nearly two thirds of the confiscated Church and monastic property had been sold off, often cheaply, to fund Henry's expensive foreign policy. This greatly increased both the size and the wealth of the landholding gentry.
- Education suffered, with the loss of monastery schools.
- Many monks and nuns became unemployed.
- Many monasteries had played a key role in their communities (e.g. offering jobs, welfare services, education and hospitals); this was all lost.

Rebellions

As in Henry VII's reign, taxation to pay for foreign wars caused unrest. There were complaints in Yorkshire in 1513 about the raising of a subsidy for Henry's campaigns and some demands had to be written off.

In 1525, there was widespread opposition to the Amicable Grant; e.g. 1000 people on the Essex–Suffolk border refused payment. The dukes of Norfolk and Suffolk faced around 4000 refusals and the king was forced to back down. Wolsey sought pardon for the protestors and the leaders were treated leniently. The unrest showed that Henry dare not press his people too hard – for his next invasion of France, he supplemented his revenue with the profits from monastic lands.

The Lincolnshire Rising and the Pilgrimage of Grace

Together, the Lincolnshire Rising and the Pilgrimage of Grace comprised the largest single rebellion in the history of Tudor England, with around 40,000 people involved.

- It began as a rising in Lincolnshire in early October 1536 and spread first into the East Riding of Yorkshire and then into parts of the West Riding.
- A second and more militant rising (the Pilgrimage of Grace) started in the Yorkshire Dales and spread west into Cumberland, Westmorland and north Lancashire, north into Durham and south-west into Yorkshire's West Riding of Yorkshire. The rebels there were more hostile towards the gentry because of the strength of their grievances against their landlords, sending out letters in the name of 'Captain Poverty'.
- Further rebellion broke out in Cumberland early in 1537.

Causes of the rebellion

The causes of the rebellion varied from place to place. There were secular motives but the main factor was resentment at Henry's religious changes, and particularly the dissolution of the monasteries.

Fears about dissolving the monasteries, e.g.:
- loss of charitable/ educational functions and the facilities/ services which monasteries offered
- loss of parish churches which were monastic properties
- fear that the north would be impoverished if monastic land was transferred to southerners

Fear for parish churches and traditional religious practices, caused by:
- Cromwell's Injunctions of 1536
- discouragement of celebration of locally important saints and of pilgrimage
- rumours that church plates and jewels, bequeathed by parishioners, would be confiscated and that parishes might be amalgamated

Religious motives → **Causes of the rebellion** ← **Secular motives**

Economic grievances, e.g.:
- resentment of taxation
- tenants' grievances (especially relevant for the extension of the rebellion into Cumberland and Westmorland)

The imposition of the Duke of Suffolk upon Lincolnshire as a magnate

A courtly conspiracy by former supporters of Catherine of Aragon, who:
- wanted to restore Princess Mary as heir
- exploited northerners' religious and financial concerns to pressurise the king

The Pontefract Articles provide the most comprehensive set of rebel demands. They incorporated a range of grievances:

- **religious**: including concerns from both common people and the clergy, and attempts to restore some of the religious houses that had been suppressed
- **regional**: including a call for Parliament to meet at York
- **specific**: such as resentment of Cromwell.

> **KEY CHRONOLOGY**
>
> **Lincolnshire Rising and the Pilgrimage of Grace**
>
> | 1536 | Oct | Lincolnshire Rising began |
> | --- | --- | --- |
> | | | Pilgrimage of Grace began in the East Riding of Yorkshire, led by Robert Aske |
> | | | Lincolnshire Rising ended by Duke of Suffolk's forces |
> | | | Northern rebels captured Pontefract Castle |
> | | | Rebels met Duke of Norfolk's forces; Norfolk offered a pardon and promised (falsely) that the dissolved monasteries would be restored and a free Parliament established |
> | | Nov | East and West Riding rebels dispersed |
> | | Dec | Royal proclamation offered a pardon to the rebels |
> | 1537 | Jan/Feb | Rebellion in Cumberland and renewed rebellion in the East Riding of Yorkshire was suppressed by Norfolk; **martial law** was declared and 74 rebels hanged (though thereafter lenient treatment was given) |

The Pilgrimage of Grace alarmed Henry VIII but did not slow the pace of religious change.

> **SUMMARY**
>
> - Henry VIII's reign saw some social change. Greater availability of land (following the dissolutions) opened up possibilities of enrichment and social mobility for both gentry and peasants; this was accompanied by a growth in the urban elites, as professional activities provided opportunities for advancement.
> - Measures were taken to create a unified state, including bringing Wales directly under Crown control.
> - Henry's religious changes, including the dissolution of the monasteries and attacks on traditional Catholic practices, caused immense social upheaval.
> - Protests against taxation, economic grievances and the unpopularity of the religious changes led to outbreaks of disorder in 1513 and 1525 and to full-scale rebellion in the Lincolnshire Rising and the Pilgrimage of Grace in 1536.

HENRY VIII, 1509–1547

APPLY

APPLY YOUR KNOWLEDGE

a To understand the difference between the social structure of Tudor society (which remained the same) and mobility within that structure, use the information in Chapter 10 to complete the following chart:

	Social change	Social structure
Nobles and gentry		
Urban elite		
Town workers		
Peasants		

b Based on your findings, which social group saw the greatest change during the Tudor period?

> **REVIEW**
> Look back to Chapter 4 to consider what the lives of peasants and town workers were like at the start of this period.

> **EXAMINER TIP**
> Even a category such as 'peasants' is quite broad and encompasses a variety of different experiences. Always try to be as specific as possible in your own writing.

ASSESS THE VALIDITY OF THIS VIEW

> **A LEVEL**: 'The key social development of the years 1509 to 1547 was the growth of the gentry.' Assess the validity of this view.

a When asked to address a 'key' development, it is important to consider what other developments occurred and to create a hierarchy of importance. Here are some of the social developments of the years 1509–47. Rank them in order of importance and add a brief comment alongside each to explain your choice.

- The gentry families of England and Wales rose to 5000 by 1540.
- The closure of 900 monasteries ended their charitable functions.
- The population of England and Wales rose from 2.1 million to 2.9 million.
- Monastic estates of 2 million acres (16% of England and Wales) were sold.
- Some peasants became yeomen or copyholders and capitalist farmers.
- Enclosure and engrossment turned many peasants into labourers or migrants.

b Use your findings to make a judgement as to whether you agree or disagree with the premise of the quotation.

c Look forward to Chapter 11 to select additional information that would be relevant in answer to this question, then plan and write the full essay.

> **EXAMINER TIP**
> Prioritisation is essential when analysing the importance of events and developments. Try also to show how such events and developments interrelate in your essay answers.

> **REVIEW**
> Look back to Chapters 4 and 5 to remind yourself of social issues under Henry VII.

EXTRACT ANALYSIS

For AS and A Level exam questions you will be given 2 or 3 extracts where you need to identify the interpretation given in each extract before deciding how convincing it is. This task helps you analyse one interpretation.

EXTRACT A

While the accumulation of capital by the wealthy merchants and gentry through the seizure of land by enclosure and engrossment continued, capitalism was secured by legal changes and the peaceful exploitation of the class who did not own land. However, there was opposition, such as the Pilgrimage of Grace. This appears to have been a reactionary, Catholic movement of the north, led by the still half-feudal local nobility and aimed against the Reformation and the dissolution of the monasteries. But if the leaders were nobles, the mass support for the rising indicated a deep discontent and the rank and file largely came from the dispossessed and from the threatened peasantry. The government had no standing army to fight the rebels and was saved only by two things. One was the support of the south and east. The other was the extreme simplicity of the rebels, who entered long negotiations with the government, during which their forces melted away and they were easily dispersed.

Adapted from A. L. Morton, *A People's History of England*, 1938

This extract might be used in a question asking you to assess how convincing its argument is in relation to the importance of social change in undermining feudal society.

a   To identify the author's argument:
   - try to pick out the part of the extract that puts forward a distinctive view on social change and how feudal society was undermined – this will be the overall argument
   - identify any other views/interpretations/arguments in the extract.

b   To assess how convincing the author's argument is:
   - find evidence that would support the overall argument and evidence that would contradict it
   - find evidence to support or criticise the other views/interpretations/arguments.

c   Now try writing an answer to the question which assesses how convincing the argument in the extract is, with reference to your own contextual knowledge.

HENRY VIII, 1509–1547

IMPROVE AN ANSWER

In an AS extracts question, you will be asked which of 2 extracts is the more convincing about the same theme. Here, you will be looking at the beginning of an answer on 1 extract – and since each extract will be shorter than those at A Level, you should read only the first part of Extract A, given on the previous page (as far as 'threatened peasantry' in line 8). This AS extracts question asks whether the extracts provide a convincing interpretation of the reasons for the Pilgrimage of Grace.

> **Answer**
> The extract's interpretation is that the Pilgrimage of Grace was non-religious. The extract says that society was becoming more capitalist and peasants were being forced to abandon their traditional feudal way of life at this time. This shows the impact of economic factors on social change and how everything was breaking down which led the pilgrims to rebel. The extract also says that although the nobles led the movement, the rank and file came from the dispossessed and threatened peasantry due to engrossment and enclosure depriving them of their land. So, this extract clearly shows the impact of economic factors on the Pilgrimage of Grace and its interpretation is very negative about society then.

> **EXAMINER TIP**
> A full answer would also need your own knowledge of context to support and criticise views.

Explain your views:

a Does this answer begin/end well?

_____
_____
_____
_____
_____

b What would you judge to be the overall strengths and weaknesses of this analysis (based on the extract only)? Could you improve on it?

_____
_____
_____
_____
_____
_____
_____
_____
_____

11 Economic development in the reign of Henry VIII

RECAP

Trade

English trade increased during the first half of the 16th century, with the encouragement of the Crown. The most important export was woollen cloth, and exports almost doubled during Henry VIII's reign. Broadcloths and cheaper fabrics, such as kersey (a lighter woollen cloth), were exported through London, although foreign merchants controlled much of this trade until the 1550s. Nevertheless the English company of the Merchant Adventurers flourished. They traded in finished cloth which was sent to their base in Antwerp (Netherlands) for dyeing and finishing, and they also controlled trade with north-west Germany. They enjoyed special privileges and in return provided the Crown with much-needed loans.

Other exports included Cornish tin, hides and furs, while wine was increasingly imported from the continent, reflecting the changing tastes and wealth of the social elites.

Exploration

Henry VIII made no attempt to build on the achievements of Cabot and the Bristol merchants at the end of the 15th century. Robert Thorne, a Bristol trader, continued his involvement in an Iceland and Newfoundland fishery but other merchants failed to procure royal support for exploration.

Prosperity and depression

Compared to earlier times, Tudor England seems to have been relatively prosperous. The woollen industry, most particularly in the West Riding of Yorkshire, East Anglia and parts of the West Country, grew in order to keep pace with increasing trade and demand. Tin mining in Cornwall, lead mining in the high Pennines and coal mining in north-east England also prospered, and new blast furnaces produced an increasing amount of iron ore in the Weald of Sussex and Kent. The growth of the population from around 1525 aided this prosperity as surplus labour could work in industry. Furthermore, debasement of the coinage (reducing the silver content), which was first attempted in 1526 and became more frequent in the 1540s (as the Crown tried to create more money to meet expenditure), created a short-term artificial boom in 1544–46 by putting more coinage into circulation.

Agricultural prices rose from the 1520s, increasing farmers' incomes. Enclosure (which increased farm size), new agricultural techniques (such as the rotation of crops and the breeding of superior cattle and sheep), and **engrossing** (amalgamating farms) benefited agriculture.

Industrial and agricultural growth did not, however, always bring prosperity for all.

- Bad harvests (e.g. 1520–21 and 1527–29) raised food prices. Food prices almost doubled across Henry VIII's reign. This brought urban poverty.
- In the countryside, some were made homeless on account of enclosure and engrossing. There was legislation to limit the practice in 1515; Wolsey established an enclosure commission in 1517, leading to some prosecutions; further legislation, in 1534, attempted to limit sheep ownership and engrossing. None of this was particularly effective.
- Debasement brought inflation and for many there had been a fall in real wages by the end of the reign as prices and rents rose.

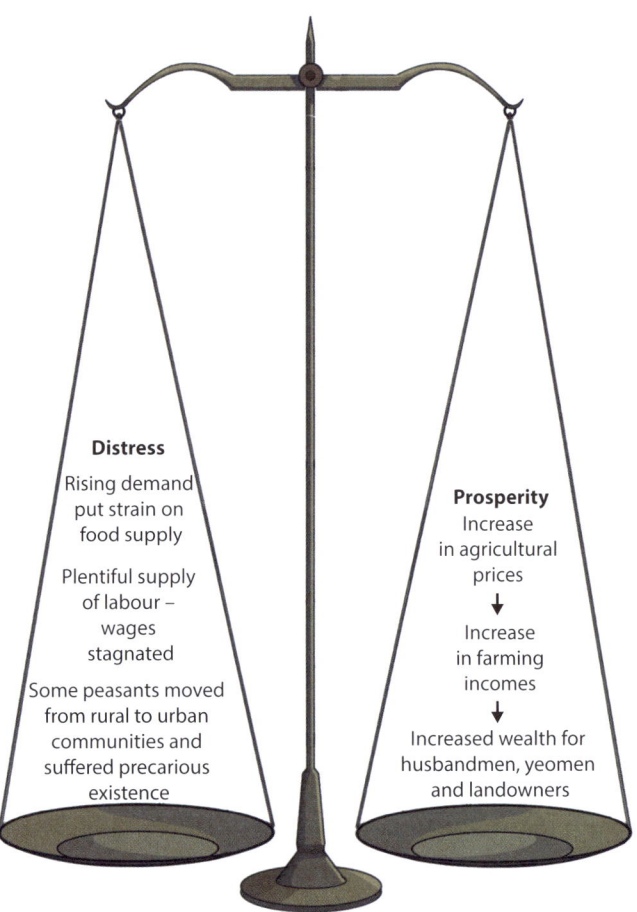

The impact of population growth

SUMMARY

- Trade (especially in cloth) increased under Henry VIII, though exploration was not pursued.
- Developments in the wool and cloth trade and in farming, coupled with a significant rise in population from 1525, brought prosperity for some; but much remained the same, and there were regular periods of depression.

HENRY VIII, 1509–1547   SB 63–123

APPLY

APPLY YOUR KNOWLEDGE

This activity enables you to contrast the achievements of Henry VII and Henry VIII in trade and exploration. Copy the diagram below and add underneath each monarch the key policies and developments in each area. When you have done this:

a Look across – which of the 2 areas was each monarch more interested in?

b Look down – which monarch made more advances in each area?

Henry VII: Trade	**Henry VII: Exploration**
Henry VIII: Trade	**Henry VIII: Exploration**

> **REVIEW**
> Look back at Chapter 5 to remind yourself about the development of trade and exploration under Henry VII.

IMPROVE AN ANSWER

AS LEVEL — 'Henry VIII failed to build on the successes of his father in his policies on exploration and trade.' Explain why you agree or disagree with this view.

Your work above effectively acts as a plan to answering this question. Here is an introduction to the question:

> **Answer**
>
> In 1509, Henry VIII replaced Henry VII as king; Henry VII had ruled for 24 years but his son ruled for 38 years. During Henry VII's time as king he did a lot for trade and exploration. He encouraged Cabot to discover Newfoundland. In trade he made lots of treaties where he helped trade, like the Intercursus Magnus. England's main trade was the wool trade and much of it went to Flanders. Henry VIII did help trade a bit during his time but as he ruled for longer than Henry VII, this meant that over the time he actually did more.

a • Identify the weaknesses in this introduction.
   • Identify the strengths.

b Write an improved version of this introduction.

> **EXAMINER TIP**
> The introduction should lead the reader into your essay so that what follows makes sense. Parts of this introduction are very detailed, yet not all is well-focused or clearly explained. Is your own version better?

> **REVIEW**
> See page 7 for further advice on how to write a good introduction to an essay.

12 Religion, ideas and reform

RECAP

Renaissance ideas

Humanism and education

Humanism gradually took root in schools such as St Paul's School, London (under John Colet) and Magdalen College School, Oxford, promoting a more secular education. At St Paul's, Colet appointed a humanist as head, chose as governors members drawn from a city guild rather than clergymen, and set out a curriculum that included works by Erasmus.

Similar concepts influenced the foundation of colleges at Oxford and Cambridge universities, e.g. Cardinal (later Christ Church) College, Oxford, founded by Cardinal Wolsey. By the end of Henry VIII's reign, humanist influences had gained a lasting hold on university curricula. University education or legal training thus came to replace the Church as the way to rise to prominence in politics. While Wolsey had been a cleric, Thomas Cromwell was a lawyer.

Erasmus visited England four times between 1509 and 1514; he was appointed as the first professor of Greek at Cambridge University, published a Greek New Testament complete with a new Latin translation in 1516, attended court, and was a friend of Fisher and More. He continued to visit England between 1514 and 1521, corresponding with his English friends while absent. His ideas, known as **Erasmianism**, influenced younger English humanists who were often described as 'Christian humanists', keen to establish the truth about Christian texts.

Henry VIII appointed humanist tutors to Prince Edward and Princess Elizabeth; and the king's sixth wife Katherine Parr, who had had a humanist education, gathered a humanist circle around her and patronised the arts and literature.

Renaissance ideas and English culture

Renaissance influence on English culture grew under Henry VIII:

Influence of the Renaissance in England:

- Classical learning spread as humanist groups formed in Oxford and Cambridge
- More schools became influenced by humanist approaches to education
- Henry VIII saw himself as a promoter of new ideas and of humanism
- English humanists became influential in government and the Church; the most important English humanist writer was Thomas More (Lord Chancellor 1530–32) who was both an intellectual and a lawyer and statesman
- Well-educated diplomats emerged, who could communicate elegantly with their counterparts abroad
- Visual culture (paintings, sculpture and architecture) combined Renaissance elements with traditional Gothic styles

Reform of the Church

Church doctrine and practices were changed between 1532 and 1540, with Henry VIII's reforms of the Church. Archbishop Cranmer played a major role in this, particularly after his appointment as Archbishop of Canterbury in 1532.

Weaknesses of the Church

The Church in England, like that on the continent, suffered from a number of abuses in the early 16th century:

- corruption, including pluralism (receiving the profits of more than one post), simony (buying Church office) and non-residence (receiving the profits of a post but being absent from that post)
- the corruption of the legal privileges of the clergy and clerical misconduct (which gave rise to some anticlericalism)
- worldly monasteries that no longer fulfilled their spiritual functions, leading Wolsey to dissolve around 20 houses in the 1520s.

Evidence of early English Protestantism

Martin Luther's attack on the Church in Germany from 1517 gave rise to Protestantism, with followers rejecting papal authority and believing in faith alone. German Protestants came to London and eastern England in the 1520s, and a group based in Cambridge included Thomas Cranmer. However, although their ideas attracted some Christian humanists, there was little committed attempt to spread Lutheran Protestantism before the 'King's Great Matter' brought discussion of religious issues.

Changes to doctrine and religious practices

Cranmer helped to reform Church doctrine with the support of Thomas Cromwell, although measures were quite hesitant at first. Protestant beliefs were introduced, such as:

- justification by faith (the belief that a person can achieve grace by faith alone, regardless of good works)
- consubstantiation (the belief that the bread and wine of the Eucharist are spiritually the body and blood of Christ without physically becoming so at the point of consecration – as opposed to the Catholic doctrine of transubstantiation).

These points of doctrine were the natural consequence of the break with Rome and the population was, often reluctantly, forced to accept Lutheran influences on their faith. As well as legislation, relics and images were destroyed and an English Bible was introduced.

Henry personally disliked the early moves towards Protestantism and was responsible (along with the conservative faction at Court, including Gardiner, Bishop of Winchester, and the Duke of Norfolk) for the Six Articles of 1539. At the time of Henry's death in 1547, the Church in England remained an odd mixture of Catholic and Protestant doctrine.

KEY CHRONOLOGY

1536	The **Ten Articles** stated that only three sacraments (penance, baptism and Eucharist) were necessary for salvation; praying to saints to forgive sins was rejected but confession was praised. This showed a mixture of Lutheran and Catholic influences
	The **first set of royal injunctions** pronounced against superstitious beliefs on pilgrimages, relics and images; they also required the clergy to teach parishioners about the Ten Articles and to teach the Lord's Prayer, creed and commandments in English
1536–40	Dissolution of the monasteries
1537	The **Bishops' Book** restored the other four sacraments (though at a lower status)
1538	The **second set of royal injunctions** ordered the removal of images, the continuance of baptisms, marriages and burials and the placing in churches of a large Bible in English. (The earliest English Bible had been published in parts by Tyndale 1525–26, but Coverdale printed the first complete English Bible in 1535)
1539	The first edition of the **Great Bible**, edited by Cranmer, was published by Coverdale, at Henry VIII's request. It was the first English Bible authorised for public use and was distributed to every church and chained to the pulpit
	The **Six Articles** reasserted Catholic doctrine and transubstantiation. (Two reforming bishops resigned)
1543	The **King's Book** revised the Bishops' Book – it was largely conservative, with some Protestant features
	The **Act for the Advancement of True Religion** restricted the public reading of the Bible to upper-class males

Dissolution of the monasteries

The dissolution of the monasteries was carried out for a variety of reasons but the lure of monastic wealth must have weighed strongly. Henry was conservative in his religious views and heavily opposed to the destruction of religious objects, so it seems unlikely that he was motivated by religious ideas, even if Cromwell and Cranmer were. Possible reasons for the dissolution are shown on page 66.

Spiritual reasons

Papal loyalty
Monks were loyal to the authority of the Pope in Rome

The monasteries were bastions of Catholic doctrine
Henry and Cromwell were keen to remove any chance of return to Catholicism on religious grounds

Perceived corruption
Some monasteries were seen as having poor standards of behaviour and piety

Non-spiritual reasons

Nobles' loyalty
Nobles' loyalty could be bought with land acquired from monasteries; they would entrench change and resist the restoration of papal authority

To finance Henry's army
A much welcome addition to the royal coffers (particularly since raising taxation could provoke rebellion)

Monasteries were outdated
The 1535 Poor Law provided support within villages, making monastic welfare outdated; printing reduced the need for scribes

Reasons for the dissolution of the monasteries

KEY CHRONOLOGY

1535 Cromwell set up the *Valor Ecclesiasticus*, a survey to assess the Church's wealth; four 'visitors' assessed monastic institutions, identifying any weakness or corruption (although they also gave some praise)

1536 Dissolution of the smaller monasteries (with an income of under £200 per annum)

1539 Dissolution of the greater monasteries (this had been carried out by March 1540)

Continuity and change in religion by 1547

Continuity

The hierarchy of the Church remained largely intact

There was little attempt to alter the interior of churches

Services remained largely traditional in form (they were still held in Latin and music was important)

The Six Articles Act in 1539 and the fall of Cromwell in 1540 weakened the cause of religious reform

Change

The jurisdiction of the Pope had been replaced by the more visible authority figure of the king

The monasteries had been dissolved – many monastic buildings fell into ruin and there had been a massive transfer of resources from the Church to the Crown through the dissolutions

Parish churches were required to possess Bibles in English

Religious doctrine had been influenced by Protestantism

SUMMARY

- Renaissance ideas in intellectual life and culture began to take hold during the reign of Henry VIII – humanism spread through schools and universities, and the king was influenced by humanist ideas.
- Between 1532 and 1547 Henry, Cromwell and Cranmer introduced sweeping changes to the Church, including the break from Rome, the dissolution of the monasteries, and the reform of traditional Catholic practices and (to some extent) doctrine.
- Despite the changes, some elements of the Church remained the same – Church structure was kept largely intact and the form of services remained mainly traditional.

KEY CHRONOLOGY

Political events

1509	Henry VIII becomes king; marries Catherine of Aragon
1514–29	Wolsey as chief minister
1532–40	Cromwell as chief minister
1534	Royal supremacy established
1535–40	Dissolution of the monasteries
1540	Henry marries Anne of Cleves; marriage quickly dissolved
1547	Death of Henry VIII

KEY CHRONOLOGY

International events

1512	First invasion of France
1513	Second invasion of France (Battle of the Spurs)
	War against Scotland; Battle of Flodden
1518	Treaty of London
1520	Field of the Cloth of Gold
1522–25	French campaign
1542	Invasion of Scotland (Battle of Solway Moss)
1544	Invasions of Scotland and France (capture of Boulogne)
1546	Peace with France

REVISION PROGRESS

APPLY

APPLY YOUR KNOWLEDGE

Below are 3 important groups from the years 1509–47. On the right are the names of some important individuals who influenced religious thought in this period. Match the individual to the group and give a one-sentence explanation of his contribution to the movement.

Desiderius Erasmus

Thomas More

Humanists

Thomas Cranmer

Catholic conservatives

Thomas Cromwell

Protestants/ reformists

Stephen Gardiner

> **EXAMINER TIP**
>
> It is important to be aware of the role of key individuals in developments. Knowledge such as this should help you to write more precisely in your essays.

HOW IMPORTANT?

A LEVEL — How important were the groups which opposed the Catholic Church in forcing change in the Church in the years 1509 to 1547?

a In the centre of a large sheet of paper, draw a box containing a list of changes in the Church between 1509 and 1547.

b Create a spider diagram around this box showing as many factors as you can think of, which helped to produce these changes.

c Highlight all the factors which relate to groups which opposed the Catholic Church.

> **EXAMINER TIP**
>
> Your diagram should help you to see the importance of the opposing religious groups (relative to other factors) visually, and so help you to reach a judgement.

> **REVIEW**
>
> For detail on the changes in the Church, look back to Chapter 8.

HENRY VIII, 1509–1547

KEY QUESTION

One of the Key Questions asks:

How important was the role of groups and how were they affected by developments?

To answer this in the context of religion, it would help to chart the development of the opposing religious groups in relation to the broader political, economic and intellectual developments in the years 1509–47.

a Look at the horizontal timeline of the 3 key periods of Henry VIII's reign: 1509–29, 1529–40, 1540–47. Record the key developments in the first 3 rows.

b In the 4th row, give the dates, names and key aims of the 2 opposing religious groups.

c Can you see a link between the growth of opposing religious groups and the political or economic situation? What intellectual ideas were affecting opposing movements at this time? Write 1–2 paragraphs giving a summary of how opposing groups were affected by the key developments of 1509–47.

REVIEW

If you find it challenging to note the key political, economic and social events and intellectual ideas, you should revisit Chapters 7–11 to consolidate your knowledge.

	1509–29	1529–40	1540–47
Political			
Economic and social			
Intellectual ideas			
Opposing religious groups			

REVISION SKILLS

You may find that making a visual diagram like this helps you to structure and remember key facts. Alternatively, you may find it more helpful to create a straight chart, with the developments in the 1st column and the 3 time periods in the 2nd, 3rd and 4th columns. Choose the revision method that works best for you – or use a variety of methods, to suit your own revision style.

REVISION PROGRESS

PLAN YOUR ESSAY

AS LEVEL 'Opposition to the Reformation of the Church in England failed in the years 1530 to 1547 because it lacked leadership.' Explain why you agree or disagree with this view.

In order to plan your answer effectively you will need to look at a variety of reasons as to why opposition to the Reformation failed.

a Create a mind-map of reasons.

b Colour all the reasons that link to the lack of leadership between the groups opposed to the Reformation in 1 colour.

c Use different colours to 'group' your remaining reasons, e.g. royal authority; succession, lack of external support; any other factors.

d Now use your colour-coded diagram to plan and write an answer to the question above.

> **EXAMINER TIP**
> Grouping factors in a suitable way helps to clarify the argument in an essay and grouping is often more successful than seeing each factor separately.

EXAM PRACTICE

AS Level extracts sample answer

REVISION PROGRESS

REVIEW

On these Exam Practice pages, you will find a sample student answer for an AS Level extracts question. What are the strengths and weaknesses of the answer? Read the answer and the corresponding Examiner Tips carefully. Think about how you could apply this advice in order to improve your own answers to questions like this one.

> **AS LEVEL**
> With reference to these extracts and your understanding of the historical context, which of these two extracts provides the more convincing interpretation of Henry VIII's actions towards the Church in England?
>
> **25 marks**

REVISION SKILLS

At AS Level, you will have to answer one extracts question which will be linked to two historical interpretations with different views. Read page 6 for details on how to master the extracts question.

EXTRACT A

Henry's greatest triumph was the establishment of supremacy over the Church, and we may doubt whether that would ever have happened had his fascination with Anne Boleyn not held him to his purpose against enormous odds. He decided to marry this woman no matter what the cost. One of the reasons was his need for legitimate children, but another was his belief in the sanctity of marriage. He was offended by loose sexual morality and criticised his sister, Margaret, when she abandoned her second husband. Until 1525 he was a conventional Renaissance prince, but thereafter his political and sexual needs drove him into uncharted waters, with extremely constructive results for the future of England.

Adapted from David Loades, *The Six Wives of Henry VIII*, 2009

EXTRACT B

Henry's failure to get rid of Catherine drove him onwards to attack Pope Clement and the Church in England, but this was not the whole explanation of his actions. There were two ideas present in his mind; one that he must procure a divorce; the other that kingship conferred on him a position in the Christian community which had been stolen by others, which he must recover. The Royal Supremacy grew with the divorce campaign, but was distinct from it. Had there been no divorce, or had Clement given up, there would probably still have been a clash between the Pope and a prince who, in the name of reform, was beginning to claim new spiritual authority.

Adapted from Jack Scarisbrick, *Henry VIII*, 1969

REVISION PROGRESS

Sample student answer

Both extracts deal with Henry VIII's actions towards the Church in England. I will explore each extract in turn and decide which is the most valuable explanation.

Extract A argues that it was Henry's 'fascination' for Anne Boleyn which drove him to marry her and so establish the Church of England. It supports this by arguing that his behaviour changed after 1525 and that Henry even criticised his sister for not keeping to her wedding vows. He needed to marry Anne not only to have 'legitimate' children but also because he believed in marriage. This in turn led him to take over the Church.

Certainly, some evidence confirms this view. Henry had been a 'Renaissance prince' before 1525, enjoying a carefree lifestyle and having at least two adulterous affairs. We know that Anne fascinated Henry as this is shown in their love letters, but Anne was not prepared to be his mistress and demanded that he marry her. This forced him to action. It was therefore Henry's 'sexual needs' which drove him to separate from Catherine and get involved in a process which led to the rejection of Papal authority and Henry's own headship of the Church in England.

However, the argument in this extract is limited because it overstates Henry's lust for Anne Boleyn as a motive for his actions towards the Church in England, and although it mentions that Henry fought against 'enormous odds', it fails to explain what these odds were. Another reason for Henry's actions was Catherine's failure to produce a son to protect the succession and establish a dynasty of Tudors.

Extract B, on the other hand, argues that 'Henry's failure to get rid of Catherine... was not the whole explanation of his actions' in attacking the Pope and the Church. More important was the fact that 'kingship' gave him a 'position in the Christian community' which he wanted to recover. The argument is that Henry's actions towards the Church in England were about 'authority' over the Church.

The extract argues that the decision to attack the Pope and the Church in England was about obtaining authority over the Church. Henry believed in the Divine Right of Kings, by which he was God's representative in England. He could therefore argue that he, and not the Pope, had the right to decide matters concerning the English Church. The reforming Archbishop Cranmer was able to provide documents to back Henry's claim to authority and this was

EXAMINER TIP

This first sentence simply repeats the question, but incorrectly uses the word 'valuable' instead of 'convincing'. There is no need for an introduction in an extracts question.

EXAMINER TIP

This paragraph correctly attempts a summary of the argument in Extract A. A more succinct summary of the interpretation would, however, have been, 'Henry was driven to take action to make himself Supreme Head of the Church of England by his determination to marry Anne Boleyn.'

EXAMINER TIP

This is a strong paragraph as it assesses the argument of Extract A with reference to relevant and reasonably detailed own knowledge.

EXAMINER TIP

This paragraph tries to introduce some balance to the evaluation of Extract A, but it never develops or explains the valid point about Henry struggling against 'enormous odds' and adds another factor somewhat randomly at the end.

EXAMINER TIP

This paragraph identifies the main argument of Extract B, showing some understanding, but it doesn't explain the interpretation and relies on overlong quotations.

EXAMINER TIP

This is a much better paragraph; it provides some explanation of the argument of Extract B and supports it with some contextual own knowledge.

an argument that was often used during the disputes over the divorce and the position of the Church.

The argument given in **Extract A** for Henry's actions towards the Church is the more convincing. Henry primarily took action to ensure his marriage to Anne Boleyn. This was why Wolsey was dismissed in 1529, and the final decision to separate from Rome was only taken once Anne Boleyn had got pregnant. Despite its emphasis on Henry's lust, the first extract is more convincing as it focuses on the king's marriage and the need for a male heir. Although the second extract suggests the need for a divorce was important, it also stresses Henry's desire for authority over his own Church. However, this seems to have been less a reason for action than an excuse. The timing of Henry's claims to supremacy suggests that the need for a divorce forced his actions and the arguments used to support this were of only secondary importance.

EXAMINER TIP

This final paragraph provides a convincing and well-explained judgement on the arguments in both extracts, with a substantiated judgement as to which is the more convincing. The good understanding shown here would help raise the level into which the answer is placed.

OVERALL COMMENT

This answer accurately identifies the key arguments in each extract and comments on them with the use of contextual own knowledge. Parts could have been fuller, however, with more development of own knowledge to both support and criticise what is said. The answer also lacks full explanations of some terms used in the extracts, such as 'enormous odds' or 'position in the Christian community'. However, the conclusion is good and shows substantiated judgement. Overall this answer would be worthy of a low Level 5.

OVER TO YOU

Take 5 minutes to read the extracts and sort out your ideas before answering this question within 40 minutes. Then, check to see if your answer avoids the pitfalls of the sample student answer as shown in the purple Examiner Tips. Have you:

❏ Used own knowledge to support the argument in each extract?
❏ Used own knowledge to criticise the argument in each extract?
❏ Ensured that all own knowledge is precise, specific and relevant?
❏ Explained the references and concepts in both extracts?

Now check Chapter 8. Are the details in your answer factually accurate? Have you missed any issues you should have raised?

PART TWO ENGLAND: TURMOIL AND TRIUMPH, 1547–1603

Instability and consolidation: 'the Mid-Tudor Crisis', 1547–1563

REVISION PROGRESS

13 Edward VI, Somerset and Northumberland

RECAP

Royal authority under Edward VI

The accession of a nine-year-old king in 1547 left the Crown insecure. Henry VIII's will had established a Regency Council that would govern during Edward's minority. Significantly, neither the arch-conservative Gardiner nor Norfolk, who was accused of treason and put in the Tower, was included.

Whether Henry named Edward Seymour, Earl of Hertford, the new king's uncle, as 'Protector' is not known, but it is possible he did so verbally. Whatever the circumstances, within days the Regency Council had delegated its power to Hertford, who awarded himself the title of Duke of Somerset and became Lord Protector (1547–49).

Administrators and lawyers

Religious conservatives such as:
Thomas Wriothesley (Lord Chancellor since 1544; made Earl of Southampton in 1547 by Somerset)
William Paulet (styled Lord St John – became first Marquis of Winchester in 1551)
Cuthbert Tunstall (Bishop of Durham)

Regency Council 16 members, supported by 12 more (who were to assist as required)

Religious reformers such as:
Edward Seymour (Earl of Hertford from 1537, Duke of Somerset from 1547)
Archbishop Thomas Cranmer
Sir Anthony Denny (MP for Hertfordshire)

The Duke of Somerset

Somerset rapidly promoted his own supporters and initially relied on:

- Archbishop Thomas Cranmer
- Sir William Paget (who had been one of Henry VIII's two private secretaries)
- John Dudley, the son of Henry VII's executed minister, Edmund Dudley; Dudley was created Earl of Warwick in 1547 (and Duke of Northumberland in 1551).

Somerset governed largely with members of his own household. He also controlled the Privy Chamber by appointing his brother-in-law, Sir Michael Stanhope, as Groom of the Stool and Chief Gentleman of the Privy Chamber, effectively making him the king's keeper. However:

- Public acceptance of Somerset's protectorate was uncertain; to stem disorder Archbishop Cranmer published 'On Obedience', to be read in parish churches, emphasising that disobedience to the king was a **mortal sin** (which could lead to damnation).

- Somerset created enemies among his former supporters through his arrogant and dictatorial manner:
  - Thomas Wriothesley, Earl of Southampton, was dismissed from the Chancellorship, losing his seat on the Privy Council.
  - Somerset's own brother, Thomas Seymour, conspired with Southampton to turn Edward VI against Somerset. Seymour was charged with treason in 1549. (Southampton was persuaded to denounce him, and was readmitted to the Privy Council.)
  - Henry FitzAlan, Earl of Arundel (Lord Chamberlain and one of the 12 'assistants' to the Regency Council) and William Paulet (Lord St John) objected to Somerset's dominance and plotted to unseat him.
- Somerset's policy failings – particularly his poor showing in the war against Scotland and his mishandling of rebellion at home in 1549 – weakened his position.

By autumn 1549, even Dudley (Warwick) was convinced that Somerset would have to go and joined the Earl of Southampton, the Earl of Arundel and Lord St John in a plot to remove him. In October, Somerset was arrested on the orders of the Regency Council and surrendered, having been promised (in a deal brokered by Cranmer) that no treason charges would be pressed against him. He was promptly committed to the Tower.

Dudley (Warwick) and Cranmer persuaded Edward to appoint some new religious reformers to the Regency Council and Privy Chamber. When Southampton tried to regain predominance, by charging Dudley with treason, the scheme backfired and Dudley had the religious conservatives Arundel and Southampton placed under house arrest. Dudley thus consolidated his power and in 1550 became Lord President of the (Privy) Council. Nevertheless, he sought reconciliation with Somerset and arranged his release and return to the Privy Council and Privy Chamber. In 1550 Dudley's son, John, even married Somerset's daughter, Anne. However, Somerset's double-dealing led to his re-arrest in 1551 and execution in January 1552.

The Duke of Northumberland

Dudley, who created himself Duke of Northumberland in 1551, initially tried to avoid the concentration of power that had caused Somerset's downfall. He made no attempt to re-establish a protectorate and presided as Lord President of the (Privy) Council.

Nevertheless, he moved away from conciliar government, and had William Paget, who had tried to draw up new guidelines, committed to the Tower in 1551. Although essentially more pragmatic and more capable than Somerset – for example he crushed the 1549 rebellions and brought some stability to the country – his record is mixed. He educated the young king in government and, like Edward, supported Protestant reform and the work of Cranmer. However, he was not universally popular and his power entirely rested on Edward's survival.

Problems of succession

Edward's health declined rapidly in 1553. Under the 1544 Succession Act, as reinforced by Henry VIII's will, Princess Mary was next in line to the throne. However if Mary succeeded, Catholicism would be restored (and Northumberland, who had supported Protestantism, would be ruined).

Northumberland therefore encouraged Edward to write the *Devyse*, to alter the succession. In June 1553 both Mary and Elizabeth were declared illegitimate, in favour of the Protestant Lady Jane Grey (grand-daughter of Henry VIII's sister Mary), who was married to Northumberland's son, Guildford Dudley. However, before Parliament could ratify this, Edward died on 6 July 1553. Without parliamentary sanction the *Devyse* had no status. Nevertheless, on 9 July 1553 Northumberland proclaimed Lady Jane Grey as queen.

The Privy Council initially agreed to this, but when the crews aboard Northumberland's ships, sent to prevent Mary sailing from Norfolk (where she was residing), changed allegiance, the cause was lost. Most of the ruling elites deserted Jane and after nine days as queen, she and her husband were committed to the Tower. Northumberland was executed in August 1553 (and Lady Jane Grey followed in February 1554).

Relations with foreign powers

Somerset inherited a state of war with both Scotland and France (who remained joined in alliance), threatening security and the succession. Despite the costs, Somerset chose to continue this, hoping to unite the Crowns of England and Scotland through a marriage between Edward VI and the infant Mary, Queen of Scots.

Somerset's armies defeated the Scots at the Battle of Pinkie in September 1547, but it proved too expensive to garrison border forts and he failed to prevent the French from relieving Edinburgh. This allowed the French to take Mary to France in August 1548, to marry the heir to the French throne.

Somerset's military strategy had proved costly and unpopular. By 1549 England was threatened with a French invasion. Northumberland therefore negotiated peace: he abandoned the remaining English garrisons in Scotland and returned Boulogne to the French. He ended the wars – but at the cost of a humiliating climb-down.

> **SUMMARY**
> - The Regency Council established to govern during Edward VI's minority was sidelined as Somerset took control as Lord Protector. However, Somerset's dictatorial behaviour, combined with failures in his foreign and domestic policy, led to his arrest in 1549.
> - From 1550, the Duke of Northumberland ruled as President of the Council; he restored stability and made peace with Scotland and France.
> - Northumberland's attempt to alter the succession to prevent the accession of Princess Mary and the restoration of Catholicism failed following Edward's death in 1553.

REVISION PROGRESS

APPLY

APPLY YOUR KNOWLEDGE

Complete the flow chart of the political changes under Edward VI below.

a Fill in key events (as given below) chronologically, with dates.

b Write an explanation of how one event led to the next.

Key events:
- Mary became queen
- Henry VIII died
- Dudley (later Duke of Northumberland) became Lord President of the Council
- Earl of Hertford (later Duke of Somerset) became Lord Protector
- Edward wrote the *Devyse*, naming Lady Jane Grey as his successor

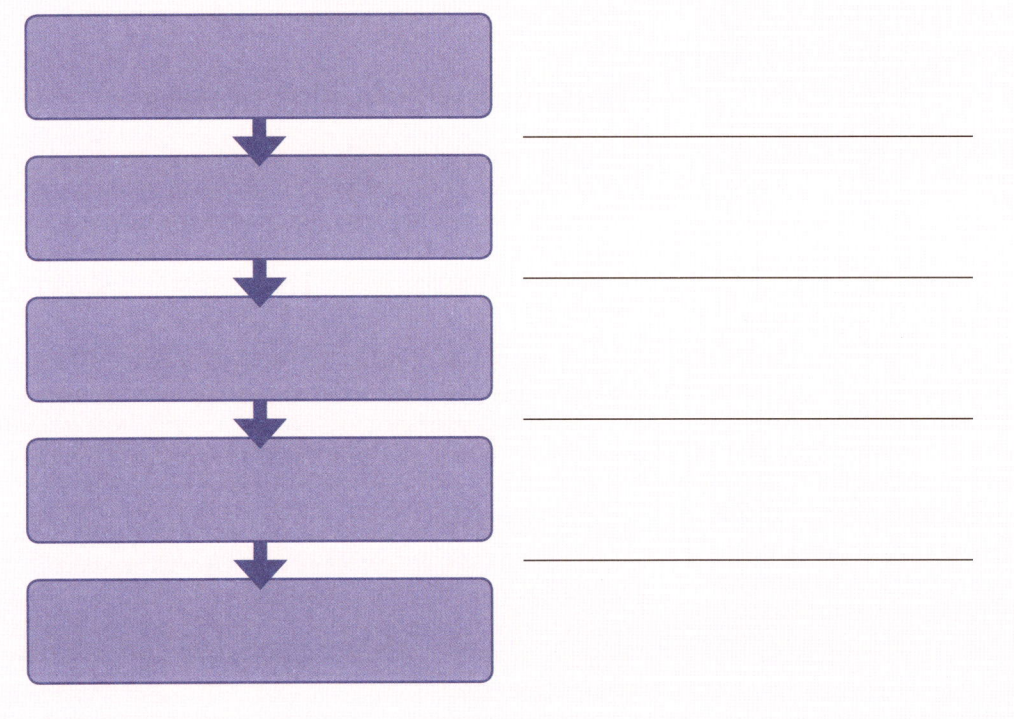

> **EXAMINER TIP**
>
> Although you will never be required to write a narrative account of events, it is very important that you develop a good grasp of chronology and understand how events relate to one another.

TO WHAT EXTENT?

A LEVEL — To what extent were Henry VIII's aims in foreign policy continued in the reign of Edward VI?

a For each, identify the ways in which Somerset and Northumberland:
- continued to carry out his aims
- partially continued to carry out his aims
- failed in or ignored carrying out his aims.

b Now plan and write an answer to the question above.

> **REVIEW**
>
> Look back to Chapter 9 for the full details of Henry VIII's foreign policy.

> **EXAMINER TIP**
>
> Part **a** should help you to plan your essay. Remember that Hertford (later Duke of Somerset) and Northumberland may not have shared exactly the same foreign policy aims.

INSTABILITY AND CONSOLIDATION: 'THE MID-TUDOR CRISIS', 1547–1563

KEY QUESTION

One of the Key Questions asks:

In what ways and how effectively was England governed during this period?

One way to study this issue for Edward VI's reign is to construct a spider diagram looking at how effective Edward was as king.

a Copy and complete the diagram opposite.

b Add labels to the lines coming from each reason that you have written, giving evidence for each reason. Add more lines and labels as required.

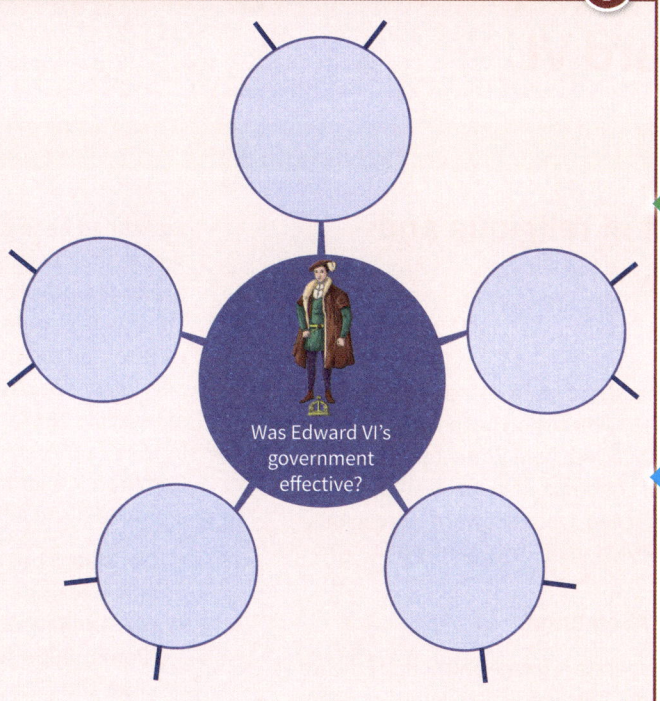

REVISION SKILLS

Spider diagrams are often used by students but many students simply add lines to show links. Annotating the diagram is essential for remembering the evidence that supports the links.

REVIEW

Before completing this chart, you need to look at Chapter 14 to see the religious and social changes under Edward VI.

IMPROVE AN ANSWER

Here is an example paragraph from a student answering an essay question asking:

> **A LEVEL** How significant was Henry VIII's legacy for the governments of Somerset and Northumberland?

> **Answer**
> Henry VIII was a king who transformed England in many ways; one of these was how he changed the Church and its relationship with the state. He wanted to divorce his first wife and so he took control of the Church. Although the Church's doctrine remained little altered, the Bible was translated into English and there was an English service, the Litany, in 1543. The monasteries were dissolved and their lands sold which required new government departments to be set up to deal with the income. After the execution of Cromwell for treason in 1540, the two main religious groups struggled for control over the government – factionalism therefore dominated with the Duke of Norfolk leading the conservatives and Edward Seymour, the uncle of the future Edward VI, leading the reformers. All of these changes show how significant the legacy was in terms of religion and the state that Henry VIII left to his son's two chief regents, Somerset and Northumberland.

a This paragraph is actually responding to a slightly different question from that actually posed. Can you suggest the question that would match the paragraph and explain what has gone wrong?

b Improve on this paragraph by linking it directly to the given question. You should not add to the evidence, but rewrite and reorder the commentary – expanding it a little if necessary.

EXAMINER TIP

Although it is important to reflect the words of the question in your answer, you need to do so in a 'thinking' manner, otherwise the meaning of the question can become lost.

REVIEW

Before attempting to write a full essay in response to this question, you will need to have studied Chapters 8–14.

REVISION PROGRESS

14 The social impact of religious and economic change under Edward VI

 **RECAP**

The social impact of religious and economic change

Religious change

Although the Church in England had been changed structurally by the royal supremacy, by 1547 there had been limited doctrinal change. There were churchmen who held Protestant views, such as Nicholas Ridley, Bishop of London; but in many areas religious beliefs had scarcely been touched. Under Edward VI, religious policy moved firmly in the direction of Protestantism.

Religious changes under Somerset

Somerset was, himself, a moderate reformer, although Edward VI had been brought up to favour more radical religious change.

- One of the first pieces of legislation passed in 1547 was a new Treason Act which allowed religious issues to be discussed and removed censorship. Protestant material could be brought into England legally for the first time.
- An Act had been passed in 1545 to dissolve chantries to secure their wealth. A subsequent Act was passed in 1547 to end the practice of masses for the souls of the dead.
- There was a spate of **iconoclasm** in London, leading to widespread destruction; the injunctions of 1538 against pilgrimages and other traditional Catholic practices were reissued in 1547.
- In 1549 Cranmer introduced the Protestant Book of Common Prayer to be used for all Church services and enforced by an Act of Uniformity. This:
  - translated the traditional services into English to enhance understanding of the key texts
  - was ambiguous in relation to the Eucharist (Communion service) using wording which might still allow the Catholic belief in transubstantiation.

Religious change under Northumberland

Northumberland favoured increasingly radical religious reforms for a number of reasons:

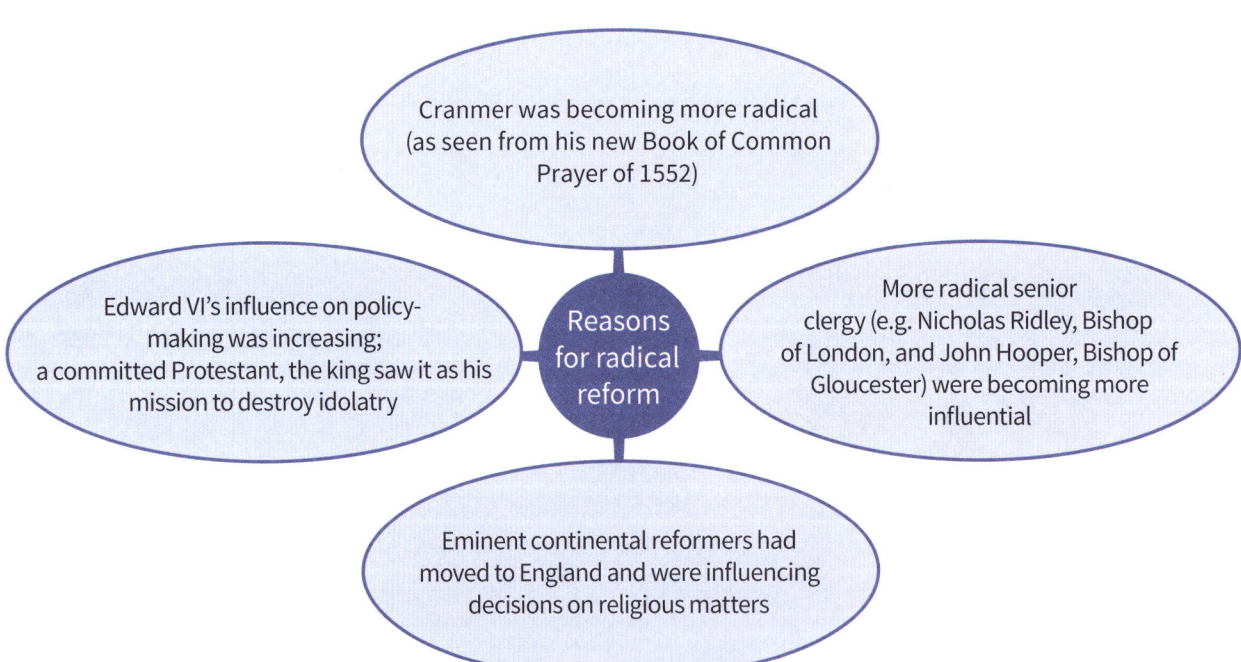

The religious changes included:

- The removal of altars and reforms to Church services, combining Lutheran and **Calvinist** elements (Calvinism being a more radical form of Protestantism put forward in Geneva by the French reformer John Calvin).
- The 1552 Book of Common Prayer (replacing that of 1549), accompanied by another Act of Uniformity. These:
  - removed remaining 'conservative' ceremonies
  - gave Protestant form to the baptism, confirmation, burial and Communion services (removing the ambiguity of the 1549 prayer book)

- banned traditional vestments (clergymen's clothes), introducing simpler replacements
- restricted Church music.
- Cranmer's Forty-Two Articles of Religion of 1553; these provided an official Protestant statement of doctrine (although Edward's death meant that they were never implemented).

Impact on society of the religious changes

Services became plainer and traditional religious practices declined. People became less inclined to leave money to their parish church, possibly for religious reasons but more probably on the basis that their bequests were likely to be confiscated. (The Church was slowly losing its wealth as land was taken from bishops and church property was seized.)

Traditional practices were not entirely destroyed; in 1550 the radical reformer John Hooper, Bishop of Gloucester and Worcester, admitted that the pace of reform was hampered by an uncooperative public. The survival of old beliefs is borne out by the speed with which traditional practices were re-adopted following the accession of the Catholic Queen Mary in 1553.

Nevertheless, the changes which took place during the years 1547–53 must have affected many people. For example, the loss of the charitable functions of monasteries and chantries, including care for the sick and elderly and the provision of education, would have impinged on many communities.

Economic changes

England's economic situation in 1547 was poor, following Henry's expenditure on war and inflation. Unemployment levels were high, partly because of the growth of the population at a time of increasing enclosure in the countryside and partly because of a fall in demand for English cloth exports in the 1540s. Both Somerset and Northumberland took steps to address the situation, including:

- Somerset's proclamation against enclosure and tax on sheep (which only harmed small farmers)
- debasement of the coinage (producing further inflation)
- Northumberland's commission to improve royal financial administration (although this took time to take effect).

Rebellion

1549 brought the Western Rebellion in Devon and Cornwall and major rebellions in East Anglia (particularly Kett's Rebellion in Norfolk).

The Western Rebellion in Devon and Cornwall was prompted in June/July by:

- **religious grievances**: the catalyst being the new Book of Common Prayer
- **the sheep tax**: seen as the imposition of an uncaring government in London hitting local farmers.

The rebels besieged Exeter but were defeated by Lord Russell's troops in August, and the revolt was suppressed.

In July, rebels led by the tanner Robert Kett captured Norwich. The rebellion was motivated by:

- hatred of local government officials
- resentment of enclosure
- local frustration about the maladministration of the Howards.

Somerset was forced to send an army under the leadership of John Dudley (Warwick). The rebellion was brutally suppressed and Kett was hanged.

There were other risings the same year, motivated by:

- inflation and high food prices
- religious grievances
- resentment of taxation.

Although they presented some danger, as Somerset was preoccupied in his dealings with Scotland and France, most died out quickly, either because of insufficient support or through prompt action from the local nobility and gentry. They did, however, contribute to Somerset's fall.

Northumberland tried to remedy the situation by ending the wars, reorganising financial administration, and passing a new Poor Law in 1552. This created a 'collector of alms' in each parish, responsible for a register of those eligible for Poor Relief.

Intellectual developments, including humanist and religious thought

The reign of Edward VI witnessed a contest between two reforming traditions: traditional Christian humanism (in the tradition of Erasmus) and a more radical approach to Protestantism (inspired by Calvinist teachings). Both sides published tracts (using the new printing press).

Stephen Gardiner had come from the tradition of Christian humanism. Its influences were also seen in much of Cranmer's work, although at times his thinking could be more radical. William Cecil (important in Northumberland's administration) encouraged humanist scholars at Cambridge and the humanist-influenced reformers Martyr and Bucer were invited to work in England (Bucer was appointed Professor of Divinity at Cambridge).

Opposing the moderates, reformers such as Hugh Latimer, court preacher 1547–50, wanted a complete change in religious doctrine and thinking. Northumberland also patronised Bishop John Hooper and the reforms of 1552 and 1553 suggested that the more radical Protestant movement was gaining ground. However, Edward VI's death destroyed both contending groups.

> **SUMMARY**
> - During Edward VI's reign, under both Somerset and Northumberland, England moved further towards Protestantism.
> - This led to significant social change (although many practices would be quickly restored after the king's death).
> - Religious change, combined with economic and agrarian grievances, provoked disorder in 1549 and two major rebellions, although stability was restored under Northumberland.
> - Christian humanism continued to flourish, but was increasingly challenged by more radical Protestantism.

REVISION PROGRESS

APPLY

APPLY YOUR KNOWLEDGE

Draw a mind-map to illustrate the impact of religious policies on England between 1547 and 1553.

> **REVIEW**
>
> When writing about the impact of religious policies on Edward VI's England, it is important to be aware of the changes that occurred as a result of Henry VIII's reformation of the Church (see Chapter 10).

EXTRACT ANALYSIS

A LEVEL Using your understanding of the historical context, assess how convincing the arguments in these three extracts are in relation to the impact of the religious reforms under Edward VI.

> **EXAMINER TIP**
>
> Although these extracts are narrower in their time-frame than would be found on a real examination paper, they nevertheless provide practice in important extract evaluation skills.

EXTRACT A

There were parishes where the Protestant reforms of Edward VI were embraced with ardour by those with influence. Even in communities where this was not so, the passage of time and the relentless push of Protestant policies had its effect. People sold off as much of their Catholic past as they could not hide or keep and called in carpenters to set boards on trestles and fix wooden forms around the Communion tables. Used to obedience, many of them accepted the changes as unavoidable. Four years of exposure to the matchless dignity of Cranmer's English services could not be without effect. Even men of profoundly Catholic convictions found themselves drawing on the rhythms of the new English Bible and prayer book to express their beliefs. Even for the traditionalists, nothing would ever be the same again. But when all that is said, in the majority of English villages, men breathed easier for the accession of a Catholic queen.

Adapted from Eamon Duffy, *The Stripping of the Altars*, 1997

EXTRACT B

What the effect of religious changes had been on the people at large by 1553 is very hard to gauge. One might guess that the short-term effect of any particular change would be negative; a change in a church service would create a good deal of resentment and gain few genuine converts. On the other hand, the long-term effect of officially-inspired Protestantism was bound to be considerable. The effects of Cromwell's vernacular bible were, under Edward VI, reinforced by the new services, gradually accustoming men to the idea that Protestant worship was not the anarchical practice of wild enthusiasts and reinforcing the evangelical beliefs fostered by scripture reading. Vested interests in the new order were increasing; those who had benefited from the sale of monastic lands were joined by the many priests who had taken the opportunity to marry. It is probably true that most people were not committed to either Protestantism or Catholicism, or even thought in such hard and fast terms. Political accident could determine England's religious future.

Adapted from C. S. L. Davies, *Peace, Print and Protestantism 1450–1558*, 1977

INSTABILITY AND CONSOLIDATION: 'THE MID-TUDOR CRISIS', 1547–1563

EXTRACT ANALYSIS

EXTRACT C

The regime of Protector Somerset has been regarded as relatively moderate yet its impact was devastating: the great majority of the decorations and rites found in English churches in early 1547 had gone by 1549. The churchwardens' accounts reveal that all the succeeding 'radical' administration of Northumberland had to do was to 'mop up' by revising the prayer book, replacing altars with communion tables and confiscating church goods. The new service was introduced in every parish within a year and the other reforms were just as thoroughly carried out. The churchwardens' accounts show that the great majority of people did not want the Reformations of Henry, Edward and Elizabeth. Catholic practices retained their vitality in the parishes until the moment they were outlawed, and few parishes acted in advance of instructions. The machinery of coercion and supervision deployed by Edwardian governments was so effective that for most parishes passive resistance to reformist changes was simply not an option for a largely Catholic population.

Adapted from R. Hutton, 'The local impact of the Tudor Reformations', in C. Haigh (ed.), *The English Reformation Revised*, 1987

a. Underline the single key statement of opinion in each extract about the effect of Protestant policies and identify the main argument.

b. For each main argument, supply 1 or more pieces of contextual own knowledge, to support and criticise that opinion.

c. What conclusion would you draw as to 'how convincing' each of the arguments is? Write a conclusion for each extract.

KEY QUESTION

One of the Key Questions asks:

How important was the role of key individuals and groups and how were they affected by developments?

It is important to understand the similarities and differences between the policies of Somerset and Northumberland. Using the following headings, write a sentence to compare the policies of each:

- Method of governing
- Attitude to Scotland
- Economic policy
- Social policy
- Attitude to France
- Religious policy

EXAMINER TIP

Comparing the policies of these 2 leaders will allow you to show an understanding of similarity and difference, which is a key concept that will add depth to your essays.

15 Mary I and her ministers

RECAP

Royal authority under Mary I

In 1553, faced with Lady Jane Grey's challenge, Mary acted bravely, decisively and quickly. She gathered Catholic supporters among the nobility and gentry and won over those who resented the brutality with which Kett's Rebellion had been suppressed. As a result she was proclaimed queen in July 1553. However, Mary was a committed Catholic in a kingdom where reforms in favour of Protestantism were well advanced. Furthermore, neither she, nor her most loyal supporters, had any real political experience.

Royal government under Mary

Although female, Mary was determined to play an active role in government. She selected a large group of Privy Councillors to help her in this, including Catholic nobles and churchmen, such as Bishop Stephen Gardiner, who became the Lord Chancellor until his death in 1555. She also called on the services of moderates from Edward's reign, such as William Paget. This brought some factional rivalry, although it provided Mary with some experienced officials.

However, the queen increasingly ignored the Council and turned instead to Simon Renard, the ambassador of Charles V and later adviser to Philip II. He acquired tremendous influence over Mary and, until her marriage to Philip of Spain in 1554, which he promoted, virtually directed English affairs. Mary also relied on Cardinal Reginald Pole, who arrived in England in 1554 and became Archbishop of Canterbury in 1556.

Mary and Parliament generally cooperated, with a few disagreements over Mary's religious policies and the succession:

Mary I

- A significant minority of MPs opposed the reversal of the Edwardian religious legislation
- MPs proved reluctant to restore ex-monastic property to the Church, out of concern for property rights (and probably self-interest)
- Parliament defeated a 1555 bill to allow the seizure of property of Protestant exiles
- There was opposition over the issue of the succession

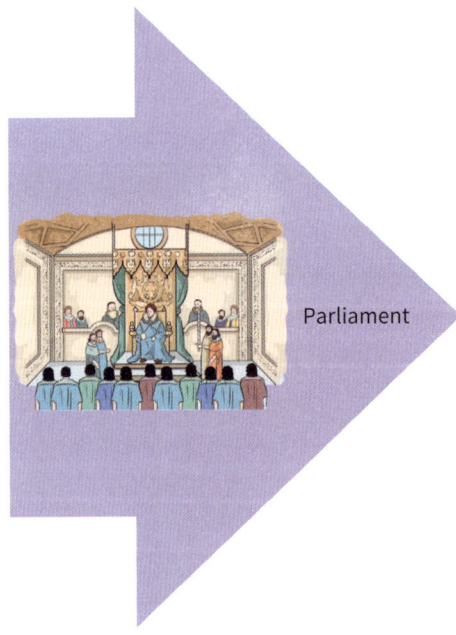

Parliament

Problems of succession

The Spanish marriage, 1554

Mary (who was already 37) wanted to marry and produce an heir as soon as possible in order to guarantee a Catholic succession.

- Gardiner suggested Edward Courtenay, Earl of Devon, but marriage to an Englishman was likely to provoke factional rivalry.
- Mary preferred her Catholic cousin, Philip of Spain (who received Paget's support), although English public opinion was hostile to a foreign marriage.

A parliamentary delegation failed to dissuade Mary, and, without consulting the Privy Council, Mary chose to go ahead with the Spanish marriage. A marriage treaty was agreed, as follows:

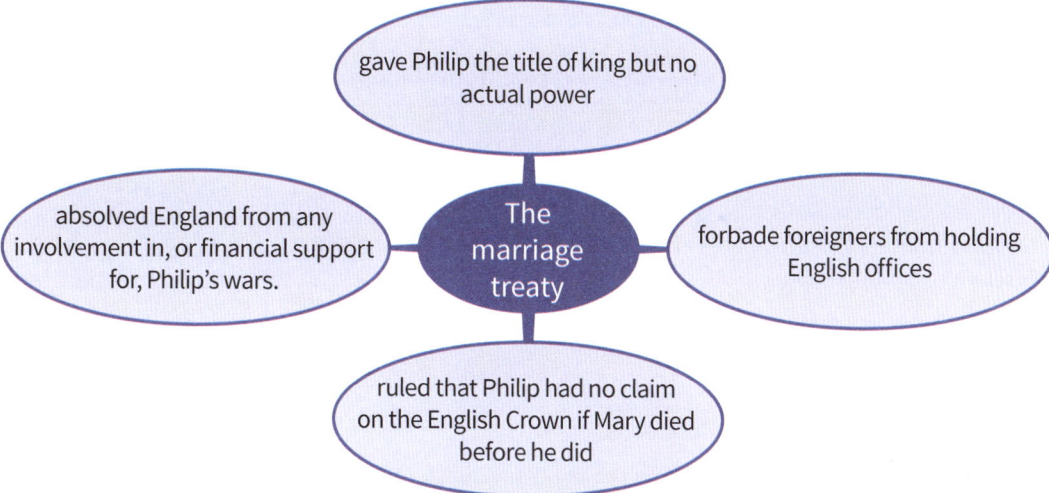

The marriage of 1554 was not a success.

- Philip found the English unwelcoming and was unimpressed by his new wife. He determined to spend as little time as possible in England.
- In 1554, Parliament rejected a bill that would have included Philip along with Mary in a proposed new law on treason.
- In 1555, Parliament prevented Philip's coronation as king.

Plans for the succession

The 1544 Succession Act, confirmed by Henry VIII's will, had provided that Mary would be succeeded by her half-sister, Elizabeth, should she die childless. However:

- Elizabeth was Protestant and likely to restore Protestantism.
- Mary resented Elizabeth as the reason for her parents' divorce. She personally believed that Elizabeth was illegitimate and without claim to the throne.

Although Mary confined Elizabeth to the Tower after a rebellion (Wyatt's) in 1554, no proof could be found of Elizabeth's involvement in that rebellion, and she was released (although carefully watched). Consequently, the childless Mary finally named Elizabeth as her successor on 6 November 1558, 11 days before she died.

Relations with foreign powers

The main influences on Mary's foreign policy concerned her desire to restore papal supremacy and to advance Philip's cause as her choice of husband. Both were achieved in 1554. However, the election of the fiercely anti-Spanish Pope Paul IV in 1555 led to renewed war between France and Spain. Despite the terms of the marriage treaty, Mary decided to support Spain, going to war against France (and, indirectly, the papacy).

Paget and others who hoped to gain credit through the war supported an expedition to northern France in 1557. Although the English successfully repulsed a minor invasion of England by the Scots the same year, the French campaign rapidly turned into a disaster, with the humiliating loss of Calais (the last English possession in France) in January 1558.

> **SUMMARY**
> - Mary's strength and determination helped her to capitalise on popular support and overcome Northumberland's attempt to alter the succession in 1553.
> - Inexperienced in politics, she relied on Catholic and moderate churchmen and councillors, and also on her husband (from 1554) Philip of Spain, Renard and Pole.
> - Her foreign relationships were largely unsuccessful: her marriage to Philip neither gained the approval of Parliament nor produced an heir, while her war against France ended in disaster.

REVISION PROGRESS

APPLY

PLAN YOUR ESSAY

A LEVEL How significant was Henry VIII's treatment of Catherine of Aragon for the failure of the marriage of Mary I and Philip of Spain?

To answer the question, you would have to consider a variety of reasons for the failure of Mary and Philip's marriage (looking at Henry VIII's treatment of Catherine of Aragon among these).

a Re-read Chapter 8 and consider how Henry treated Catherine of Aragon. You need to think of the implications for England's relationship with Spain.

b Review this chapter and make a spider diagram to show the reasons for the failure of the marriage of Philip and Mary, considering both the English and Spanish perspectives and showing links to the points you made in part **a**.

c Add numbers to show the most to least significant of your reasons.

d Using the information in the previous steps, create an essay plan to the essay question.

EXAMINER TIP

When answering a question like this, you would need to define what is meant by significant. It would also be helpful to think of long- and short-term reasons for failure.

IMPROVE AN ANSWER

Here is an example paragraph, on the years 1547–58, from a student answering an essay question asking:

A LEVEL 'England was better governed by ministers and regents than by monarchs.' Assess the validity of this view of the years 1513 to 1558.

> **Answer**
> The reigns of Edward VI and Mary provide a vivid contrast between the two forms of government. Edward as an infant had to rely on two regents, the Dukes of Somerset and Northumberland, whose periods of government almost led to disaster. They tried to exploit their position for their own advantage one way or another and they showed the problem of ruling by ministers when the ministers were self-seeking and plainly incompetent. On the other hand, Mary was a much more effective ruler of the country. She never employed a chief minister and so, despite qualms about her capacity to govern as a woman, she ultimately made all the key decisions herself. Her decisions, taken on the whole, were far better than those of Somerset and Northumberland and had she been spared beyond her 42 years, her decisions would probably have had time to become far more effective and permanent. This clearly shows that in the latter part of the period at least, monarchs were far more effective rulers than ministers.

a Identify the opinions that are being expressed in this paragraph.

b Identify the evidence that is provided to support these opinions.

c Suggest pieces of evidence which would support the opinions more effectively.

KEY QUESTION

This essay question is addressing the Key Question 'In what ways and how effectively was England governed during this period?'

REVIEW

Look back at Chapters 13–15, which provide information relevant to this activity.

KEY QUESTION

One of the Key Questions asks:

How did relations with foreign powers change and how was the succession secured?

The material in this chapter could be used to address this Key Question. Complete the Venn diagram below to show the ways in which Mary pursued her foreign policy and succession objectives during her reign. The overlap should show the ways in which the two objectives overlapped; other details within the circles should relate to the key area of policy concerned, using dates where relevant.

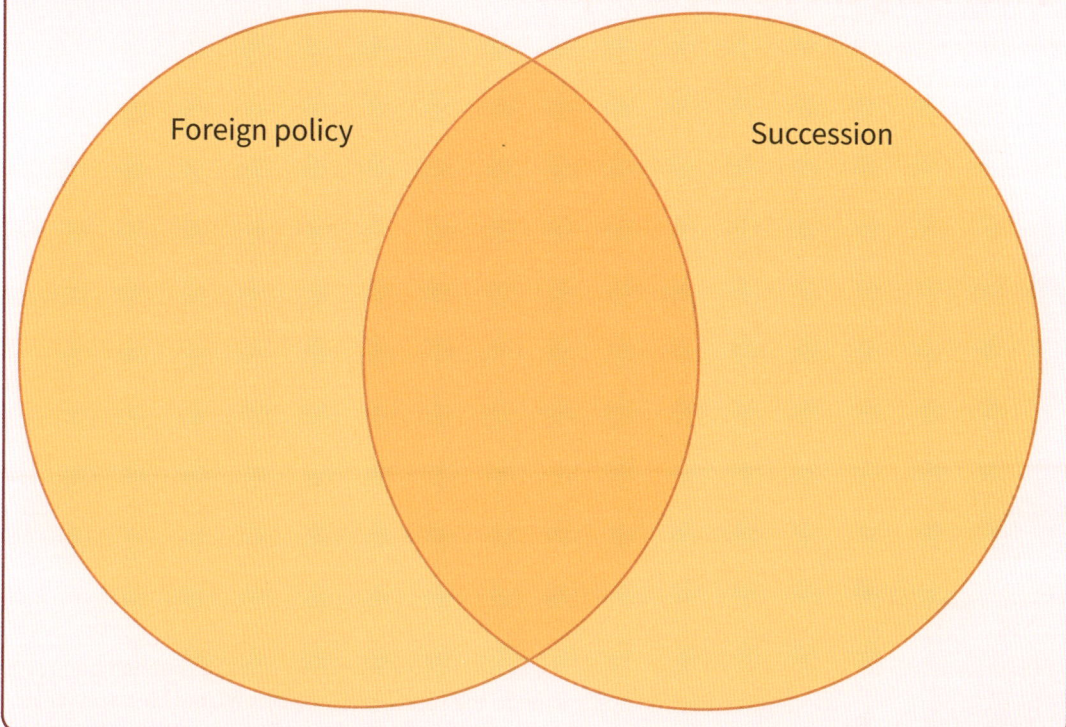

APPLY YOUR KNOWLEDGE

If you were required to write a breadth essay evaluating the importance of succession in foreign policy in the years 1534–58, you might include a paragraph assessing its role under Mary. Look at the material given in this chapter, and:

a Write an opening sentence for the paragraph which gives an overall assessment of the role of succession in foreign policy under Mary.

b Choose 4 pieces of relevant information which could be used to determine its importance in her reign.

c Write this paragraph in full.

REVISION PROGRESS

16 The social impact of religious and economic changes under Mary I

RECAP

Religious change under Mary and its social impact

Mary's greatest desire as queen was to restore the Catholic faith and Church in England. This desire was not unpopular. In many areas, local people began restoring Catholic practices even before Mary's government ordered religious changes, showing that Protestantism was far from entrenched in 1553. However, Mary proceeded cautiously as a number of problems had to be resolved.

Problem	Actions
A strong Protestant minority in London and other parts of the south Reformed Protestant Church of England had been established by statute law Many members of the political elites, on whose support Mary depended, had acquired Church land and had no desire to return it	**Beginning of reign:** • Some prominent Protestant clergy, including seven bishops, were deprived of their livings • Foreign Protestants were ordered to leave the country • Around 80 MPs voted against the religious changes of Mary's first Parliament **First Parliament (Oct 1553):** • Edwardian religious legislation was repealed but the legal status of the Church of England was upheld • The Church was restored to its state of 1547 • Clergy who had married could be deprived of their livings
Pope Julius III demanded that the Church submit to Rome *before* dispensations to landowners of ex-Church property could be granted	**1554:** • Pope Julius agreed not to try to claim back Church land that had been sold (this reduced opposition to the return of Catholicism from MPs and local landowners) • Cardinal Pole was sent to England, as legate and Archbishop of Canterbury, to facilitate a change to Catholicism
Act of Repeal provoked furious debates particularly directed against Pole Paul IV (Pope from 1555) dismissed Pole as papal legate, April 1557	**Third Parliament (Nov 1554 – Jan 1555):** • This restored the heresy laws (1554); these made it punishable by death to deny papal supremacy • Act of Supremacy (1555) made the Pope the leader of the Church again

Mary's key religious reforms

In 1553, Mary repealed earlier religious legislation and reinstated the Catholic faith. Under the heresy laws, Mary persecuted Protestants, including the Oxford martyrs (Cranmer, Ridley and Latimer). Around 280 Protestants (mainly men but also women) were burnt at the stake, most in the south-east and East Anglia. Because of this, Mary has become known as 'Bloody Mary'.

The persecutions under the heresy laws increasingly turned people against Mary. While facing opposition only from a small number of ardent Protestants at the beginning of her reign, by the end she was widely unpopular.

Other religious reforms

Pole tried to introduce reforms into the Church and increase the number of priests. He appointed new bishops, who were to reside in their dioceses, to preach and to oversee carefully the religious life of their parishes. He also proposed that each cathedral should have a seminary for training priests. However, Mary's reign was too short for these reforms to have much impact and while some areas (such as Catholic Durham and Lancashire) enthusiastically embraced his reforms, many others did not.

Economic change and its social impact

Mary inherited a serious economic situation in 1553, and this grew worse during her reign as inflation continued, culminating in serious distress in the years 1556–58. There was a series of bad harvests and the population suffered bouts of various epidemics, including the plague.

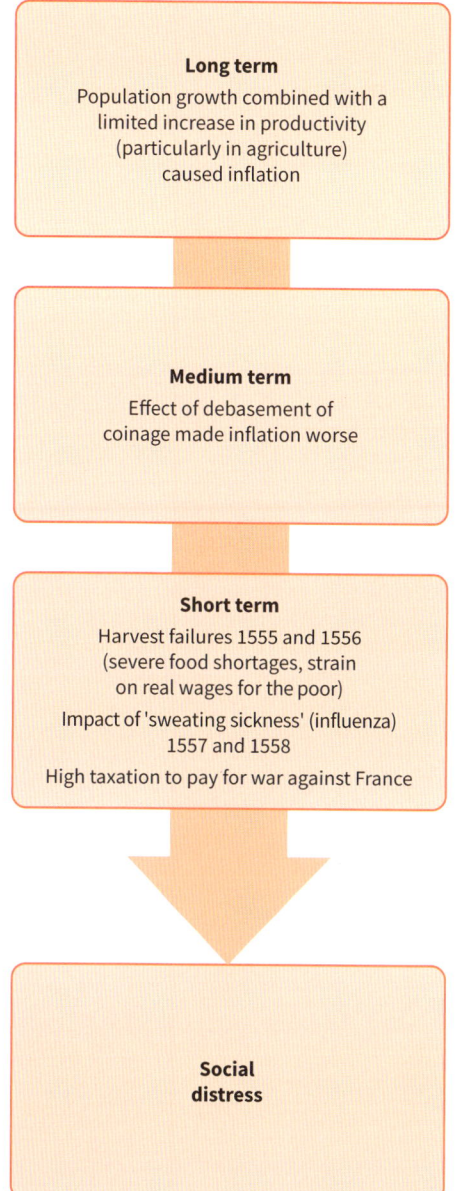

The government made some attempt to address the issues:

- 1556–58: re-coinage plans were drawn up (although not carried out until Elizabeth was queen).
- 1555: the Poor Law Act extended the Act of 1552 and ordered licensed beggars to wear badges; this was intended to encourage fellow parishioners into donating more alms for poor relief.
- Encouragement was given to the conversion of pasture land to crop farming.
- Movement of industries from town to countryside was discouraged in an attempt to reduce urban unemployment.

Not all measures were a success, however, and any benefits were not realised until Elizabeth's reign.

One area of economic success was in the reorganisation of the administration and finance of the navy; six new ships were built and others were repaired, laying the foundations for the powerful navy of Elizabeth's reign.

Wyatt's Rebellion

Mary's determination to marry Philip II of Spain produced a rebellion in 1553–54. Not only was there strong anti-Spanish sentiment in the country, some rebels were also provoked by Mary's religious outlook and determined to prevent pro-Catholic change. Social and economic grievances are also likely to have played a part. The rebels hoped to unseat Mary, in favour of either Elizabeth or Jane Grey, whose father was involved in the rebellion.

There were four simultaneous risings: in Devon (led by Edward Courtenay – Gardiner's candidate for Mary's husband), Hertfordshire, Leicestershire and Kent. However, the only serious rising was in Kent where Sir Thomas Wyatt raised a force of about 3000 men. Wyatt's rebels tried to march on London, but were repelled and Wyatt was forced to surrender within a month.

Although the rebellion failed, it demonstrated the extent of popular hostility to the Spanish marriage, and showed that Protestant religious opinions could not be ignored. It resulted in the execution of Lady Jane Grey and the imprisonment of Princess Elizabeth in the Tower of London. However she was released when it was proved that she had not been involved.

Intellectual developments, including humanist and religious thought

The reintroduction of Catholicism weakened the influence of humanism; Pope Paul IV regarded the Catholic humanist Erasmus as a heretic and banned Catholics from reading his books.

Religious thought was largely centred on Catholic reform at a parish level. Edmund Bonner, Bishop of London, published *A Profitable and Necessary Doctrine*, which explained the faith in a straightforward manner, and a new book of homilies.

Protestants, who were forced into exile, were divided in their thinking. Some were happy to use the 1552 prayer book and to operate within existing structures, while others (such as John Knox) wanted to move in a yet more radical direction.

> **SUMMARY**
> - Although most of the country remained Catholic in sentiment, the shortness of Mary's reign, coupled with a delay in restoring the structure of the Catholic Church, meant that Mary was unable to restore Catholicism fully.
> - Economic and social distress worsened under Mary I, culminating in severe hardship in 1556–58.
> - Wyatt's Rebellion demonstrated that neither Mary's foreign marriage nor her religious reforms enjoyed universal support; the kingdom remained divided.

REVISION PROGRESS

APPLY

APPLY YOUR KNOWLEDGE

Mary wanted to restore the Catholic Church in England but she encountered many obstacles. Nine of these are listed below, in no particular order. Look at these then copy the 'diamond 9' shape shown and complete the following tasks:

a Rank the obstacles in their order of importance from top to bottom and right to left.

b Explain why you have chosen your most important obstacle in the 'why' box at the top.

c Explain why you have chosen your least important obstacle in the 'why' box at the bottom.

Obstacles encountered in restoring the Catholic religion

- Protestant opposition
- Ownership of former Church lands
- Lack of papal support
- Married priests
- Reaction to persecution
- Need to repeal reforming legislation
- Influence of Church reformers
- Succession problems
- Shortness of the reign

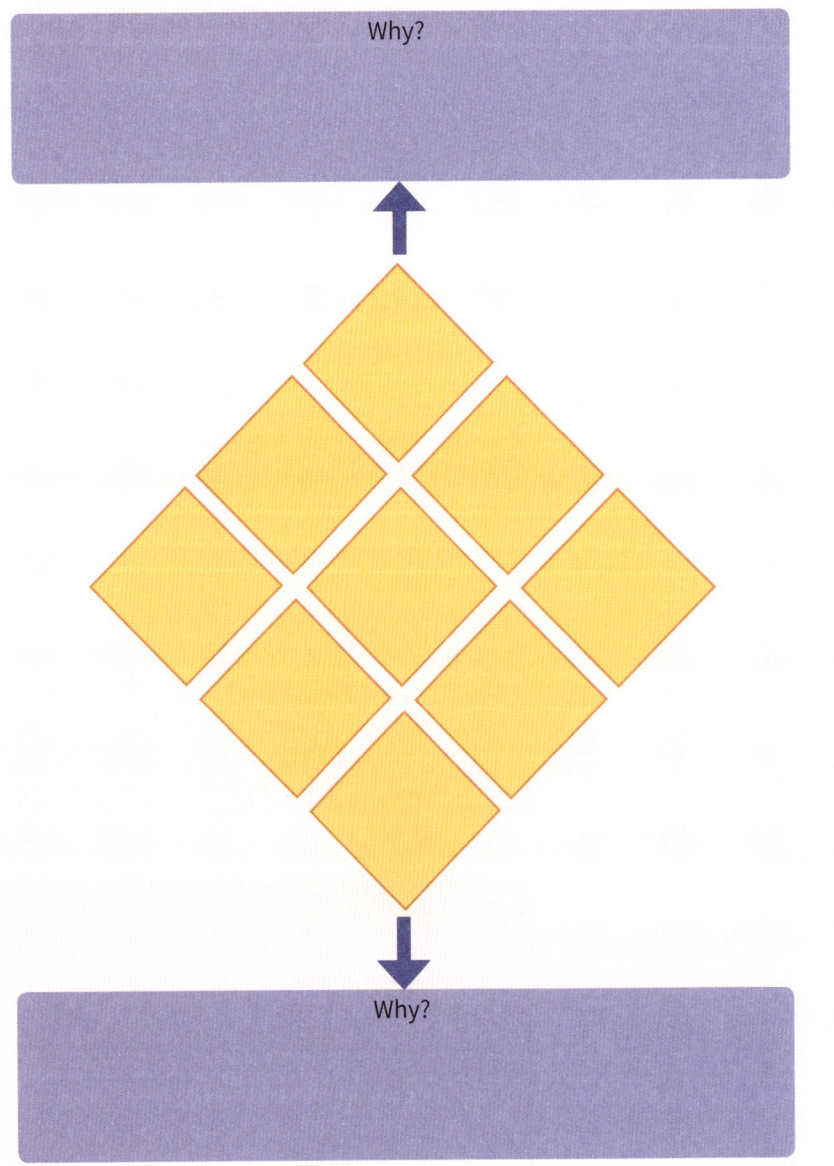

INSTABILITY AND CONSOLIDATION: 'THE MID-TUDOR CRISIS', 1547–1563

KEY QUESTION

One of the Key Questions asks:

In what ways and how effectively was England governed?

The following groups and persons all played a role in how England was governed during the period of Mary's reign:

- advisers
- the Privy Council
- Parliament
- Philip II
- Mary

For each group or person, explain their role, their influence, and whether they helped England to be governed effectively or not.

REVIEW

To complete this activity, you need to look at Chapter 15 as well as Chapter 16.

APPLY YOUR KNOWLEDGE

Draw a mind-map to illustrate the impact of economic change on social policy under Mary, 1553–58.

EXAMINER TIP

Start by identifying the problems posed by the economic situation in 1553 and add those that developed in 1556–58. Lead out to the social policies adopted to address these issues.

REVISION SKILLS

Sections 3 and 4 of this Revision Guide trace developments in Tudor England between 1547 and 1603. To support your revision of this period, create a 56-year timeline and record key events on it as you meet them. Colour code your entries: red: political/government, green: religion, blue: economic, yellow: social, black: international; 1547 has been started for you. Note that you may not be able to fill in a specific event for every year of the timeline.

1547	Edward VI becomes king
	Earl of Hertford (later Duke of Somerset) becomes Lord Protector
	Battle of Pinkie (Sept)
	Military and Church decrees (Dec)
	Unemployment and inflation are high
	Chantries dissolved and injunctions reissued (Dec)

EXAMINER TIP

Your timeline will be an essential revision aid. Use it to check context for extract work, and to ensure accurate chronology and an appreciation of change and continuity in essay answers.

17 Elizabeth I: character and aims

RECAP

The character and aims of Elizabeth I

Elizabeth was 25 (much younger than Mary) when she came to the throne. She was well educated and had learned from personal experiences (including imprisonment in the Tower as a consequence of Wyatt's Rebellion). She was shrewd and proved a good judge of character. However, her difficult existence, as a Protestant during Mary's reign, had made her cautious and, even as queen, she was reluctant to take final decisions.

Elizabeth believed God had saved her to be his queen and she derived much comfort from her faith. Although a Protestant with a firm belief in royal supremacy, she had conservative views in matters of church ceremony.

On coming to the throne her short-term aims were:

- to consolidate her position
- to settle religious issues
- to end war with France.

Elizabeth I's consolidation of power

Elizabeth swiftly consolidated her power:

- Mary's councillors accepted Elizabeth's succession; many of them personally assured her of their loyalty. She was proclaimed queen in November.
- William Cecil was appointed Principal Secretary.
- Elizabeth presented herself to the people from the Tower of London.
- Her coronation took place in January.

The Elizabethan religious settlement

It was clear that the English Church would again be broken from Rome, and that Elizabeth would seek to re-establish royal supremacy over the Church in England. However, it was less clear what form Elizabeth's Church would take. The Elizabethan Church Settlement of 1559 provided the framework for this, creating a 'via media' (middle way) between Catholicism and Protestantism. The settlement, enacted in Elizabeth's first parliament, January–April 1559, not only established the royal supremacy, but also set out the way the Church was to be organised and the content and conduct of services.

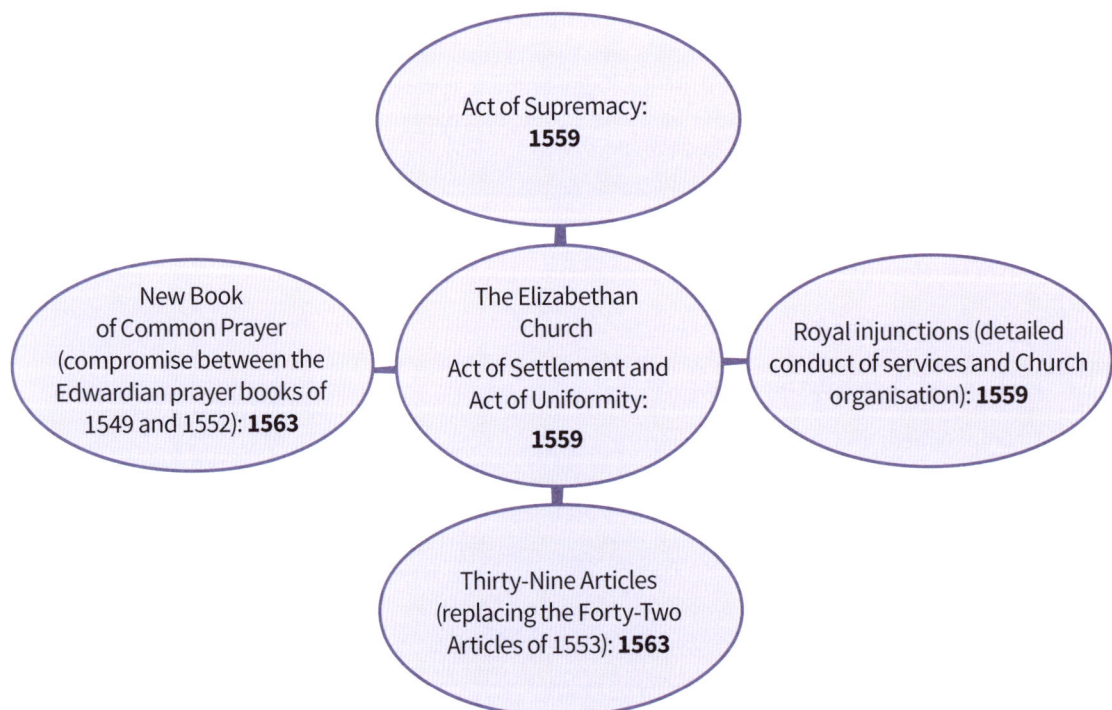

The Act of Supremacy, 1559

This Act:

- repealed the papal supremacy and Marian heresy laws
- reinstated the religious legislation of Henry VIII's reign and revived the powers of royal visitation of the Church
- made the queen 'supreme governor' (rather than 'supreme head') of the Church of England
- demanded an oath of supremacy from all clergymen and church officials.

The Act of Uniformity, 1559

As well as demanding that everyone should go to church once a week or pay a fine of 12 pence (a considerable sum), this established the use of the new Book of Common Prayer. The 1559 prayer book was a version of that of 1552, to make it more acceptable to traditionally minded worshippers. For example, it was carefully worded to allow variations in Eucharistic belief.

The royal injunctions, 1559

A set of royal injunctions nominated 'visitors' to inspect the Church and gave specific instructions such as:

- the removal of 'things superstitious' from churches
- the purchase of an English Bible and a copy of Erasmus's Paraphrases by every parish church
- the celebration of the Eucharist at a simple Communion table (not altar)
- the suppression of Catholic practices (e.g. pilgrimages and the use of candles)
- the requirement that any prospective wife of a clergyman had to produce a certificate, signed by two JPs, to indicate her fitness for the role.

The Thirty-Nine Articles, 1563

The Thirty-Nine Articles, drawn up by the Church in convocation in 1563 (and confirmed by Act of Parliament in 1571) sought to define the doctrine of the Church of England.

Based on Cranmer's earlier articles, they broadly supported reformed doctrine. For example, they denied teachings concerning transubstantiation and affirmed that Scripture was the final authority on salvation. They stated that both bread and wine should be served to all in the Communion service and that ministers could marry.

The significance of the settlement

The settlement was a compromise. It is not known whether it was intended as an end in itself or as a precursor to further reform. Certainly, Elizabeth was placed under pressure from two extremes:

- a 'Puritan choir' of radical clergymen and MPs, who may have forced her to accept a more Protestant prayer book than she had really wanted
- Catholic bishops and conservative peers in the House of Lords, who strongly opposed the uniformity bill, believing the settlement too Protestant.

England's relations with foreign powers, 1558–64

The Treaty of Câteau-Cambrésis, 1559

Elizabeth ended the French war with the Treaty of Câteau-Cambrésis (April 1559). This stated that France would retain Calais for eight years; thereafter, France would pay England 500,000 crowns (around £125,000) or return it.

Intervention in Scotland

In June 1559, Henry II of France was succeeded by Francis II, whose wife was Mary, Queen of Scots – Elizabeth's cousin and the main Catholic claimant to the English throne. The new king sent French troops to garrison Scottish fortresses.

John Knox, the radical Calvinist, and his political allies, the Lords of the Congregation, who were seeking power in Edinburgh, requested assistance from their fellow Protestants in England. Elizabeth was reluctant to intervene, but Cecil strongly supported intervention as he wanted to secure England's borders and weaken the influence of Mary, Queen of Scots.

England initially sent money and armaments but from December 1559 became more directly involved.

KEY CHRONOLOGY
Intervention in Scotland

1559	Dec	The navy was sent to the Firth of Forth to stop French reinforcements from landing
1560	Mar	An army was sent north and blockaded Leith, where most of the French force was situated
		The French fleet was damaged by storms, leading to its withdrawal
	July	The Treaty of Edinburgh brought peace and a Protestant Scottish government
	Dec	Francis II died; Mary had to return to Scotland, where she was forced to accept the political and religious power of John Knox and the Lords of the Congregation

Cecil had succeeded – the interests of Scottish Protestants had been protected and Mary's political influence had been reduced.

Intervention in France

In 1562, conflict broke out between Catholics and Protestants (known as Huguenots) in France; Robert Dudley encouraged Elizabeth to put military pressure on the French Crown so as to ensure the return of Calais. Elizabeth provided the Huguenot leader, the Prince of Condé, with men and money, but his army was defeated and Condé captured.

The English were forced to accept the Treaty of Troyes, 1564, by which the loss of Calais was confirmed as permanent.

SUMMARY
- With Cecil's assistance, Elizabeth skilfully managed her accession and coronation, and achieved a compromise religious settlement.
- Despite mixed results in her foreign policy, by 1563 she had firmly established herself as queen.

APPLY

APPLY YOUR KNOWLEDGE

This chapter sets out the 3 short-term aims Elizabeth set herself. One way to revise a topic is to look at the aims of a monarch and assess whether they were achieved or not, by using a see-saw diagram.

a Copy the diagram below 3 times, 1 for each aim:
  - Consolidate her position
  - Settle religious issues
  - End war with France

b Add points on the 'Yes' side to suggest they were achieved, and on the 'No' side to suggest they were not.

c Rank the 3 aims in terms of how feasible it was to achieve them and explain your prioritisation.

Aim:
_____

Yes   No

APPLY YOUR KNOWLEDGE

Look back through this section and Section 2, and create a timeline/ flow chart to record the main developments in foreign policy from 1540 to 1564. For example:

 1540–47
 1547–49
1549–53
1553–58
1558–64

REVIEW

Look back to Chapters 9, 13 and 15 to remind yourself of the development of foreign policy before Elizabeth's reign.

EXAMINER TIP

The difference between a middling and a high-level answer is often the certainty of dates and chronology, and the use of specific facts and evidence when addressing change over time. Also, remember that breadth questions will cover 20 years or more, so make sure you think about the short reigns of Edward and Mary in the context of a longer period of time.

INSTABILITY AND CONSOLIDATION: 'THE MID-TUDOR CRISIS', 1547–1563

ASSESS THE VALIDITY OF THIS VIEW

It is important to break essay questions down, so that you examine all aspects. For example, you might be asked:

> **A LEVEL** 'The Elizabethan religious settlement was a balanced response to twenty years of religious division.' Assess the validity of this view.

To answer this question, you would need to think about:
- the nature of the religious divisions
- the history and impact of these divisions over 20 years (dates and details)
- the nature of the settlement
- whether the settlement was 'balanced' between reformists and Catholics
- a 'balanced response' suggests a considered policy; was this a considered policy or the result of events?

a Breaking down the question should help you to formulate a response to it. Which of the following first sentences would you use in your introduction? (If you are not happy with any of them, provide your own.)

- 'The Elizabethan religious settlement was certainly a balanced response to a twenty-year old religious division.'
- 'The Elizabethan religious settlement was neither balanced, nor a response to a twenty-year old religious division.'
- 'The Elizabethan religious settlement was not balanced, but it was a response to a twenty-year old religious division.'
- 'The Elizabethan religious settlement may have been balanced, but it was certainly not a response to a twenty-year old religious division.'

b Now write a full introduction to this essay, building on your chosen opening sentence to explain your choice of view and to refer to the words of the question.

EXAMINER TIP

It is easy to ignore parts of questions when focusing on the main issue, e.g. the word 'balanced' in this quotation. To achieve high marks, you should try to analyse all aspects of questions and show a clear judgement about those aspects.

KEY QUESTION

One of the Key Questions asks:

How important was the role of key individuals and groups and how were they affected by developments?

The following groups were involved in the Elizabethan religious settlement of 1558–64:
- radical clergymen and MPs
- Catholic bishops and Conservative peers
- William Cecil and the mainly Protestant Privy Council
- Elizabeth herself.

For each group, explain their view of the religious settlement. Then decide the importance of each in the eventual religious settlement.

18 The impact of economic, social and religious developments in the early years of Elizabeth's rule

The impact of economic and social developments, 1558–63

In 1558, the economy was in a poor state and a fall in real wages meant that there was considerable social distress. MPs were particularly concerned about the number of masterless (unapprenticed) men in towns, and reports of increasing vagabondage and escalating crime.

Date	Problem	Elizabethan action	Results
1561	Inflation, due to debasement of the currency	Plan put forward to replace the debased coins (which contained only 25% of the silver content of their face value) with soundly minted ones	Had only limited effect in the short term, because households tended to hoard the good coinage and pay their debts with the old debased coinage
1563	Vagabonds in towns, increasing crime, and workers demanding higher pay Concerns about increasing numbers of masterless men and vagabondage	**Statute of Artificers** • sought to fix prices, impose maximum wages, restrict workers' freedom of movement and regulate training • made local magistrates responsible for regulating agricultural wages • established a compulsory seven-year apprenticeship in order to follow a craft	Proved very difficult to enforce, even for JPs within their own communities
1563	Increasing poverty, made worse by inflation and poor harvests Lack of support for 'deserving poor' with reduction in Church-sponsored welfare	**Poor Law Act** • extended the previous Act of 1555 • laid down fines for those who refused to contribute to poor relief when requested to do so	Had limited impact

The impact of religious developments, 1558–63

The Elizabethan settlement of 1559 was clearly Protestant. In December 1559, all but one of the Marian bishops refused to consecrate the new Archbishop of Canterbury, Matthew Parker, a Cambridge University don of moderate views. Their positions were filled by Protestants exiled under Mary, such as Edmund Grindal, who became Bishop of London in 1560.

However, Elizabeth herself was more conservative than her strongly Protestant supporters. She disapproved of clergy marrying, distrusted preaching, and favoured the musical culture of the cathedrals and university colleges.

- The queen viewed the settlement as an act of state, defining the relationship between Crown and Church but not 'making windows into men's souls'.
- Others (including Cecil and Dudley) believed the settlement was the starting point for the development of a Puritan Church (i.e. a radical Protestant Church, following Calvinist ideas and totally rejecting Catholic teaching).

While the Elizabethan settlement reformed doctrine, it did not go far enough to please leading Protestants in its reform of the Church's structures, disciplinary procedures, services and clerical dress. In essence, the Church of England was becoming Calvinist in doctrine but only 'half reformed' in its structures.

INSTABILITY AND CONSOLIDATION: 'THE MID-TUDOR CRISIS', 1547–1563

A mid-Tudor crisis?

Historians for a long time promoted the concept of a mid-Tudor crisis. According to this view, the reigns of Edward VI and Mary I (and to some extent the last years of Henry VIII's and the first few years of Elizabeth's reign) were unproductive and marked by religious strife, inefficiency in government, economic and social distress, and failures in foreign policy. This marked them out from the achievements of the reigns of Henry VIII and the later years of Elizabeth.

More recent historians have emphasised the positive features of the period 1547–58 and have argued that more negative features, such as rebellions and social dislocation, were just as apparent in, for example, the mid 1530s.

SUMMARY

- The early years of Elizabeth's reign saw some attempts to address problems of social distress but these were of limited effect.
- Religious development proceeded in the direction of Calvinist Protestantism, although the queen's conservative tendencies meant that many Catholic practices were retained.

KEY CHRONOLOGY

Political and religious events

1547	Edward VI succeeds
1549	First Book of Common Prayer introduced; Fall of Somerset
1552	Second Book of Common Prayer introduced
1553	Forty-Two Articles of Religion published; Edward VI dies, Lady Jane Grey proclaimed queen; Mary I succeeds
1553	Edwardian religious laws repealed
1554	Mary marries Philip of Spain; Wyatt's Rebellion
1558	Death of Mary; Elizabeth succeeds
1559	Elizabethan religious settlement
1563	Thirty-Nine Articles of Religion published

KEY CHRONOLOGY

International events

1547	Battle of Pinkie against Scotland
1557	England declares war against France
1558	England loses Calais
1559	Treaty of Câteau-Cambrésis ends war with France
1559–60	English intervention in Scotland
1562	English intervention in France on the side of the Huguenots
1564	Treaty of Troyes makes peace with France

REVISION PROGRESS

APPLY

APPLY YOUR KNOWLEDGE

The mid-Tudor crisis is a key concept in this period of history, but not all historians agree on whether it existed. If they do think a crisis occurred, there is often debate about when to date it from. Complete the chart below; in the 2nd column record events which could be seen as the start (in red) or end (in green) of the possible crisis; in the 3rd column suggest why it could be seen as the starting point or the final point of the crisis.

	Event	Reason
1534		
1540		
1547		
1558		
1559		
1563		

APPLY YOUR KNOWLEDGE

One way to view the religious changes in Tudor England 1540–63 is to think of them as a pendulum swinging from Catholicism to various kinds of Protestantism. The diagram below marks out key elements of the kind of Church you would find at each point.

a Copy the diagram, then on the curved orange line place a coloured dot and a year next to where the Church in England would be at the following points, and draw a line to connect them in order:

- 1547 The end of Henry VIII's reign
- 1549 The end of Somerset's Lord Protectorship
- 1553 The end of Northumberland's Lord Presidency
- 1558 The end of Mary's reign
- 1564 After the Elizabethan religious settlement

b Note when the line makes its biggest change of direction and write a sentence to explain why this was.

c Note where the position of Elizabeth's religious settlement is and write a sentence to explain why it is often called the 'via media' (middle way).

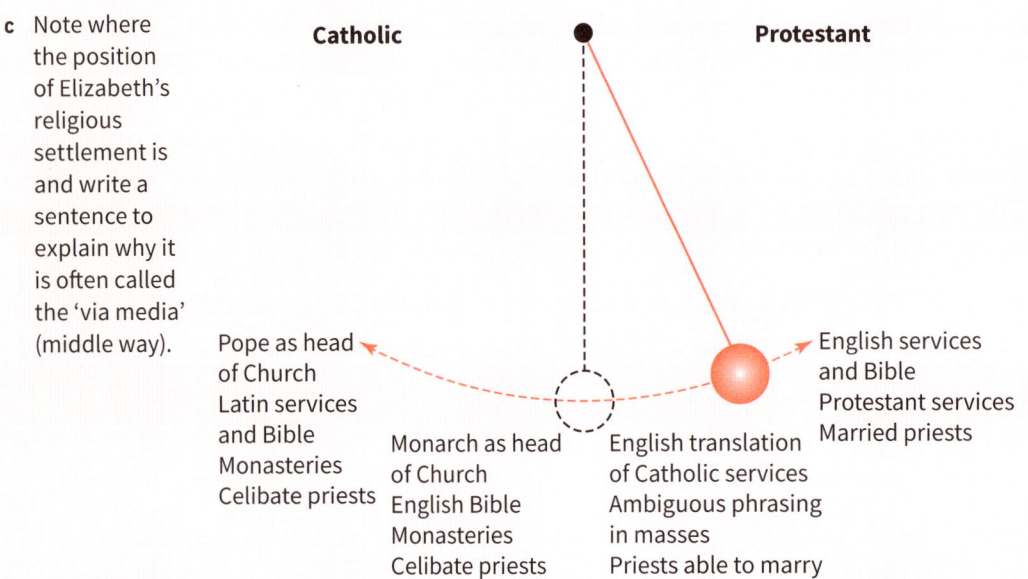

INSTABILITY AND CONSOLIDATION: 'THE MID-TUDOR CRISIS', 1547–1563

KEY QUESTION

One of the Key Questions asks:

How did English society and economy change and with what effects?

To assess the ways in which society and the economy changed between 1540 and 1563, and ascertain the effects, review Sections 2 and 3 of this Revision Guide. As you read through the sections, copy and complete the table below. Add up to 3 social and 3 economic changes in each period. In the last column, list the overall effects of these social and economic changes.

Ruler	Social	Economic	Effects
Henry VIII from 1540			
Edward VI			
Mary			
Elizabeth I to 1563			
Overview			

REVIEW

You will need to read Chapters 10 and 12 to gain information on social and economic changes in the later reign of Henry VIII, Chapter 14 for those under Edward, and Chapter 16 for those under Mary.

ASSESS THE VALIDITY OF THIS VIEW

 'A state of crisis existed in England between 1540 and 1563.' Assess the validity of this view.

One way of approaching this question is to work out what you think is meant by a 'crisis', and then test to see whether it applies to the statement.

a Below is a list of events which could be described as a crisis. Write down those which could be useful criteria for this essay:

- A serious threat of a civil war within the country
- Profound religious differences leading to deaths and conflicts
- Social and economic problems leading to disease, death and disturbances
- The likelihood of the seizure of power by one group of politicians from another
- Weak government
- A change in the line of succession
- A serious threat of foreign invasion and conquest
- Bad harvests
- Arguments in the government about policy

b Now write down the key event that corresponds with the beginning and end dates of the question. Do these events suggest you have selected appropriate criteria?

c Complete the table below.

Criteria	To what extent apparent	Evidence

d Now write down a short paragraph where you state your overall judgement and your key reasons.

EXAMINER TIP

When 2 dates are given in an exam question, make a point of explaining their significance. Remember that within a time span there may be periods of crisis and periods of calm. You need to form a judgement about whether the periods of crisis outweigh the periods of calm in duration or seriousness – and show this debate in your answer.

EXAMINER TIP

Whenever a key term is given in an essay always explain what it means. In this case a definition of 'crisis' will help your answer.

EXAM PRACTICE

A Level essay sample answer

REVISION PROGRESS

REVIEW

On these Exam Practice pages, you will find a sample student answer for an A Level essay question. What are the strengths and weaknesses of the answer? Read the answer and the corresponding Examiner Tips carefully. Think about how you could apply this advice in order to improve your own answers to questions like this one.

> **A LEVEL**
> 'Despite a change in authority, England remained a largely Catholic country in belief and structure between 1547 and 1564.' Assess the validity of this view.
>
> 25 marks

REVISION SKILLS

At A Level you have to answer two of the three essay questions you are given. You have 45 minutes to answer each one. Read page 7 for details on how to master the essay question.

EXAMINER TIP

This introduction addresses the question, is accurate and explains the approach to the answer. It also states a clear view in relation to the question.

Sample student answer

England saw many religious transformations between 1547 and 1564. Henry left a Church which was largely Catholic but the Pope had been replaced as the leader. Edward's regents turned the Church in England into a more reformist organisation in two stages. Mary reversed this so much that it was as Catholic as it was before Henry's seizure of control. Elizabeth returned the Church to a middle way between reformists and Catholics. This seems to suggest that England did not remain a largely Catholic country in belief and structure throughout this period. However, despite the changes in authority, the formal structure of the Church under bishops and priests was untouched while the beliefs of most 'ordinary people', although difficult to assess, seem to have remained quite Catholic.

In terms of formal authority the Church see-sawed dramatically. However, it was only for a very short period that the Church was not Catholic in belief — between 1552 and 1553 — when the use of the second Book of Common Prayer was enforced. The services were made reformist and simpler so that ordinary people could understand. However, even then there were elements of Catholicism in the Church's structure, as bishops and archbishops remained. Moreover, for most of the period, there were always elements of Catholicism in the established Church. For example, the words of the Communion service were designed so that both Catholics and Protestants could say them honestly and priests were allowed to wear decorative vestments in services.

It could be argued that, apart from Mary's reign, the Church in England was more Protestant than Catholic. Catholic institutions such as chantries and monasteries disappeared, which undermined

EXAMINER TIP

This paragraph builds on the first one with some focused comment and detailed evidence.

the Catholic Church structure, and practices such as priests being allowed to marry and English Bibles and services predominated, reinforcing the idea of a new 'Protestant' Church. However, many priests took wives in England even though it was against Catholic Church teaching and the services were largely translations of Latin ones. So it could be argued that the Church had always contained a mixture of Catholicism and Protestant ideas since the time of Henry VIII's reformation and it is impossible to say that the Church was entirely Catholic or largely reformist. The best way of viewing it is the way in which Elizabeth's Church was established and viewed – as a 'via media' throughout this period.

However, it can also be argued that the 'ordinary people' never lost their Catholic beliefs at all. Even in Edward's time a radical reformer admitted that 'uncooperative public' hampered reform. This is also shown by the speed with which traditional practices were re-adopted following the accession of the Catholic Queen Mary in 1553 and the confidence of the conservative nobility who blocked a more Protestant settlement in 1558. The key turning point between England being Catholic and Protestant was probably not until the 1570s and it certainly took a long time before the old beliefs died out, if they ever did.

In conclusion, Catholic beliefs and structures remained in England after 1547, and although ideas had begun to change by 1564, there was still some way to go before England could be described as a truly Protestant country. However, reaction to the burnings at the stake by Mary meant that England was more of a Protestant country than it had been by 1558, and Elizabeth's 'via media' helped establish a Church that combined Catholic and Protestant structure and beliefs successfully.

> **EXAMINER TIP**
> This paragraph is trying to address counter arguments and to offer an individual argument and judgement in an analytical way. However, it lacks some precision in relation to terminology and the degree of change and continuity over time.

> **EXAMINER TIP**
> This paragraph tries to explore the views of the 'ordinary people' but lacks development and the idea of a 'turning point' in the 1570s comes as an afterthought and goes beyond the finishing date of the question.

> **EXAMINER TIP**
> This conclusion is well developed, although the reference to Mary's burnings is not clearly integrated or consistent with what has gone before. It provides some judgement.

OVERALL COMMENT
After a strong start, the essay falls away and despite its overall understanding, the points made are not always well-developed nor effectively substantiated. There is analysis and balance, together with some supporting evidence and reference to both aspects of the question. However, the explanation of the main ideas is thin, permitting only a low Level 4.

OVER TO YOU
Take 45 minutes to write your answer, then review it using the following checklist:
☐ Does each paragraph address the question?
☐ Have you provided focused comment backed by specific evidence in your answer?
☐ Have you offered a counter argument to give balance to your answer?
☐ Have you given a clear judgement in relation to the question at the outset, which is subsequently well substantiated and repeated in the conclusion?

Review Chapters 14, 16 and 17 again. Are the details in your essay factually accurate? Have you missed any issues you should have raised?

The triumph of Elizabeth, 1563–1603

19 Elizabethan government, 1563–1603

> **RECAP**

The royal court and Privy Council

The royal court was not just the monarch's home, but also the centre of government. The court travelled with the queen and came under the jurisdiction of the Lord Chamberlain. The Privy Council, the main formal body in which the queen's principal ministers met, was based at this court and work and pleasure were often combined as the queen met with ministers in both a formal and informal setting.

Elizabeth wanted to be an active ruler and deliberately chose a much smaller Privy Council than that of Mary's reign. This was intended to reduce opportunities for faction-fighting and improve efficiency. Consequently, around ten members usually attended its regular meetings. Some of Mary's councillors were chosen to continue in service, but Elizabeth also added her own choices, giving the Council a new dynamism.

The Privy Council was responsible for policy advice and administration, and its principal functions were:

- to discuss and advise on state matters, helping to formulate policies
- to manage Crown finances
- to manage Parliament
- to oversee the regional councils and local officials (e.g. JPs and borough councils)
- to oversee national defence
- to enforce the 1559 religious settlement
- to act as a court of law (when sitting as Star Chamber).

Despite some disagreements over foreign policy and the execution of Mary, Queen of Scots, for most of the reign Elizabeth and the Council worked well together.

The role of ministers and factional rivalry

Elizabeth's chief adviser was William Cecil (who became Lord Burghley in 1571). Cecil had served under Edward VI; he twice became Principal Secretary (1550–53 and 1558–72) and was also Lord High Treasurer from 1572. Other members of the Privy Council included Sir Nicholas Bacon, Francis Russell (Earl of Bedford) and Sir Francis Knollys. More conservative ministers included the Duke of Norfolk and the Marquis of Winchester, and the earls of Sussex and Shrewsbury, while Elizabeth's favourite, Robert Dudley (who became Earl of Leicester in 1564), joined the Council in 1562.

Despite Elizabeth's good intentions, the Council experienced some factional rivalries. For example, the Earl of Leicester and Cecil, two of Elizabeth's key ministers, disagreed over the queen's potential marriage and were frequent rivals in political matters, with competition between the Dudley (Leicester) and Cecil factions at court. Nevertheless, these factions largely balanced one another out and disagreements were matched by issues of agreement.

In the 1570s, the influence of the traditional conservatives was reduced, as a result of perceived disloyalty in the 1560s; Norfolk was executed and Winchester died. A nucleus of firmly Protestant councillors subsequently emerged, including Sir Francis Walsingham, who became Elizabeth's Principal Secretary 1573–90 and acted as her chief spy master. Working with Lord Burghley, Walsingham devised an effective spy network in the later years of Elizabeth's reign. He was also instrumental in convincing Elizabeth to execute Mary, Queen of Scots in 1587.

Sir Walter Mildmay, the Earl of Leicester and his brother the Earl of Warwick, Sir Francis Knollys and the Earl of Bedford joined Walsingham and Burghley to form an 'inner ring' of strongly Protestant councillors, although there were still some conservative figures, such as Sir James Croft and Sir Christopher Hatton and Thomas Radcliffe, Earl of Sussex.

For the most part Elizabethan ministers of all persuasions worked together to give coherence to government. It was not until the 1590s that faction-fighting became problematic, as Robert Cecil clashed with the Earl of Essex.

Problems of government in the 1580s and 1590s

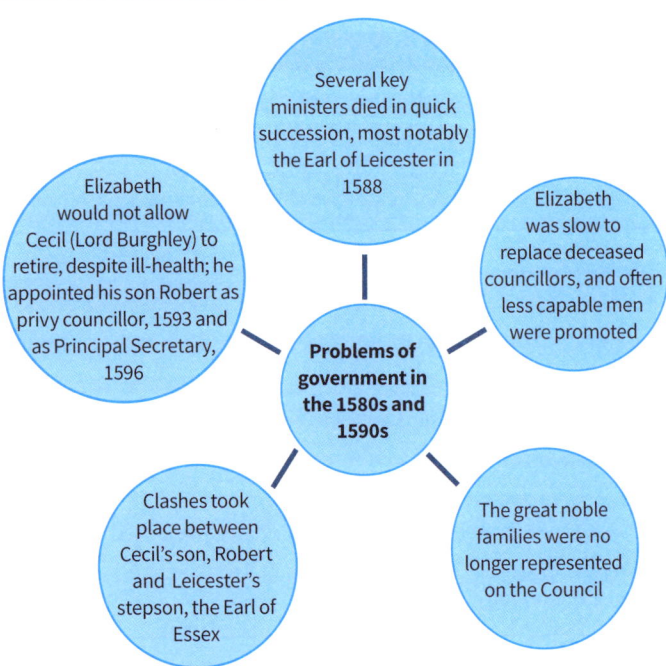

Problems stemming from Cecil–Essex faction-fighting culminated in the Essex 'rebellion' of 1601, when Essex (who had failed in his bid to defeat Irish rebels and had been banished from the court by Elizabeth, because of his arrogant manner) tried to revive his declining influence by mounting a coup against Cecil. This attempt failed and he was tried and executed. Essex lacked political judgement, but his attitudes nevertheless reflected increasing wider discontent with the rule of Elizabeth and Cecil.

Parliament

Parliament had always been a less important feature of government than the Privy Council and this continued under Elizabeth. In a reign of 44 years, Parliament held only 13 sessions and most lasted around three months. Parliament was primarily called to:

- **grant taxation:** 11 out of 13 parliaments were asked to grant revenue
- **make statute laws:** 438 Acts were passed by Elizabeth's parliaments, notably the Acts of Supremacy and Uniformity in 1559 and the poor laws of 1597/8 and 1601.

Within Parliament, the House of Lords was more important than the House of Commons and all bills were first discussed there. Parliamentary sessions were carefully managed. Cecil was active in preparing bills, assisted by the Crown's representatives in the House of Commons (initially Sir Francis Knollys and from 1576 Sir Christopher Hatton) and privy councillors often began parliamentary sessions by outlining the Crown's priorities. When parliaments were invited to discuss legislation, all debate was closely controlled by the Speaker. Cecil managed the Commons, which was expected to be respectful and not hinder parliamentary business with undue debate, with the help of supportive MPs (typically lawyers), and generally this tactic seems to have succeeded. Nevertheless, the Queen's assent was needed before any measure became law and Elizabeth refused royal assent to over 60 bills that had passed through both houses.

The royal prerogative and parliamentary clashes

Elizabeth would not allow uninvited debate or opposition on any matter which she regarded as her prerogative. Such matters included marriage and the succession, religion and foreign policy. This brought about several clashes between the queen and her parliaments.

KEY CHRONOLOGY	
1559	Parliament raised the issue of marriage but Elizabeth deflected it
1563	Parliament met at a time when it was feared that Elizabeth would die of smallpox. The queen opposed the discussion of the succession; she survived her illness
1566	Parliament (encouraged by Cecil and Leicester) pressed Elizabeth to marry: the queen responded angrily and banished Leicester from the court
1571	At the opening of the 1571 Parliament, Elizabeth sent explicit instructions to the Commons, not 'to meddle with matters of state'. When William Strickland tried to introduce a radical religious reform bill he was forced to leave the chamber
1572, 1576	The Commons took action against its own members for speeches that were felt to have gone too far regarding Mary, Queen of Scots and religion
1576	Peter Wentworth made an appeal for freedom of speech and was committed to the Tower by order of the House. (He was later readmitted but imprisoned again in 1587 and again in 1593 for defying Elizabeth's restrictions on freedom of speech concerning both religion and the succession)
1585	Speaker John Puckering delivered a message from Elizabeth banning religious debate

Nevertheless, until 1593, relations between queen and Parliament were generally cordial. Most MPs apparently accepted the restrictions she imposed and those who did not were punished severely. Protests like Wentworth's were exceptional.

From 1593, however, relations between Crown and Parliament deteriorated:

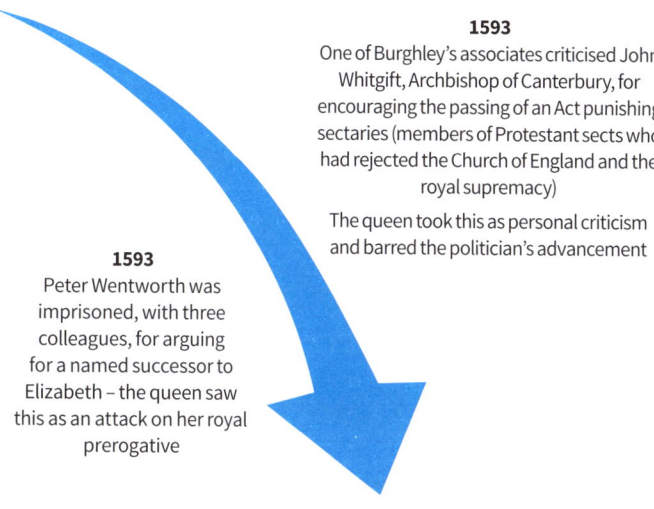

1593
Peter Wentworth was imprisoned, with three colleagues, for arguing for a named successor to Elizabeth – the queen saw this as an attack on her royal prerogative

1593
One of Burghley's associates criticised John Whitgift, Archbishop of Canterbury, for encouraging the passing of an Act punishing sectaries (members of Protestant sects who had rejected the Church of England and the royal supremacy)

The queen took this as personal criticism and barred the politician's advancement

1601
The relationship between Elizabeth and her parliaments broke down in the debate over monopolies (whereby the sole right to sell or manufacture a particular commodity was bought by an individual or company)

A compromise was achieved and the parliamentary session ended with the queen's emotionally moving Golden Speech (essentially a farewell) to a crowded gathering of MPs

SUMMARY

- In general, government during Elizabeth's reign was well conducted, especially over the first 30 years of the reign, and there was a broad consensus (except on religion) concerning royal policies and their enforcement.
- Elizabeth chose her key ministers well, and was rewarded by the services of talented individuals, such as Cecil, Walsingham, Mildmay and Hatton.
- Towards the end of the reign, the coherence of government began to break down as these experienced ministers died and were replaced by less able officials; a renewal of factional rivalry, between Robert Cecil and the Earl of Essex, indicated a decline in effective government.

REVISION PROGRESS

APPLY

APPLY YOUR KNOWLEDGE

a Draw a mind-map to illustrate the problems in the relationship between the queen and Parliament. The diagram below gives you an example.

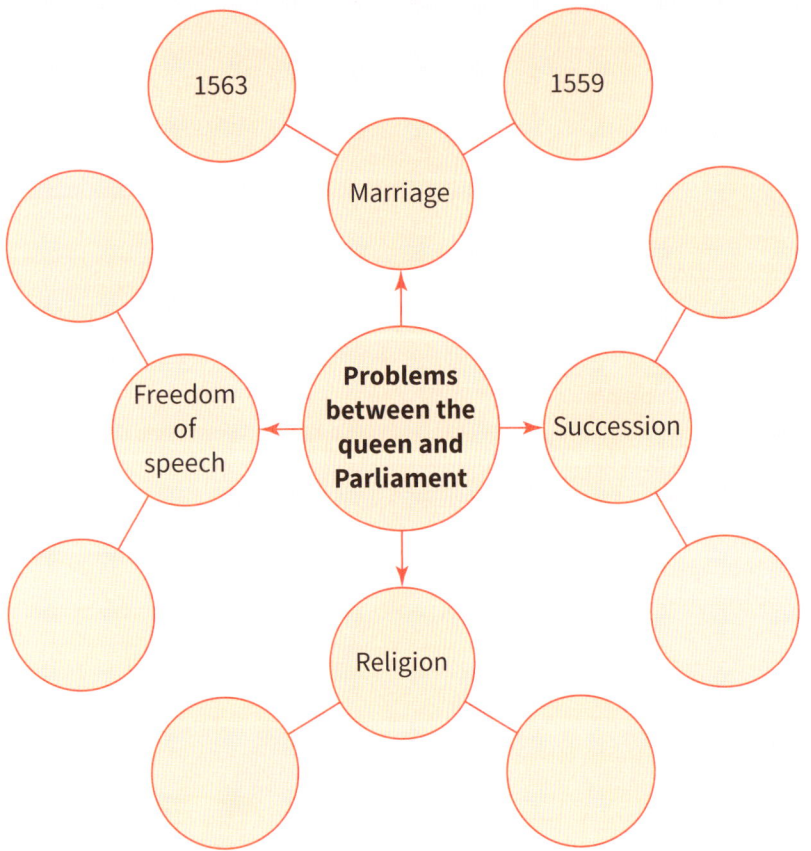

b Beneath your diagram, write a definition of the term, 'royal prerogative'.

EXAMINER TIP

It is often helpful to use historical terminology, such as royal prerogative, in essays, but you should never use terms that are not properly understood.

APPLY YOUR KNOWLEDGE

Elizabeth used various methods to control Parliament.

a Re-read this chapter, paying attention to the sections on Parliament, the royal prerogative and parliamentary clashes and make a list of the methods Elizabeth used to control her parliaments.

b Rank the methods in order of effectiveness and explain the reasoning behind your prioritisation.

c From your results in part **b**, is there a single reason which stands out for the continued problems Elizabeth faced with Parliament?

EXAMINER TIP

You could use this activity to respond to a question asking how effectively Elizabeth managed her parliaments.

THE TRIUMPH OF ELIZABETH, 1563–1603

KEY QUESTION

One of the Key Questions asks:

In what ways and how effectively was England governed during this period?

Review this chapter, paying special attention to the sections dealing with the ministers and Parliament 1563–90. Then complete the following table about the role of the Privy Council in serving the queen from 1563–90 by adding a general comment in each box, followed by specific example(s).

Issues	Issues well managed	Problems
Maintaining a working relationship		
Working together to provide constructive advice		
Management of Parliament		
Loyalty about religion		
Protection of queen		
Foreign policy		

REVIEW

In finding specific examples for the last row (on foreign policy), you will find it helpful to read Chapter 20.

IMPROVE AN ANSWER

A LEVEL 'Elizabeth's management of government could be described as 30 years of success, followed by 15 years of decline.' Assess the validity of this view.

An essay evaluating this exam question would require a paragraph on the relationship between the queen and the Privy Council in the first 30 years. Here is a sample paragraph:

> **Answer**
>
> The queen appointed Cecil as her Principal Secretary in 1558 although he was not a leading civil servant. She used Cecil and the Privy Council to manage Parliament. The Privy Council was also used to discuss foreign affairs. One of her privy councillors was her favourite, Robert Dudley, and rumours abounded about their relationship. She had a portrait of him in her bedroom bearing the words 'My love'. When Dudley was alleged to have killed his wife, this caused problems in the Privy Council and she had to remove him from court for a while. However, she managed this factionalism well, partly because William Cecil shared out the benefits of service to the state fairly between factions. Generally the Privy Council managed Parliament well, but allowed it to push its own agenda at times because it wanted to put pressure on the queen; this is shown in several ways. Both Parliament and the Privy Council wanted Elizabeth to get married and name a successor. Also, they both wanted her to execute Mary, Queen of Scots. One of the few times the Privy Council acted beyond their powers was when they sent the order to execute Mary before the queen was ready to do so. The queen also promoted able people to the Privy Council which protected her from many Catholic plots. This shows that, during the first 30 years, the queen and the Privy Council worked well together and produced effective government.

a   Sections of this paragraph are irrelevant; score them out.
b   The paragraph is poorly ordered, with the comment on effective government coming last instead of first. Rewrite the first sentence.
c   The information in this paragraph is presented either very descriptively or assertively. Rewrite the paragraph to improve the answer and make the given information more relevant to the question.

EXAMINER TIP

The order and way in which you present your material within a paragraph is very important. Facts followed by a concluding sentence will never provide as convincing an argument as an opinion supported by facts.

20 Foreign affairs

RECAP

Issues of succession

Marriage issues

Elizabeth's marriage was an issue of great concern for her ministers and those who represented her people in Parliament. It was initially assumed she would marry – probably a powerful European prince – so enhancing England's status and producing an heir to guarantee the succession. The alternative – of marriage to a member of the English nobility – posed potential problems in terms of faction-fighting.

While she remained without an heir, her natural successor was Mary, Queen of Scots; but Mary was a devout Catholic. Fear of a Catholic inheritance was strong among Elizabeth's Protestant nobility and Elizabeth's death without a successor could bring civil war, foreign invasion and religious strife. However the queen felt that issues of marriage and succession lay within the royal prerogative and were not areas for discussion either in Parliament or even by the Council. The queen was not short of suitors – both from within England and from abroad.

For Elizabeth, the issue of her marriage gave her a bargaining tool which she could use to England's advantage in foreign policy.

Mary, Queen of Scots

The Catholic Mary had fled south in 1568 (after a breakdown in her relationship with the Protestant lords had culminated in a brief civil war), and was living in captivity in England.

Mary represented a continuous threat to Elizabeth, since some English Catholics saw her as the rightful monarch. This problem increased when Elizabeth was excommunicated in 1570, meaning that the Pope freed her Catholic subjects from the need to obey her.

Mary became the focus of four plots to overthrow Elizabeth between 1571 and 1586. The last of these, the Babington Plot of 1586, resulted in a trial at which she was found guilty. Although Elizabeth was reluctant to authorise the execution of another anointed monarch, Cecil convinced her that it was necessary for her personal safety and the security of the Protestant State. Mary was beheaded in 1587. This provided an excuse for Philip II, whose suit of Elizabeth had broken down by the 1570s, to send an Armada against England in 1588.

By the 1580s, Elizabeth was well past childbearing age, although she refused to name a successor right up to her death. She was succeeded by Mary Queen of Scots' son, James VI of Scotland, who had the best hereditary claim, was Protestant, and already had two sons by 1600. Councillors such as Essex (who died himself in 1601) and Robert Cecil had already made contact with James when Elizabeth died in 1603, paving the way for a smooth transition.

England's relations with Spain

Relations to 1585

Anglo-Spanish relations began cordially in the 1560s as Philip proposed marriage with Elizabeth. However, they had deteriorated by the 1570s and became steadily worse during the rest of Elizabeth's reign.

- John Hawkins' trading activity threatened the Spanish trading monopoly in the Caribbean.
- In the Netherlands, the Catholic Philip II (who controlled the Netherlands) clashed with Dutch Protestants. Protestant councillors pressurised Elizabeth to aid the Protestants. She was reluctant to support rebels but her expulsion from English ports of the Sea Beggars (Dutch pirates) in 1572 sparked a revolt in the Netherlands against Spanish rule.
- 1568 – the English seized Spanish vessels, driven by a storm into English ports, and confiscated the money they carried, which was intended to pay Philip's army in the Netherlands.
- Philip supported the Northern Rebellion (1569) and the Ridolfi Plot to replace Elizabeth with Mary, Queen of Scots (1571).
- 1570s and early 1580s – Philip's success in the Netherlands were of concern to Elizabeth; relations continued to deteriorate as privateers captured considerable quantities of Spanish bullion on its way to Europe from the New World.
- 1584 – Philip's Treaty of Joinville with the Catholic League in France proved the final straw and an Anglo-Spanish war broke out in 1585.

The Anglo-Spanish War, 1585–1604

- To counteract the terms of the Treaty of Joinville, Elizabeth made the Treaty of Nonsuch with the Dutch Protestant rebels and sent troops to the Netherlands under the command of the Earl of Leicester. However, the English commanders quarrelled among themselves and the troops were ill-disciplined.
- 1587 – the English successfully attacked Spanish ships at Cadiz ('singeing the King of Spain's beard'), delaying the launch of the Spanish Armada (invasion fleet).
- 1588 – Leicester returned to England. Philip's huge Armada set sail with plans to load a Spanish army in the Netherlands, for an invasion of England. It was sighted off Cornwall; engaged in indecisive battle (by Drake) in the English Channel; and forced by unfavourable winds to round Scotland and Ireland, losing many ships to rocks and storms.

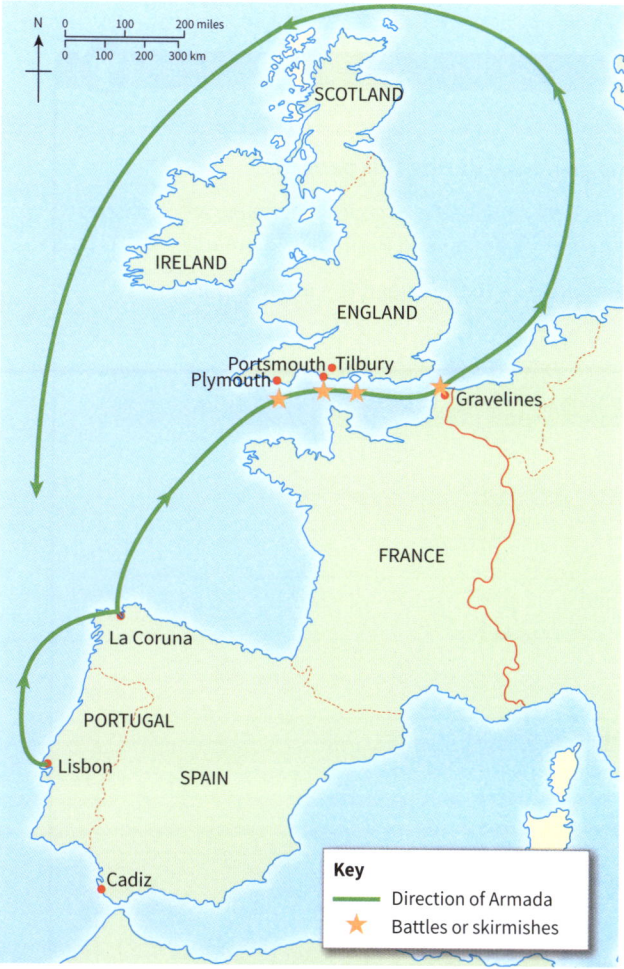

- The war was fought both at sea, off western Europe and in the Caribbean, and on land (including in Ireland, where it was connected to a revolt against Elizabeth's rule). It dragged on at great expense.
- 1589 – Sir Francis Vere was made commander of the English forces in the Netherlands. He worked effectively with the Dutch Protestants so that the Spanish were expelled from the north by 1594; the country was divided into an independent Protestant north and Catholic south, the latter under Spanish sovereignty.
- Attacks on Spanish shipping mounted both by professional seamen such as Hawkins, Drake and Frobisher, and by courtiers such as Walter Raleigh, achieved some financial gains but little strategic success.
- Philip ordered another invasion of England in 1596 but the fleet was defeated by storms.
- The war was finally concluded in 1604 after the deaths of both Philip and Elizabeth.

SUMMARY

- The issue of marriage and the succession caused tension at home and affected policies abroad.
- Elizabeth's foreign policy was broadly successful, although costly. Dynastic considerations were coupled with the desire for glory and the national interest.
- The conflict with Spain was long-running, expensive and brought limited gain.

REVISION PROGRESS

APPLY

APPLY YOUR KNOWLEDGE

Look at the diagram of Elizabeth's suitors on page 104, and make a simplified form of the diagram with just the suitors' names. Then draw an outer circle. From each suitor draw 2 lines to the outer circle labelled 'For' and 'Against'. For each suitor write in at least 1 point in favour of the marriage (For) and 1 point against it (Against).

EXAMINER TIP

Marriage was a vital issue for a queen in the 16th century, as Mary found to her cost. Therefore, it is important to make sure you understand the issue.

KEY QUESTION

One of the Key Questions asks:

In what ways and how effectively was England governed during this period?

Marriage was a key issue as it would affect how effectively England was governed. Below are 7 reasons why Elizabeth might not bow to pressure from the Privy Council and Parliament to marry.

a Rank the statements below in order of their importance to the queen (1 = most important, 7 = least important).

Reason	Rank and explanation
A It would interfere with royal prerogative.	
B She had seen what problems marriage had caused her sister, Mary.	
C Elizabeth did not want to risk having a child as a male heir as he might be a rival to her position.	
D In a male dominated world, marriage would restrict her power.	
E Marriage was a bargaining tool that could only be used once.	
F All the eligible foreign suitors brought serious problems.	
G Marrying Dudley (probably her preferred choice) would have led to faction-fighting in England.	

b Write a sentence to explain why you think your first choice was the most important reason.

c Write 2–3 bullet points showing what impact not getting married had on how effectively she was able to govern.

106

THE TRIUMPH OF ELIZABETH, 1563–1603

TO WHAT EXTENT?

A LEVEL — To what extent was the execution of Mary, Queen of Scots in 1586 the key turning point in England's relationship with Spain in the years 1558 to 1603?

Since this essay addresses a turning point, you should plan it by considering other potential 'turning points'. Recording the information in chart form will enable you to make a judgement.

a Complete the planning chart below – the first row has been completed. You might also pick other dates/events as possible turning points.

Year: Potential turning point	Case for	Case against
1569: Northern Rebellion	Philip for the first time acted against Elizabeth; because of this, the Pope excommunicated Elizabeth in 1570, confident of Spanish support. Plots followed	There was no active war between the 2 nations; alternatively, Elizabeth had already soured relations by seizing some Spanish bullion ships in 1568
1584:		
1587:		
1588:		

b Decide on your judgement. You could then write the opening sentences of your paragraphs – or a full essay.

EXAMINER TIP
Remember that when you write your essay, you should ensure that the case for and against each turning point (columns 2 and 3) is fully assessed. This is a high-level skill which examiners will look for in good essays.

REVIEW
To contrast this Elizabethan period of declining relations between England and Spain with previous good relations, look back at Chapters 9 and 15. Also, learn more about the Northern Rebellion in the next chapter.

KEY QUESTION

One of the Key Questions asks:

How did relations with foreign powers change and how was the succession secured?

Review this chapter and write 3 bullet points about:
- the improvement or deterioration in relations with France, Spain and Scotland
- how the succession was secured.

Compare the two sets of points. Is there any connection between the two?

REVISION SKILLS

Create a timeline of key foreign policy events from this chapter, and the earlier Tudor periods. Colour code references to specific countries.

REVISION SKILLS
This timeline can help inform your understanding of change and continuity in Tudor foreign policy.

21 Society in Elizabethan England

RECAP

Society: continuity and change

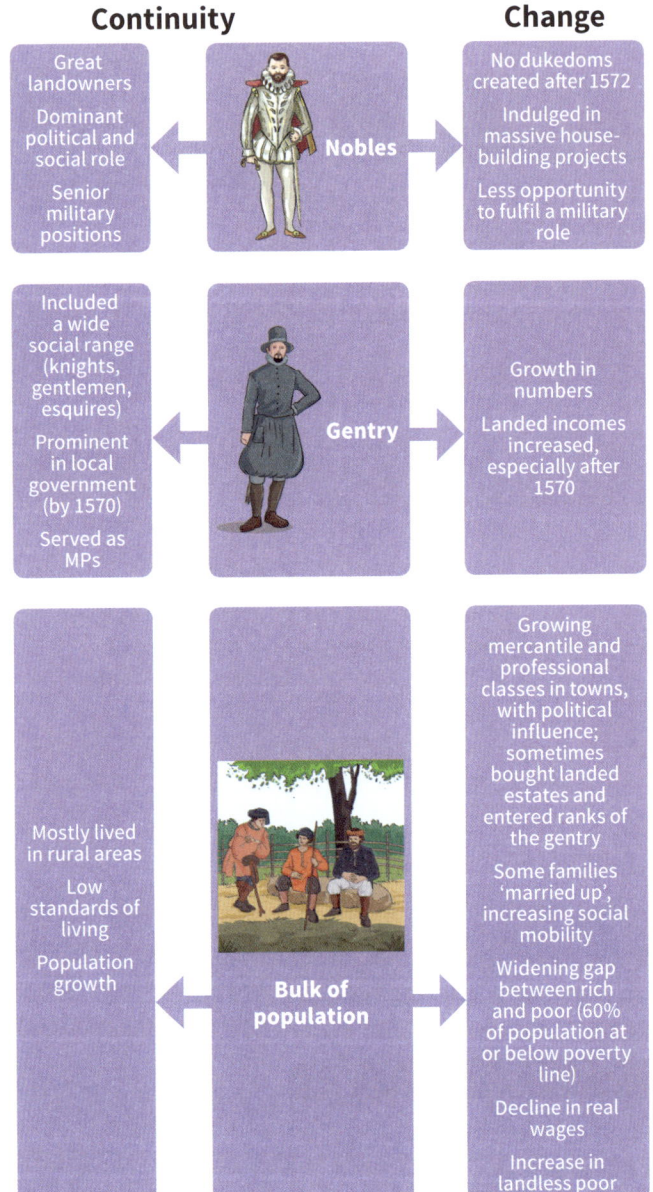

Nobles
- Continuity: Great landowners; Dominant political and social role; Senior military positions
- Change: No dukedoms created after 1572; Indulged in massive house-building projects; Less opportunity to fulfil a military role

Gentry
- Continuity: Included a wide social range (knights, gentlemen, esquires); Prominent in local government (by 1570); Served as MPs
- Change: Growth in numbers; Landed incomes increased, especially after 1570

Bulk of population
- Continuity: Mostly lived in rural areas; Low standards of living; Population growth
- Change: Growing mercantile and professional classes in towns, with political influence; sometimes bought landed estates and entered ranks of the gentry; Some families 'married up', increasing social mobility; Widening gap between rich and poor (60% of population at or below poverty line); Decline in real wages; Increase in landless poor

Poverty and poor relief

The increase in the numbers of poor impelled further measures to relieve poverty, since destitution and vagrancy were seen as potential sources of crime and disorder:

- 1572 – Act required local ratepayers to pay a rate for the relief of their own poor.
- 1576 – Act required towns to make provision for employment for the deserving poor.
- 1597/8 – Act provided a code for poor relief establishing overseers of the poor.
- 1601 Elizabethan Poor Law – created a national system for poor relief based on the parish (poor relief would be conducted on a local basis until 1929):
  - Each parish was required to raise the rates for, and administer, poor relief through an overseer of the poor.
  - The impotent poor (those unable to work) were to be cared for in a poorhouse.
  - The able-bodied poor were to be given work in a 'House of Industry'.
  - The idle poor and vagrants were to be sent to a 'House of Correction' or prison.
  - Pauper children were to be apprenticed to a trade.

Although the treatment of the undeserving poor was harsh, the creation of a national system showed a more enlightened attitude to relief than that of earlier reigns. This system was further complemented by an increase in donations from wealthy secular benefactors who gave or left money to found almshouses, schools and hospitals.

Problems in the regions

England under Elizabeth I was relatively unified and peaceable, although there was trouble in Ireland and one serious rebellion in England – the Northern Rebellion of 1569 (which quickly collapsed). That the aristocracy largely abandoned their fortified castles and built comfortable country houses suggests social stability and order.

Ireland

Elizabeth's government wanted to impose English control in both religious and secular matters. Elizabeth was proclaimed Supreme Governor of the Church of Ireland in 1560. However, Ireland was largely Catholic, spoke mostly Gaelic and had customs and laws that differed from England's; this made it

KEY CHRONOLOGY

Ireland

1569–73	Rebellion against English rule in the south
1579–82	Rebellion linked to a Spanish incursion into County Kerry. Brutally suppressed
1595	Earl of Tyrone led rebellion in Ulster, linked to Anglo-Spanish War
1598	Rebels victorious at the Battle of Yellow Ford; Tyrone and allies controlled most of Ireland 'beyond the Pale' (with Spanish support)
1599	Earl of Essex sent to Ireland as Lord Lieutenant. Essex made a truce with Tyrone (against orders) and returned to court; on expiration of the truce, Tyrone moved south, hoping to link up with a Spanish army
1601	Over 3000 Spanish troops landed in support of the rebellion; rebels were defeated by the new Lord Lieutenant, Lord Mountjoy
1603	Peace concluded, following Elizabeth's death

difficult to enforce Protestantism. The behaviour of English incomers and the frequent use of martial law soured relations with the Irish lords.

The troubles were a financial drain on the English Crown as well as destroying and impoverishing much of Ireland, leaving a legacy of bitterness among the native population.

Wales

By Elizabeth's reign, Wales was well integrated into England, although some linguistic and cultural differences remained.

- The Council of Wales and the Marches continued to police the border so conflict there was no longer an issue.
- The Welsh language (widely spoken among the Welsh people) was no longer used in government. Nevertheless, the Book of Common Prayer and the Bible were translated into Welsh, and Welsh dictionaries and grammars were published.
- Much of Wales remained poor.

Scotland

For the most part, England remained on reasonable terms with Scotland, where the Protestant Lords of the Congregation held sway.

When rebellion broke out in the north of England in 1569, some of the English rebel leaders evaded capture by escaping into Scotland. Moreover, when the grip on power of the Protestant lords in Scotland was uncertain, the English position was less secure. Nevertheless, order was mostly maintained by the border lords while the Council of the North based in York also tried to curb lawlessness on the border.

Social discontent and rebellions

Elizabeth's reign was mostly a period of social stability. However, there was still religious division, particularly after Elizabeth's excommunication in 1570 which ultimately led to the introduction of the recusancy laws in 1593. These imposed punishments on those who refused to attend Anglican services.

There was also economic discontent which led to sporadic food riots. The 'Oxfordshire rising' of 1596, for example, was provoked by high food prices after a harvest failure. It was led by four men who were desperate enough to seize weapons and march on London. The authorities responded harshly to such incidents, although they were genuinely concerned about the poor, giving rise to the poor law legislation.

The Northern Rebellion, 1569–70

The Northern Rebellion took place mainly in Durham and the North Riding of Yorkshire in 1569, with a subsequent rising in Cumberland in 1570. It was headed by the leading northern nobility, the earls of Northumberland and Westmorland, and was largely a 'noble' rebellion. Motives included those shown in the following diagram.

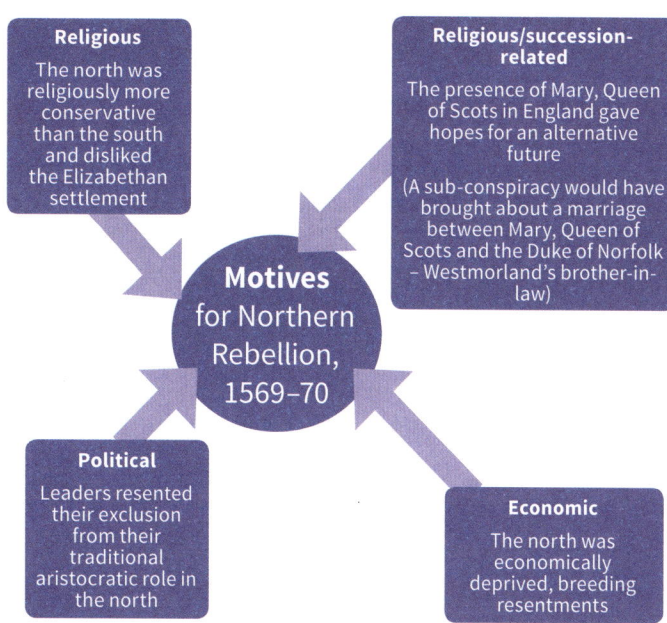

The rebels marched as far as York, before heading northwards again and taking Barnard Castle, in the county of Durham. However, they suffered from a lack of clear objectives, disorganisation and poor leadership. They did not get a mass popular following and they failed to gain foreign support. The Crown acted decisively and sent a force north, at which the earls disbanded their forces and fled into Scotland. A subsequent rebellion in Cumberland was also put down.

The government ordered mass executions of the rebels; Northumberland was executed in 1572 and Westmorland exiled to the Spanish Netherlands. The Crown took over the rebel leaders' lands.

The rebellion revealed the London government's lack of comprehension of the differences between north and south and of the problems of managing the localities. The Council of the North was reconstituted in 1572, under the Earl of Huntingdon, an outsider with no local ties, who owed his influence entirely to Elizabeth. Otherwise, the Crown mostly relied here, as elsewhere, on the Lord Lieutenants and JPs who took responsibility for defence and order.

SUMMARY

- The structure of society changed little under Elizabeth, except that the gentry class increased in size and wealth and a consumer class began to arise from the landed, mercantile and professional classes.
- The gap between rich and poor continued to widen, but a succession of poor laws attempted to alleviate poverty by introducing nationwide measures for poor relief.
- The kingdom was generally peaceable and social order was maintained, although repeated rebellion in Ireland proved difficult and costly.
- The only serious rebellion, the Northern Rebellion of 1569–70, was geographically limited and quickly suppressed.

REVISION PROGRESS

APPLY

APPLY YOUR KNOWLEDGE

Define the following words and terms, in relation to Elizabethan society, and write a sentence to show your understanding of each in context:

- vagrancy
- undeserving/impotent poor
- martial law
- almshouses
- house of correction
- poor relief
- parish

> **EXAMINER TIP**
> Using these terms correctly in an exam question will help you to demonstrate your understanding of key concepts.

ASSESS THE VALIDITY OF THIS VIEW

 'Rebellion sparked by religious belief was more dangerous to rulers than courtly conspiracies in the years 1536 to 1569.' Assess the validity of this view.

a Underline the key words and dates in this question. Which terms will require clarification?

b Below is a two-column plan, with a row for each of the 4 monarchs:

	Rebellion sparked by religious belief	Courtly conspiracies
1536–47		
1547–53		
1553–58		
1558–69		

- Record in the chart examples of each of the 2 forms of opposition and whether these posed a significant threat or not.
- Decide which type of opposition posed the greater danger.
- Make a judgement and write an introduction to this essay, setting out your view and clarifying what you understand as 'dangerous to rulers'.

> **EXAMINER TIP**
> Never assume the reader shares your understanding of key words in essay questions. In this essay you would need to clarify how you will judge whether an action/behaviour is 'dangerous'.

> **REVIEW**
> For the various rebellions and courtly conspiracies, look back to Chapter 10 for the Pilgrimage of Grace, Chapters 13–14 for opposition in the time of Edward VI, Chapter 15 for details of Mary's reign as well as this chapter for the Northern Rebellion.

THE TRIUMPH OF ELIZABETH, 1563–1603

ASSESS THE VALIDITY OF THIS VIEW

A LEVEL — 'Rebellions against Tudor rulers were totally ineffective in the years 1536 to 1569.' Assess the validity of this view.

Whatever judgement you choose to adopt in response to an essay question, you will always need to show 'supported' argument in your essay. Comments should be supported by relevant, precise and specific evidence.

a Support each of the following arguments with at least two pieces of evidence:
   - Rebellions were ineffective.
   - Rebellions had some effect.

b Choose an example from the evidence you provided in part **a**, and write a supported paragraph to this essay based on the argument you find most convincing. You could argue either way, but your paragraph should use the evidence you would have included in your essay to back the argument.

PLAN YOUR ESSAY

A LEVEL — To what extent was the transformation of society under Elizabeth I accomplished without any social disorder?

EXAMINER TIP
Be careful in cases like this where there are 2 terms to assess – in this case, social disorder and transformation. Make sure that both elements are addressed in your answer.

This will activity help you write a conclusion to an essay. When you answer an essay question, make sure you leave enough time to write a conclusion that provides a substantiated judgement.

a Provide 2–3 pieces of evidence to substantiate each of the following judgements:

There was a 'transformation of society' under Elizabeth	
There was not a 'transformation of society' under Elizabeth	
There was no social disorder	
There was social disorder	

b Write a conclusion to this essay based on one of these 4 judgements. Make sure your conclusion summarises the arguments you would have made in your essay.

22 Economic development in Elizabethan England

RECAP

Trade

Trade grew considerably during Elizabeth's reign. Nevertheless, foreign trade was surpassed in value by internal trade. For example, although export of coal to France increased, there was an even greater growth in the shipping of coal from the River Tyne to the River Thames to supply the London market.

External trade involved:

- **a flourishing cloth trade with the Netherlands:** however, in the 1580s, the main markets for English wool moved from the southern to the northern Netherlands, as William Cecil encouraged trade with (Protestant) Amsterdam rather than with Antwerp which was under (Catholic) Spanish control

- **a broadening of overseas markets:** there was an increase in trade with the Ottoman Empire; trade links were established with India and trading routes extended into Russia; a wider range of foreign luxury goods was imported in return

- **three expeditions by John Hawkins:** to Guinea, in Africa, from 1562; he acquired slaves to transport to South America in exchange for other goods, and was backed by London merchants and prominent courtiers, including the Earl of Leicester; Elizabeth gave support (selling ships), but the third expedition suffered a Spanish blockade in Mexico in 1568 – Hawkins's activities worsened relations with Spain, but even Elizabeth saw the potential gains in riches abroad

- **the formation of a number of trading companies:** these had varying degrees of success in widening England's trading interests (see table).

Date	Company	Area(s) with which it was set up to trade	Degree of success
1555 (under Mary I)	Muscovy Company	Russia and northern Europe	Failed in the long term to compete effectively with the Dutch
1579	Eastland Company	Baltic	Had limited success
1581	Turkish Company (became the Levant Company)	Ottoman Empire	Reasonably successful
1600	East India Company	Asia	In the short term, found it difficult to compete with the better-funded Dutch East India Company

By 1603, these were still relatively modest organisations. However, there was a significant change in that all except the Eastland Company were **joint-stock companies** owned by their shareholders – this model would determine future capitalist development.

Exploration and colonisation

Colonial activity in North America was inspired by different events, as shown in the following diagram.

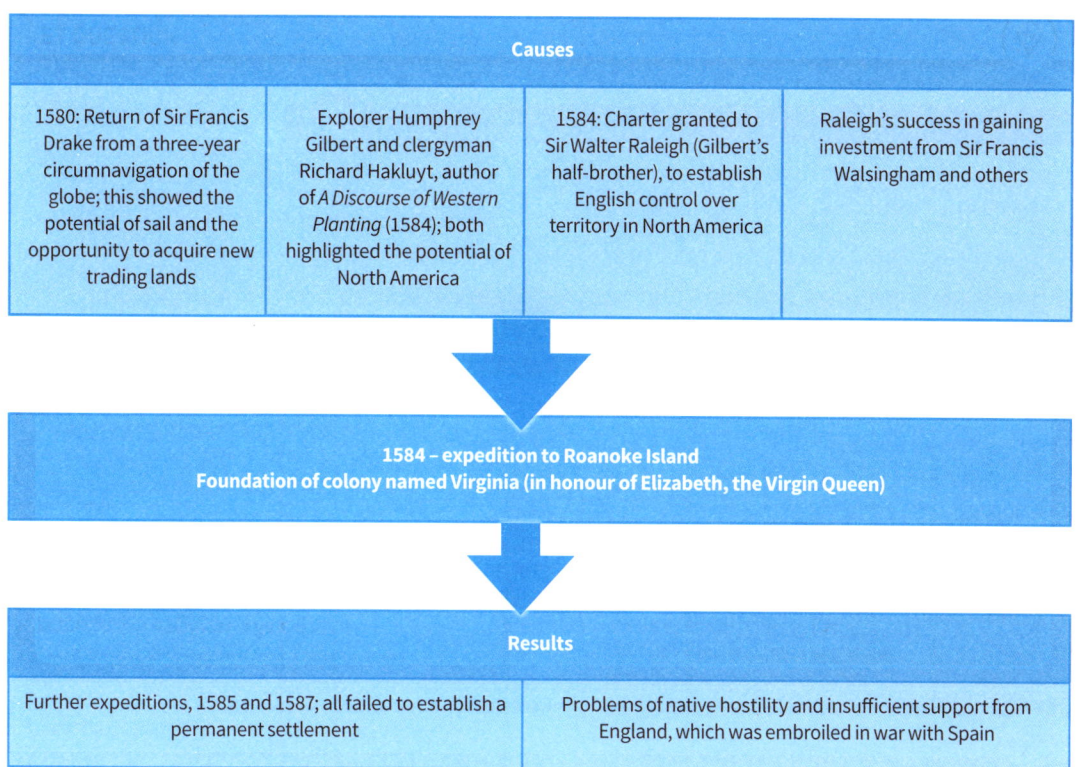

Prosperity and depression

Prosperity

- Agricultural production increased overall (although bad harvests provided interruptions to this trend).
- Cloth-making in rural areas increased; but some old-established cloth towns, such as Stamford and Winchester, declined.
- New urban settlements developed, thriving on a broad range of manufacture (e.g. Manchester and Plymouth).
- London grew and provided a market for internal goods (e.g. coal from Newcastle upon Tyne).
- Shipbuilding and its associate ports grew and prospered with the growth of trade.
- The south-east flourished, followed closely by Norfolk, Suffolk and the 'inner West Country' counties of Somerset, Gloucestershire and Wiltshire. (The poorest counties were those of the north and in the West Midlands.)
- Legislation to regulate trade and industry proliferated. This was a sign of the government's awareness that the taxes and duties which could be levied on manufacturers brought wealth to the country as a whole:
    - Acts to regulate trade in cloth, leather, coal, iron, grain and timber
    - two Navigation Acts to promote the use of English ships
    - Statute of Artificers (1563), to fix prices, regulate wages, restrict workers' freedom of movement and control apprenticeships (this replaced a number of the functions of the old guilds).

Depression

Despite the many signs of growing prosperity, harvest failure could be disastrous; four successive bad harvests 1594–97 led to some serious poverty. By 1596 real wages had collapsed to less than half the level of nine years earlier, and 1596–97 saw a subsistence crisis. Distress was widespread, but particularly bad in the far north, where people died of starvation, both in remote rural areas and in Newcastle (to which the poor and needy from further afield gravitated).

> **SUMMARY**
> - During Elizabeth's reign trade increased and its patterns changed, with mixed success.
> - Prosperity and depression varied across the country, with the north of the country faring less well than the more prosperous south.

REVISION PROGRESS

APPLY

APPLY YOUR KNOWLEDGE

Based on the previous 2 chapters, summarise the results of economic change in the years 1558–1603 using the following table.

	Trade	Exploration and colonisation	Industry	Agriculture
Successes and achievements				
Failures and limitations				

EXAMINER TIP

This table would be useful for an essay addressing consequence and demanding an evaluation of the nature of economic development. It is important that you can follow developments over an extended period for breadth essays.

REVIEW

You may find it helpful to look back at Chapter 20.

APPLY YOUR KNOWLEDGE

Look at the summary table you have just compiled of the results of the economic changes 1558–1603. Then look back the social changes described in Chapter 21.

a Make a list of the key social changes on the left hand side of a sheet of paper.

b Then on the right hand side write which economic changes might link with them.

THE TRIUMPH OF ELIZABETH, 1563–1603

EXTRACT ANALYSIS

EXTRACT A

The cities were filled with poor who led passive, unpleasant lives. Rogues and unemployment were accepted as part of the seamier side of life. The unemployed were deemed potentially dangerous and both local and national authorities took action accordingly. Ultimately it was accepted that responsibility must be taken for the all the poor including the able-bodied, but the numbers rarely exceeded five per cent of the population. Those that were supported were absolutely destitute. Many others were kept from this state by charitable bequests or loan funds for tradesmen set up by wealthy townsmen. Merchant interest dominated in this area and it stemmed from a mixture of pangs of conscience and fears of social disturbance. Whatever the key motive, the government was in control of the situation. It was only at times of dire distress that the average working man reacted violently and this was usually within reasonable bounds. Both poverty and vagrancy were fairly well contained and did not create a dangerous national situation.

Adapted from John Pound, *Poverty and Vagrancy in Tudor England*, 1971

Read the extract.

a Look at the list of statements below: does the extract support or oppose each of them?
  - Poverty was prevalent in Tudor towns.
  - The government always accepted the need to take responsibility to help the unemployed.
  - Merchants acted purely out of fear of threats to their social position.
  - Charity kept many people out of destitution.
  - The poor were out of control in the Tudor period.
  - Poverty was addressed both at the local and the national level.
  - The poor behaved with a surprising lack of violence.

b Explain the overall argument of the extract in relation to poverty and vagrancy in Tudor times and find 1 piece of contextual evidence to support and 1 to challenge this argument.

KEY QUESTION

One of the Key Questions asks:

How did English society and economy change and with what effects?

a Create a mind-map to show how English society and economy changed during Elizabeth's reign. Colour code your map to indicate which changes were largely beneficial (green) and those which were harmful (red).

b Use your diagram to assess the extent of social and economic change and write a three-sentence summary.

REVISION SKILLS

You may find it useful to equip yourself with sheets of A3 paper and card, for producing mind-maps like this, so that you have plenty of space to write what you want. These can then serve as posters in your workroom.

23 Religious developments and the 'Golden Age' of Elizabethan culture

RECAP

Religious developments

The majority of the population supported the royal supremacy and after the legislation enacting the Elizabethan religious settlement of 1559, there was broad acceptance of the 'via media'. Most worshippers accepted the changes which occurred in their parishes as churches lost some of their statuary and plate, and plain Communion tables were erected. It is hard to know how ordinary people felt about all this and the more rural the community, the more conservative it was likely to be. However, there were some who had strong religious convictions and actively worked against the settlement. These included:

- recusants (Catholics who paid fines rather than attend Anglican services)
- Puritans (a new group, opposed to all Catholic practices, which emerged in the 1560s).

From 1570, when the Pope excommunicated Elizabeth, the English Church became more Protestant and those who failed to conform could be punished. Nevertheless, a Puritan faction grew and contained:

- Presbyterians, whose ideas derived from Calvinism and who wanted to remove the bishops
- Separatists, who were dissatisfied with the pace of Protestant reform and wanted to go further.

Similarly, the Catholic faction became more active:

- it linked up with movements on the continent for counter-reformation in the 1570s and 1580s
- it supported the activities of English priests trained abroad (e.g. at Douai from 1568) and Jesuits who came to England to reconvert it (these were harshly treated by the authorities).

Harsh penal laws against Catholics and the 1588 defeat of the Spanish Armada, which reduced the perceived threat of Catholicism, helped Puritans reconcile themselves to the Elizabethan settlement in the later years of Elizabeth's reign. By the time of the queen's death in 1603, religion was no longer a serious political issue and the 'godly' Puritans were accepted within the Church.

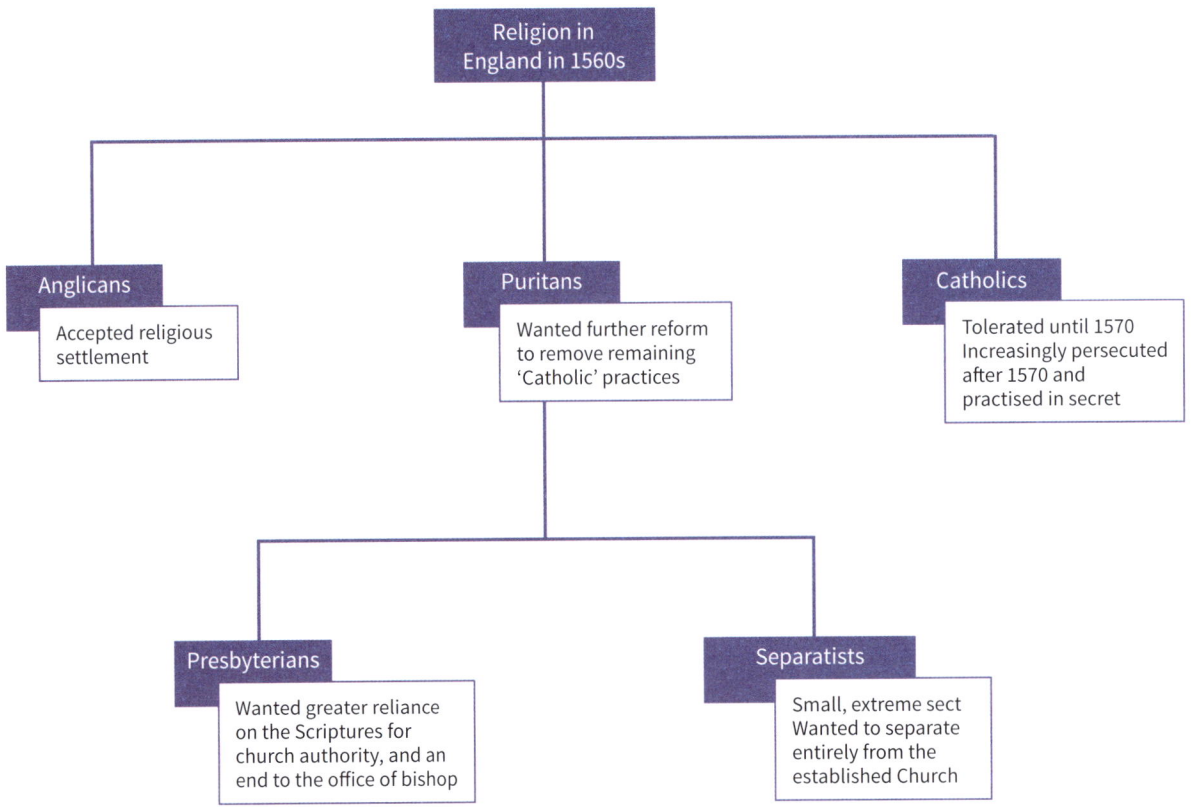

Puritanism

Puritanism arose after the 1563 Convocation of Canterbury failed to go further in its reform of the Church.

1566: the Vestiarian controversy occurred when Archbishop Parker issued his Advertisements making certain vestments compulsory. This angered some Protestants (Puritans), particularly in London, and some Puritan ministers were deprived of their livings.

1583: Archbishop of Canterbury, John Whitgift issued Three Articles. These demanded acceptance from the clergy of:

- the royal supremacy
- the prayer book
- the Thirty-Nine Articles.

Few Puritan clergy were prepared to break with the Church by refusing the Three Articles.

1595: The Lambeth Articles, approved by Whitgift, reaffirmed the fundamentally Calvinist beliefs of the Church of England and proved acceptable to both Puritans and their opponents.

Presbyterianism

Presbyterianism was a Puritan sub-set which developed after the Vestiarian Controversy. It attracted some important supporters, including the Earl of Huntingdon and the Earl of Leicester, but was generally a fringe movement in London, the south-east and parts of the East Midlands.

1572: The *Admonition to Parliament* by John Field and Thomas Wilcox (London clergymen) demanded greater reliance on the authority of the Scriptures and church government by ministers and elders rather than bishops. (Its authors were imprisoned.)

1583: Some Presbyterians stood out against the Three Articles.

1584 and 1587: Peter Turner and Anthony Cope, respectively, introduced bills in Parliament to replace the Book of Common Prayer with a new prayer book stripped of 'popish' elements. Neither bill was passed.

Late 1580s: Presbyterianism declined as Parliament's rejection of Cope's proposed prayer book suggested further reform was unlikely.

Separatism

Separatism was the most extreme form of Puritanism. Its adherents wanted to separate from the Church of England altogether and create independent church congregations, without the queen as Supreme Governor.

The movement emerged in the 1580s but had only small followings, for example in Norwich and London.

1593: Act against Seditious Sectaries (members of sects which had separated from the Church of England) brought arrests of separatists. The leaders of the London movement were tried and executed for circulating 'seditious books'.

Catholicism

Initially, Catholics were tolerated but:

- they had to pay recusancy fines if they failed to attend Anglican services (many outwardly conformed, despite their inner beliefs)
- all (except one) Catholic bishops refused to conform to the 1559 Oath of Supremacy
- many Catholic intellectuals went into exile; some priests survived as private chaplains to Catholic nobles.

1571: Following Elizabeth's excommunication (1570), the publication of papal bulls in England became treasonable.

1575–85: Catholic priests trained abroad came to England to uphold and spread Catholicism. They operated in secret from the country houses of Catholic gentry and aristocracy. Some were trained at a new college in Douai (Spanish Netherlands), from 1568.

1580: Jesuit priests also arrived, led by Robert Parsons and Edmund Campion. (The latter was captured and executed in 1581.)

1581: Act to Retain the Queen's Majesty's Subjects in their Due Obedience made:

- non-allegiance to the queen or Church of England treasonable
- saying Mass punishable by a heavy fine and imprisonment
- the fine for non-attendance at church £20 per month.

The missions had limited success. Fifteen Catholic priests were executed in 1581–82 and a further Act in 1585 made it treasonable for Catholic priests to enter England. Catholicism became more of a 'country-house religion' than the popular faith it had been in the 1560s.

The culmination of the English Renaissance and the 'Golden Age' of art, literature and music

Many aspects of English culture flourished in Elizabethan England. The patronage of queen, courtiers, nobility and gentry ensured that the arts thrived. Some courtiers, such as Sir Philip Sidney and Sir Walter Raleigh, even composed poetry themselves. Many of the arts celebrated the Virgin Queen. Plays, paintings and literature became propaganda for Elizabeth, who was sometimes known as 'Gloriana'. The 'high' culture of the elites also transformed popular culture. Increased educational opportunities led to the emergence of a literate audience, and Shakespeare's plays, for example, appealed to all sections of society.

Around 30 grammar schools were established in Elizabeth's reign and increasing numbers of young noblemen attended Oxford and Cambridge – not necessarily to acquire a degree but to perfect their cultural education. (This replaced the more traditional 'apprenticeships' in the household of another noble.) It was in such a context that the Elizabethan 'Golden Age' was able to flourish.

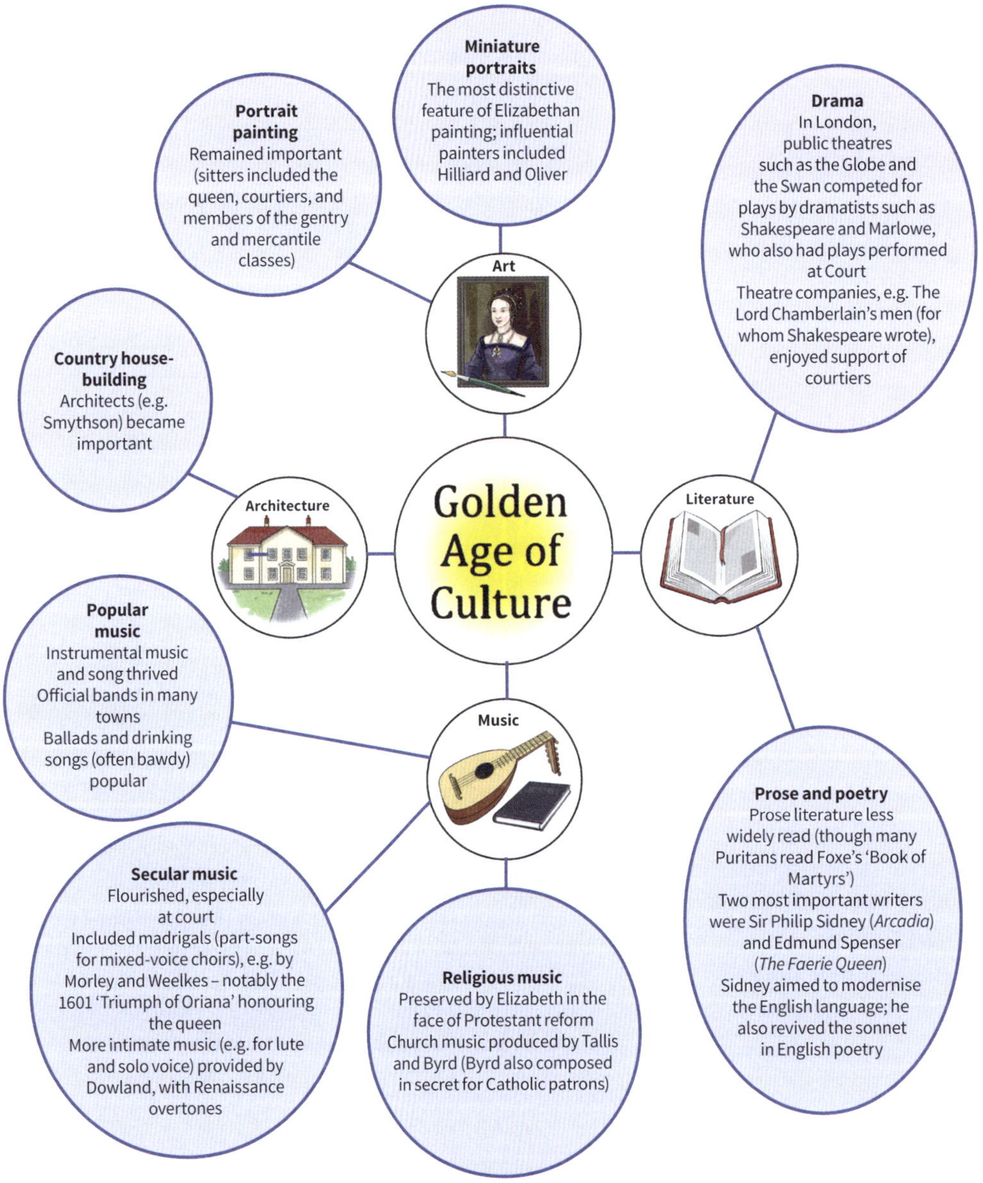

Golden Age of Culture

Art

- **Portrait painting**: Remained important (sitters included the queen, courtiers, and members of the gentry and mercantile classes)
- **Miniature portraits**: The most distinctive feature of Elizabethan painting; influential painters included Hilliard and Oliver

Architecture

- **Country house-building**: Architects (e.g. Smythson) became important

Literature

- **Drama**: In London, public theatres such as the Globe and the Swan competed for plays by dramatists such as Shakespeare and Marlowe, who also had plays performed at Court. Theatre companies, e.g. The Lord Chamberlain's men (for whom Shakespeare wrote), enjoyed support of courtiers
- **Prose and poetry**: Prose literature less widely read (though many Puritans read Foxe's 'Book of Martyrs'). Two most important writers were Sir Philip Sidney (*Arcadia*) and Edmund Spenser (*The Faerie Queen*). Sidney aimed to modernise the English language; he also revived the sonnet in English poetry

Music

- **Popular music**: Instrumental music and song thrived. Official bands in many towns. Ballads and drinking songs (often bawdy) popular
- **Secular music**: Flourished, especially at court. Included madrigals (part-songs for mixed-voice choirs), e.g. by Morley and Weelkes – notably the 1601 'Triumph of Oriana' honouring the queen. More intimate music (e.g. for lute and solo voice) provided by Dowland, with Renaissance overtones
- **Religious music**: Preserved by Elizabeth in the face of Protestant reform. Church music produced by Tallis and Byrd (Byrd also composed in secret for Catholic patrons)

SUMMARY

- By the end of Elizabeth's reign England had been transformed both religiously and culturally.
- Religious disagreements between religious conservatives and those who wanted further reform (the Puritans) had subsided, while Catholicism survived essentially as a minority religion. The Elizabethan Church was generally accepted.
- Elizabeth's reign also demonstrated a great flowering of culture.

APPLY

APPLY YOUR KNOWLEDGE

Copy out the list below and decide which religious group or groups shown in the diagram 'Religion in the 1560s' (page 116) would agree with each statement.

- The Church should have bishops.
- There should be a state Church.
- Brightly coloured vestments should not be worn by clerics.
- The Pope is not the spiritual head of the Church.
- The Bible and services should only be in Latin.
- The Church should be governed by ministers and lay elders.

EXAMINER TIP

It is worth taking time to learn the names and beliefs of the many religious groups flourishing in England at this time. You can then use the names with confidence in your essays.

KEY QUESTION

One of the Key Questions asks:

How far did religious ideas change and develop and with what effect?

To consider this question, it would be helpful to reflect on the material in this chapter and complete the following chart:

Area of impact	Influence of religious ideas
Religious settlement	
Foreign policy	
Popular culture	

EXAMINER TIP

When considering change in this period of history, it is always useful to remember that the religious ideas of individuals and groups will play a varying part. Sometimes they are the prime movers of change, but at other times they are almost forgotten and more circumstantial factors predominate. Understanding the place of religious ideas can add weight to your arguments.

REVIEW

For further detail on religious ideas, look back at Chapters 6, 12, 14, 16 and 18.

REVISION PROGRESS

KEY QUESTION

One of the Key Questions asks:

How far did intellectual ideas change and develop and with what effect?

Consider this key question again.

a   Each of the following are ways in which Elizabethan rule encouraged the arts. Write a sentence to explain each of them:
  - the context of Elizabethan peace and stability
  - patronage
  - propaganda.

b   Each of the following are alternative reasons to explain the flourishing of the arts. Write a sentence to explain each :
  - growing numbers of schools and increased literacy
  - demand from all classes.

c   Write a sentence giving your judgement as to whether Elizabeth herself was the main reason or not for the Elizabethan 'Golden Age'.

> **REVISION SKILLS**
>
> When revising the topic of the Elizabethan Golden Age take care to ensure that the focus is on historical issues rather than long descriptions of various works of art.

> **REVIEW**
>
> Use your knowledge gained from Chapters 18–23, which cover Elizabethan foreign, social, economic and religious policies, to help you answer this question. Also, Chapters 6, 12, 14 and 16 will remind you of religious changes before Elizabeth's reign.

PLAN YOUR ESSAY

 How important were government policies and actions in the decline of Catholicism in England between 1558 and 1603?

When tackling how important a factor was in leading to a historical development, you should ask yourself – was it very important, not particularly important or not at all important?

You can provide a balanced analysis by considering the ways in which this factor was important and balancing these comments against the ways it was not – so arriving at a substantiated judgement.

Alternatively, you might want to consider the importance of other factors and compare these with the factor given in the question. Often you will want to combine the two approaches.

One way of sorting out your ideas is by making a chart like this one:

The decline of Catholicism	Government policies and actions	Weaknesses of Catholic Church	Tolerance because of 'via media'	Other alternative factor
Important				
Not important				
Overall conclusions				

a   Re-read this chapter and consider the alternative factors you could put forward. You can add any others in the last column. You will need to re-read Chapters 17 and 18.

b   In your chart, insert evidence for 'important' and 'not important' for each factor, and complete the last row to show your overall conclusion about each factor.

c   Think about the judgement you will put forward based on your completed chart.

d   Now write your essay.

> **EXAMINER TIP**
>
> All good essays should show balanced analysis. Thinking your essay questions through carefully before you begin writing will enable you to provide sound judgement and support it effectively.

24 The last years of Elizabeth

RECAP

The political condition of England by 1603

England had enjoyed broadly effective and successful government during most of Elizabeth's reign. However, royal authority and the quality of administration declined during the 1590s, because of:

- diminishing talent following the death of Elizabeth's long-standing ministers (Leicester 1588; Burghley 1598)
- increasing factional rivalry in government as younger courtiers sought power; the conflict between Essex and the Cecil faction – involving the Essex 'rebellion' of 1601 – illustrated the problems
- problems of an aging queen who could no longer control her courtiers as effectively as in the past
- anxieties over the succession
- economic problems.

By the time of her death, in 1603, Elizabeth was not as popular as she had been, and the prospect of a new king was welcomed.

The economic condition of England by 1603

England had enjoyed considerable economic growth during the 16th century, with the expansion of trade and industry.

By 1603 some of the structures that would contribute to England's commercial domination within Europe in the 17th century had been established – e.g. trading companies to challenge Spanish/ Portuguese/ Dutch domination, and the beginnings of an interest in the Americas.

Domestic demand thrived. Cottage industries such as nail making, hosiery, soap manufacturing and brewing flourished, and total production rose substantially during Elizabeth's reign.

Although inflation was a problem, the stability of the Elizabethan era did much to aid commercial prosperity.

The state of society in England by 1603

England remained socially divided, with huge differences in living standards between the wealthy few and the poor majority. Nevertheless, in contrast with many continental societies, the nobility were subject to taxation and for the majority of the time, most people could be fed. The lives of those at the lower end of society were still highly dependent on uncontrollable forces such as the weather, orders and taxation demands from central government and the localities, and the problems of wartime. However, many survived through thrift, multiple employments and hard work. There was only one subsistence crisis, in the 1590s. The distress of those years led to the reforms of the poor law enacted in 1598 and 1601; these limited the worst effects of poverty, at least for the deserving poor.

The state of religion in England by 1603

By the end of Elizabeth's reign, there was a broad consensus surrounding the Church of England, which ensured a substantial degree of religious unity.

Catholicism

Church of England (Anglican Church)

Most people could identify with/accept the Anglican Church

Popular Catholicism had declined

Puritanism had faded; most Puritans had become assimilated within the mainstream Church

English Catholics divided between a majority who tried to be loyal to both Crown and faith and a minority who sought a Catholic succession

Separatism had virtually disappeared

SUMMARY

- By 1603, the glories associated with the earlier years of Elizabeth's reign had faded and faction-fighting and rebellion damaged her government.
- The reign had brought continued economic growth and some social improvement.
- Although Elizabeth's later years saw increased persecution of Catholics, the Elizabethan religious settlement came to be widely accepted and the Puritan threat had been contained.

KEY CHRONOLOGY

Political developments 1563–1603

1563	Statute of Artificers
1566	Vestiarian Controversy
1569–70	Northern Rebellion
1570	Pope Pius V excommunicates Elizabeth
1585	Start of Anglo-Spanish War
1588	Spanish Armada
1601	Poor Law
1601	Essex 'rebellion'
1603	Death of Elizabeth

THE TRIUMPH OF ELIZABETH, 1563–1603

APPLY

APPLY YOUR KNOWLEDGE

To consider the success of Elizabeth I as Queen of England, review the Key Chronology of political developments given on page 122.

a Create 9 revision cards: on each card, write 1 political development, and points to explain the development and its significance. Write corresponding date(s) on the back. For example:

Front of the card

Development:
What is it?
-
-
-

Significance:
-
-
-

Back of the card

Date:

b Sort the 9 cards into a 'diamond 9', ranked by importance for the development of Elizabeth's England.

c Re-sort the cards in chronological order to test your understanding. (You will be able to check this by turning them over.)

> **EXAMINER TIP**
> This activity will help you to both prioritise relevant information and ensure chronological understanding. Both skills are essential for essay questions in examinations.

> **REVIEW**
> To check the detail, look back at Chapters 18–23.

> **REVISION SKILLS**
> The 'diamond 9' is a useful way of prioritising detail. Look back to page 53 to remind yourself of how it works.

ASSESS THE VALIDITY OF THIS VIEW

> **A LEVEL** 'The economy of England was in a much stronger position in 1603 than it had been in 1558.' Assess the validity of this view.

a Completing the change and continuity chart below will help you to assess the degree to which the economy was strengthened (or otherwise) between these dates:

	Situation in 1558	Situation in 1603
Positive changes		
Trade and commerce:	• • •	• • •
Agriculture:	• • •	• • •
Continuity		
Trade and commerce:	• • •	• • •
Agriculture:	• • •	• • •
Negative changes		
Trade and commerce:	• • •	• • •
Agriculture:	• • •	• • •

> **EXAMINER TIP**
> In an essay you should substantiate your argument with some precise examples. In a question like this, it is important to compare directly between the dates given, and distinguish between 'trade and commerce' and 'agriculture'.

b Use your diagram to help you to decide whether the economy got stronger, stayed the same, or worsened.

c Write a conclusion to this essay, offering a judgement on the view given.

> **REVIEW**
> To remind yourself of the economic situation at the beginning of the period, look back at Chapters 16, 18 and 22.

REVISION PROGRESS

EXTRACT ANALYSIS

EXTRACT A

There were two reigns of Elizabeth I, each with distinctive features. Her 'first' reign ended about 1585, with the dispatch of an English force to the Netherlands. This reversal of the queen's non-interventionist policy was followed by the trial and execution of Mary, Queen of Scots, and the outbreak of war with Spain and the French Catholic League. Mary's execution resolved one political and constitutional crisis but caused another. The costs and casualties of the resulting war was high and England was often threatened with conquest. The crown's poverty and the competition for patronage kindled factionalism and sparked Essex's attempted coup. The turmoil created by rising prices and bad harvests caused resistance to the crown's fiscal and military demands. This triggered an authoritarian reaction with an obsessional emphasis on state security and fear of religious nonconformity. There was also a change of personnel between Elizabeth's 'first' and 'second' court with the deaths between 1588 and 1590 of four key men – Leicester, Warwick, Mildmay and Walsingham.

Adapted from John Guy, *The Reign of Elizabeth I: Court and Culture in the Last Decade*, 1991

a **Comprehension**: Read the extract carefully.
- Pick out 3 key turning points between the 'first' and 'second' reign of Elizabeth.
- Pick out 2 other references that are factually correct.
- Summarise the overall view of this extract.

b **Evaluation**: Write an answer to the question: With reference to this extract and your understanding of the historical context, assess how convincing the argument is, in relation to Elizabeth's 'second' reign (1585 to 1603).

REVIEW

To remind yourself of the context of Elizabeth's reign, look again at Chapters 18–23 as well as this chapter.

EXAMINER TIP

You should spend around 15 minutes on this exercise. As always, begin your answer with a summary of the overall argument and then look at any sub-arguments. All should be supported and criticised with reference to the text and your own contextual knowledge, and you should arrive at a substantiated judgement.

REVISION SKILLS

Now that you have completed your revision of The Tudors: England 1485–1603, you should extend and add to the revision activities suggested in this guide to encompass the whole of the content. These are:
- Key Question cards (Chapter 1).
- Revision chart of change and continuity – adapt the general subject headings to each monarch's period, e.g. 'Society in the reign of …' instead of 'English society at the end of the 15th century' (Chapter 6).
- Revision chart to show the state of the country in 1553, 1558 and 1603 (Chapter 8).
- Colour coded thematic timeline (Chapter 16).

EXAMINER TIP

These 4 activities will ensure your awareness of all the major elements of the Component 1 Breadth Study exam paper: appreciation of the Key Questions; appreciation of key topic areas; specific understanding of chronology linked to the major themes.

REVIEW

You will need to look back through the whole of the Revision Guide to complete these activities.

EXAM PRACTICE

A Level extracts sample answer

REVISION PROGRESS

REVIEW

On these Exam Practice pages, you will find a sample student answer for an A Level extracts question. What are the strengths and weaknesses of the answer? Read the answer and the corresponding Examiner Tips carefully. Think about how you could apply this advice in order to improve your own answers to questions like this one.

 A LEVEL Using your understanding of the historical context, assess how convincing the arguments in these three extracts are in relation to Elizabeth I's rule in England.

30 marks

REVISION SKILLS

The A Level exam paper will have one extracts question which you must answer. It will be made up of three extracts with different views on a common theme. This question is worth 30 marks unlike the essays which are each worth 25 marks. Unlike the AS extracts question, you do not need to compare the value of the extracts but simply comment, in turn, on how convincing the arguments are. Look back at page 6 for details on how to master the extracts question.

EXTRACT A

Elizabeth brought real dramatic talent to the role of Virgin Queen and freed herself from some of the restrictions of her sex. But the production in which she starred ran for 45 years: she had no understudy and she had to appear in every show; it was a constant strain. Her performances were not flawless; she disliked her part in her early years when she hoped to marry Dudley; she was bored with it in 1579 when she thought of marrying Alençon, and she could not quite carry it off in her last decade. She lost confidence in the interpretation of the part in 1585 and allowed her leading man to persuade her into a more aggressive version for foreign audiences. But hers was an award-winning performance. The metaphor of drama is an appropriate one for Elizabeth's reign, for her power was an illusion. She projected an image of herself which brought stability and prestige to her country.

Adapted from Christopher Haigh, *Elizabeth I*, 1988

EXTRACT B

It is easy to be taken in by Elizabeth's love of theatricality. Elizabeth's political aims and style of government were more complex than her image makers and admirers have admitted. In addition, her popularity with her subjects can no longer be taken for granted, especially during the last decade of her reign. Nonetheless her achievement as a ruler should not be underestimated. Despite enormous difficulties and several major crises, she survived as monarch with her Protestant religious settlement intact, while her realm was preserved from successful invasion and the civil wars which afflicted her neighbours, Scotland, France and the Netherlands. Fifteen years of warfare created stresses certainly but not the financial collapse or large scale political unrest which often came in the wake of war. The stability and security which England enjoyed owed much to Elizabeth's firm but flexible leadership, and her conservative and relatively cautious policies.

Adapted from Susan Doran, 'Elizabeth I', *The Historian* (No. 54), 1997

EXTRACT C

In the making of the cult, images and presentation were as important as policies and patronage. Elizabeth certainly capitalised on all the qualities commonly attributed to her sex and the court was the natural setting for the cult of Gloriana with its conspicuous displays in the queen's honour. The queen was also always anxious to reach out to the nation at large, hence the royal progresses. It is certainly true that many contemporaries equated the monarch's fame with the emergent English nation. After the triumph over the Armada, Elizabeth I became enshrined in the myths of the Virgin Queen and Gloriana, as the symbol of England's greatness. However, there is more to the successes of Elizabethan England than Elizabeth's leadership. Moreover, England in 1603 still had unresolved constitutional problems between queen and Parliament and grave economic difficulties with over 40 per cent of the population living below subsistence level. The queen's subjects had suffered unrelieved taxation for two decades, so the Elizabethan age ended for many in despair and disillusionment.

Adapted from John McGurk, *The Tudor Monarchies 1485–1603*, 2010

Sample student answer

Extract A argues that the queen relied on drama during her rule in England. It claims that her image brought 'stability and prestige' to the country despite occasions when she failed to live up to her role. Certainly, Elizabeth relied on image, as shown by the mass manufacture of her portrait as the Virgin Queen, and her ability to make effective speeches was shown at Tilbury before the Armada and by the Golden Speech in the previously disastrous last Parliament of 1601. However, Elizabethan rule depended on more than this. Walsingham prevented many Catholic plots against her. Her armed forces were successful against the Spanish and the Irish rebels at the end of her reign. The extract is persuasive and illustrates the argument with evidence; but it is limited because it overlooks other elements which gave the country stability and prestige.

Extract B argues that stability and security came from Elizabeth's 'firm but flexible leadership' and her 'cautious policies'. It has some balance, admitting her loss of popularity in her later years, especially among the Essex faction and those hard pressed by taxation paying heavy taxes on monopolies. It is true that the last fifteen years of warfare exacerbated her problems. However, these were due to a decline in her leadership and the dominance of the Privy Council which implemented the death warrant for Mary, Queen of Scots and pushed Elizabeth into war with the Dutch. So, while this extract is well supported by evidence, it provides only a limited explanation of circumstances by the end of her reign.

Extract C takes a negative view of Elizabeth's reign. It paints a gloomy picture of England by 1603, pointing out the economic and constitutional problems that she left at the end of her reign which left many in despair. However, the extract is convincing because it talks about how the image of Gloriana became a symbol of England's greatness, which was certainly the case in, for example, the paintings produced to glorify England's victory against the Armada. It suggests images and presentation were as important as policies, which may be an exaggeration but which is corroborated by knowledge of Elizabeth's popularity in her earlier years. The decline in image would therefore seem to account for the deterioration in her rule after the Armada.

> **EXAMINER TIP**
>
> This identifies (at least in part) the interpretation in the extract and applies some contextual own knowledge to consider its strengths and limitations. However, it is slim in relation to the content of the extract and the limitations are purely seen in terms of what is omitted. There is also no overall judgement given.

> **EXAMINER TIP**
>
> This paragraph misses some key points in the interpretation and focuses only on the comments relating to the later years of Elizabeth's reign. It offers some own knowledge to support and criticise but, again, much is left unsaid and undeveloped.

> **EXAMINER TIP**
>
> This shows some understanding of the interpretation of Extract C but the application of contextual knowledge is limited, and there is no explicit criticism of the view given.

EXAM PRACTICE: A LEVEL EXTRACTS SAMPLE ANSWER

OVERALL COMMENT

This answer shows some awareness of how to respond to the question and some understanding of what each extract has to say. However, it is very limited in development. The overall interpretation of each extract is not succinctly defined at the beginning of each evaluation so it is not always clear that the whole extract has been properly understood. There should also have been reference to sub-arguments and interpretations. Still more importantly, very little contextual own knowledge has been used to assess the strengths and limitations of the extracts in relation to the question. This answer would therefore be placed in Level 3.

OVER TO YOU

Take 5 minutes to read and plan your answer and 50 minutes to write it. Then review your answer using the following checklist. Have you:

☐ Identified the overall interpretation of each extract at the beginning of each evaluation?

☐ Identified sub-arguments and interpretations?

☐ Referred explicitly to the detail in the extracts?

☐ Applied your own knowledge to support and to criticise interpretations?

☐ Given a clear judgement on how convincing the argument is at the end of each of the three evaluations?

Now check Chapters 17–24, especially Chapter 23. Are the details in your answer factually accurate? Have you missed any issues you should have raised?

Activities: Suggested answers

The answers provided here are examples, based on the information provided in the Recap sections of this Revision Guide. There may be other factors which are relevant to each question, and you should draw on as much own knowledge as possible to give detailed and precise answers. There are also many ways of answering exam questions (for example, of structuring an essay). However, these suggested answers should provide a good starting point.

Chapter 1

Apply Your Knowledge

Problem:
- Yorkist opponents
- Few allies in important positions
- Weak claim to the throne

Actions:
- Henry dated his reign from the day before Bosworth so those who had fought against him could be treated as traitors under Acts of Attainder.
- Henry appointed his main supporters to key positions.
- Henry arrested the Earl of Warwick, he was crowned before Parliament met to show his claim was by hereditary right, and he married Elizabeth of York to exploit the union of the houses of Lancaster and York.

Assess the Validity of This View

Factors to show that Henry's claim was insecure:
- There were always other claimants to the throne who launched rebellions and de la Pole was at large.
- While the children of Henry had a strong claim through having Elizabeth as their mother, Henry's own claim was unaltered and insecure.

Factors to show that Henry's claim became secure:
- Many of the rival claimants were killed or imprisoned by 1506.
- Henry's marriage to Elizabeth of York strengthened his claim as unifying the 2 houses.

Changes that occurred during Henry's reign
- Henry married Elizabeth of York in 1486
- Earl of Lincoln defeated and killed at the Battle of Stoke in 1487
- Perkin Warbeck was executed in 1499
- Edmund de la Pole was made Henry's prisoner in 1506

Improve an Answer

Answer 2 is the better example because:
- it avoids narrative description
- it begins with a clear comment on the question
- it contains clear and wide-ranging information with further analytical comment.

Revision Skills

You should produce your own set of revision cards for this activity.

Chapter 2

Apply Your Knowledge

a **courtier** – a person who attends a royal court as a companion or adviser to the monarch

magnate – a member of the higher ranks of the nobility

bonds and recognisances – a bond bound an individual to behave in a certain way, or to pay a sum of money if they failed to do so; a recognisance acknowledged a debt or other obligation which could incur a financial penalty

prerogative rights – rights or powers which the monarch could exercise without requiring the consent of Parliament

personal monarchy – a monarchy in which the political power and influence of an individual depended on their relationship with the monarch

Chamber – the private areas of the court; also a key department for the efficient collection of royal revenues; remodelled in 1495 into the Privy Chamber

Privy Chamber – created by Henry VII, the close personal servants of the monarch; its members had direct access to the monarch

Act of Attainder – an act declaring a landowner guilty of rebelling against the monarch

tonnage and poundage – the right to raise revenue for the whole reign from imports and exports

extraordinary revenue – money raised by the king from additional sources as one-off payments when he faced an unforeseeable expense of government

feudalism/feudal aid – medieval system by which the nobility held lands from the Crown, originally in exchange for military service; feudal aid was the right of the Crown to tax tenants for the knighting of the eldest son, the marriage of the eldest daughter or to ransom a lord

b These terms could be used to explain and comment on political authority and government (courtier, magnate, prerogative rights, personal monarchy, Chamber, Privy Chamber, Act of Attainder, feudalism), maintenance of law and order (bonds and recognisances, Act of Attainder) and Crown revenue (tonnage and poundage, extraordinary revenue, feudal aid).

Plan Your Essay

a **Successes of financial policies:**
- Revenue from Crown lands increased
- Profits from feudal dues increased (increase in profits from wardships, feudal aid granted in 1504)
- Revenue increased from customs revenue (tonnage and poundage), pensions from other powers, profits of justice (including fines and income from bonds)

Failures of financial policies:
- Henry's financial demands made him unpopular with landowners upon whom he depended for support
- Caused disagreement with Parliament (in 1504, had to agree not to raise any more funds through extraordinary revenue)
- Weakened government (Empson and Dudley unpopular with other key ministers)
- Raising of extraordinary revenue helped cause rebellions in 1489 and 1497

Issues raised:
- Financial issues (increase in Crown's finances)
- Political issues (unpopularity of Henry and his ministers, tensions with Parliament)
- Social issues (social distress, leading to rebellion)

b You should use the points you have identified in part **a** of this activity to help you plan your essay.

Key Question

You should create 1 flashcard for each individual.

Assess the Validity of This View

Was Henry VII an expert financial manager?
Yes:
- Replaced Court of Exchequer by the Chamber
- Revived feudal dues
- Gained income from effective foreign policy
- Used bonds and recognisances

No:
- Empson and Dudley's financial expertise important

Should Henry be praised for increasing royal income?
Yes:
- Made Crown more independent of Parliament by not needing to call it for raising taxes
- Left no debts for son

No:
- Provoked rebellions
- Alienated nobility – his main supporters

Conclusion: An expert financial manager but prioritised increasing finances over political security which may not deserve praise

Your judgements might suggest:
- Henry was an efficient financial manager – he appointed Empson and Dudley and 'managed' finances.
- Financial benefits may be outweighed by the political problems; if Henry's methods caused rebellions, they may be considered to be counter-productive – provoking discontent and rebellion.
- Whether Henry deserves praise depends on your view of what was important to the king.

Try to support your judgement with precise evidence.

Chapter 3

Apply Your Knowledge

1485–95: Anglo-Scottish relations were tense – poor

1495–96: James IV provided a small army to invade England – close to bottom line

1497: Truce of Ayton – neutral

1502: Truce of Ayton – a little better than neutral

1503: James IV married Margaret Tudor – strong

Assess the Validity of This View

a You should produce a mind-map for this activity. For an example of a good mind-map see pages 12 and 64.

b You may conclude that dynastic motives outweighed economic ones, as Henry was willing to jeopardise economic motives for dynastic goals as in Burgundy.

 Improve an Answer

Some of the problems with this answer:
- Overall it is too dogmatic and generalised – it lacks balance and precision.

ACTIVITIES: SUGGESTED ANSWERS

- The first sentence refers to the question partly but suggests that there will be no examination of other aims.
- Precise supporting evidence is lacking – which marriages? When? Was the future Henry VIII always the succession he was considering? Also the 'twice' section is not precise.
- Its claims are too broad – for example, 'all of the leading powers in Europe'. Scotland was not a leading power and no marriage involved the HRE.
- It mostly focuses on the question at the end but is too assertive and there is some drift.

Key Question

1485–1509:

- Brittany: Allowed to become part of France for dynastic and financial reasons
- Burgundy/Netherlands/HRE: Improved – trading agreement
- France: Improved – financial gains
- Spain: Improved by marriage but still in the balance
- Scotland: Improved by marriage and treaty
- Ireland: Improved to having a reasonable level of control

The rest of the chart should be completed in a similar fashion.

Chapter 4

Apply Your Knowledge

a and **b** Your answer should include examples of both actions which weakened or did not weaken the nobility. These could include:

Reduced noble powers:

- Used bonds and recognisances: to make the nobles financially dependent on their good behaviour towards the king
- Limited the numbers of retainers: reduced their power to raise armed forces
- Used spying network: made it hard to plot against Henry
- Used lesser magnates to govern: meant the nobles had less control over government
- Dated his reign from the day before Bosworth: left those lords who had fought against him in a vulnerable position
- Used Acts of Attainder to take estates: could be used either to remove the power of magnates or at least threaten to do so

Maintained noble powers:

- Did not create many new peers: preserved the status of existing peers to influence government in the House of Lords and ambitious new men were kept under Henry's control

c Your judgement is likely to be that the nobility was weakened during Henry VII's reign but not completely so.

- The nobility retained their political position in Parliament.
- They retained their control over regional councils.
- Most had not lost their estates and so had the potential to be strong again.

How Important?

Examples of the Church's importance to society:

- The Church was a great landowner.
- Leading churchmen sat in the House of Lords.
- The Church's influence varied by area – the Bishop of Durham controlled a palatinate.
- The Church had its own courts.
- Leading churchmen such as Morton and Fox were important government administrators.
- The Church had a major spiritual role in people's everyday lives via the parish church.

Examples of the nobility's importance to society:

- Nobility served the Crown as part of government.
- The 50–60 leading peers sat in the House of Lords.
- They controlled important regional councils on the borders.
- They were higher in the feudal system than the gentry.
- They were large landowners and wealthy.
- They had military power.

Plan Your Essay

Key points might include:

- Both were important politically – they held leading political positions in the regions and were important in the House of Lords.
- However, the power of the nobility was under attack from Henry VII with bonds and recognisances, for example, and churchmen were often used as councillors.
- Economically both were very important as major landowners.
- Both had areas of specific strength – the Church had a major influence on people's spiritual lives but the nobility had potential military power.

Your judgement may well depend on what you consider was the most important – the spiritual influence of the Church on everyday life in an age when everyone seems to have been sincere believers, or the military and political power of the nobility.

Chapter 5

Apply Your Knowledge

a and **b Navigation Acts (1485 and 1489):** these limited the movement of certain goods to England to English vessels to boost shipbuilding and profits for English merchants.

The embargo on trade with the Netherlands (1493): although this harmed trade, Henry wanted to force the rulers of the Netherlands to stop supporting Warbeck.

The depression in the cloth industry (1493–1496): this harmed cloth workers, the merchants and the farmers who kept sheep to supply the trade with wool.

Intercursus Magna (1496): this ended the trade embargo and aimed to open up and regulate trade with Flanders.

John Cabot's discovery of Newfoundland (1497): this voyage was intended to find new fishing grounds to help Bristol merchants in particular.

Weston's expedition to the New World (1499): this was another voyage trying to find trading opportunities in America.

Sebastian Cabot's journey to find a 'north-west passage' to Asia (1508): this was an attempt to find a short cut to Asia around the north of America to encourage trade.

To What Extent?

You should produce a mind-map for this activity. For an example of a good mind-map see pages 12 and 64.

Extract Analysis

a Extract A summary: Henry's commercial policy was a very limited start to the development of trade. He did open up new markets but this did not produce extra customs revenue for him. Shipping and the cloth trade did expand but they were small-scale in comparison to other countries. Expansion of trade was always secondary to dynastic considerations.

- The Intercursus Magna and treaties like that with Spain did open up trade. However, the openings he forged with Venice for example were very limited.
- Increasing customs revenue was a key aim of Henry VII's as part of trying to make himself financially secure.
- England was a much smaller state than Spain and so it was likely on pure size it would be smaller. This may not be a fair criticism.
- Dynastic concerns did dominate foreign policy; however generally Henry did assist economic growth and was far more proactive than his predecessors or immediate successors.

Extract B summary: Henry's policies showed 'economic wisdom' that allowed further economic growth. His main policies were to concentrate trade in English ships and to expand international trade. When he failed to achieve fixed traditional trading rates for English merchants he used treaties to gain trade with individual countries. His investments in the cloth trade increased trade and tax revenue.

- Economic growth did occur but the investment in the alum trade was the only example of encouraging manufacturing directly
- The cloth trade was important and did have an economic impact on ordinary people especially in the South East of England in towns like Lavenham.

Extract C summary: Henry did not really have a policy of 'economic nationalism'. He did encourage the cloth trade actively but he only acted against foreign merchants for financial or dynastic reasons. His actions 'greatly assisted' commercial revival but it made little impact on his income from customs.

- The Hanseatic League dominated trade to the Baltic and so this was a market which Henry failed to open up.
- The rise in the woollen cloths exported (cited in Extract B) supports his view that there was economic growth.
- Much always depends on how statistics are expressed. As a percentage, customs revenue increased by 15%; this is far more impressive than the way Elton represents the increase.

b A good answer will identify the overall argument of each extract clearly and will both support and criticise this argument using relevant contextual own knowledge. It is also likely to look at sub-arguments and interpretations within the extract to provide a rounded and convincing judgement on 'how convincing' the extract is.

A good answer will evaluate each extract in the way suggested for A Level but will need a clear judgement as to which one is more convincing based on the detail of the extracts and own knowledge. Extract A is more balanced than Extract B, and its view of the dominance of dynastic influences is also supported by the Intercursus Malus and the Earl of Suffolk in 1507.

Chapter 6

Apply Your Knowledge

Humanists

- were probably few in number as it was only an intellectual movement
- were drawn from the educated elite
- influenced a minority of the educated nobility and gentry; however, humanists patronised educational institutions which influenced the children of the wealthy and humanist ideas were spread by printing

Religious orders

- large numbers of men were monks (1% of population) or friars

129

- they were drawn from a wide section of society, especially friars
- they were often remote (like Cistercian monasteries) or in decline (like the friars) – but the latter did work among lay people

Assess the Validity of This View

a **Examples of the Church being stable:**
- There was no other organised Church in England except the Catholic Church.
- Its teaching could be seen as a successful form of indoctrination and propaganda.
- It was bolstered by the religious orders which included large numbers of people.
- The Church was an essential part of daily life so people accepted it.
- The Church's teaching about the threat of hell and purgatory greatly influenced behaviour.

Examples of the Church not being stable:
- There were Lollards who attacked the Church who wanted the Bible to be read in English.
- Humanism was gaining a growing influence.
- The monasteries were often remote from people and the number of friars was in decline.
- There was some criticism of the Church.
- Printing allowed the spread of new ideas like humanism which challenged the Church's teaching.
- The Church's traditional ceremonies were under threat.

Possible judgement:
- Lollards were a small minority and in decline.
- Humanism only gained an influence among the educated.
- On balance, most people accepted the Church and gave money to it.
- Anti-clericalism was not widespread.
- Few people were literate but in the long run humanist education would have an impact.

b A good introduction will:
- Make clear that the Church had many strengths at this point. This might be linked to the fact that there was only one international Church throughout western Europe under the Pope, who also did not interfere much.
- Mention areas where there was some challenge to the Church. This could be supported by mention of the Lollards, the humanists, and the development of printing and education.
- Emphasise that, in broad terms, much remained the same. This could be linked with the lack of education and literacy at the time.

The introduction will need to convey a judgement. This is likely to state that the Church was largely stable and the premise of the quotation is largely acceptable despite there being some threats.

Key Question

a **Change:**
- Humanists had gained ground among some socially important people.
- New ideas circulated more due to changes in education and printing.

Continuity:
- The Church as an institution remained intact.
- The Church commanded the support of the vast majority of the population.

b **Impact:**
- Only relatively few people were affected and while they did have some influence there was no question of anything but reforming the Church from within as yet.

- Old ideas were also circulated due to education and printing.

The balance between changes and continuities:
You should have found it very easy to list 2 continuities. The impact of the changes had not really taken root – yet. Clearly continuity was far more important than change under Henry VII.

Revision Skills

You should produce a chart using your own judgement to select the most important key facts for each entry.

Chapter 7

Apply Your Knowledge

Henry VII:
- Fought hard to get rid of pretenders
- Was prudent with money
- Oppressed the nobility
- Used councillors but never had a chief minister

Henry VIII:
- Fought for glory and enjoyment
- Spent heavily on war and entertainment
- Jousted with the nobility
- Used a chief minister to help him govern

Assess the Validity of This View

a **Henry VII's aims:**
- wanted to be prudent with money
- wanted to control the nobility
- wanted to have close personal control of government

Henry VIII's aims:
- wanted to be a warrior king
- wanted good relations with the nobility
- wanted to control government, through ministers

Shared aims:
- wanted to retain control over the nobility
- wanted to be stable financially
- wanted to establish the succession
- wanted good relations with other countries
- wanted to promote trade

b Your answer may include the idea that clearly the two Henrys were very different in approach – but any monarch would share some political aims. Both wanted to control the nobility and both excluded them. Both wanted to establish the succession. However, their aims in foreign, economic and financial policies were very different. You are likely to conclude that although they shared some similar political aims, these differences are too great to support the second part of the quotation in the question.

Chapter 8

Apply Your Knowledge

a The timeline should include the following approximate dates for the key turning points:
- Henry decided that Catherine would not have more children – c1525
- Henry decided that Wolsey would not get the divorce – c1529
- Henry forced the English Church to pay a fine of £100,000 for the crime of *praemunire* – c1531
- Henry decided that he must start the process of the break with Rome to ensure the succession – Jan 1533

b As well as considering the Pope's opposition, you would also need to examine other reasons for the break with Rome, including:
- Henry VIII's need for a son
- Henry's belief that he had religious grounds for the divorce
- Charles V's control over the Pope and his relationship to Catherine of Aragon
- Thomas Cromwell's encouragement
- Anne Boleyn's decision to sleep with Henry and try for a son.

Plan Your Essay

a **Enforcing law and order:** Successes – Chancery and the Court of Star Chamber were used to uphold fair justice. Failure – Wolsey's efforts were rarely effective.

Increasing royal authority: Successes – royal courts increasingly used; local law officers and regional councils increased authority outside London; minions in Privy Chamber more controlled by Eltham Ordinances.

Raising finance for the king: Success – royal tax commissioners; reformed Privy Chamber's finances. Failure – Amicable Grant.

Resolving the 'King's Great Matter': Success – did get the Pope to hold a legatine court. Failure – could not get the Pope to rule in the king's favour.

b **Enforcing law and order:** Limited success despite good intentions.

Increasing royal authority: Success – the power of the nobility was clearly reduced although they remained important at court.

Raising finance for the king: Failure – despite the successes, the failure of the Amicable Grant was a humiliating blow to the king and emphasised the king's problems in raising money.

Resolving the 'King's Great Matter': Failure – although this seems to have been an impossible dilemma without breaking with Rome, this led to his removal from office and ultimate failure.

c **Possible sentence starters:**
- Wolsey's actions as Lord Chancellor were intended to improve the fairness of justice…
- While fairness was an important aim, increasing the power of the Crown was even more so after the era of overmighty nobles…
- Despite increasing royal authority, Wolsey was not able to convert this into improving the king's finances effectively…
- Wolsey's failure in the Amicable Grant was outweighed ultimately by his failure to resolve what became the king's main aim – the 'King's Great Matter…
- Wolsey certainly had successes in his aims but these were undermined by his failure to deliver on the king's key concern…

Extract Analysis

a Overall argument highlighted in yellow.

b Useful references highlighted in purple.

The changes in government under Cromwell were revolutionary, if that term may be applied to any changes which profoundly affect the constitution and government of a state even when no systematic and entire destruction was involved. The essential ingredient of the Tudor revolution was the concept of national sovereignty which Cromwell summarised in the Act of Appeals of 1533 by using the phrase 'this realm of England is an empire'. Previous kings like Edward I had claimed to rule an empire but the meaning here is different. Instead of a claim based on ruling a large extent of land, the Act said that Henry was the 'one supreme Head and King'. The

ACTIVITIES: SUGGESTED ANSWERS

royal supremacy over the Church virtually replaced the Pope in England by the king but the Reformation statutes demonstrate that the political sovereignty created in the 1530s was a parliamentary one. Cromwell's administrative reforms – like the Privy Council – provided the machinery for the new state he had started to construct.

c You should use the points you have identified in the earlier parts of this activity to help you plan your essay.

Revision Skills

You should produce a chart using your own judgement to select the most important key facts for each entry.

Chapter 9

Apply Your Knowledge

Most important: Succession

Why? All of Henry's actions at home and abroad were dominated by this – 5 of his marriages and the break with Rome revolved around succession. He married Catherine of Aragon to have a son with powerful relatives; the annulment's importance 1525–34 was only because he needed a son. Military glory by gaining lands in France was important – this is why he fought the war in France 1544–46 when very ill. Other factors like Scotland were only important for short periods.

Then: Annulment; Military glory

Then: Land in France; Attempting to outdo Francis I; Conquest of Scotland

Then: Alliance with Protestants; Control of Ireland

Least important: Trade

Why? Unlike his father, Henry VII, the acquisition of money only really mattered to Henry as a means of achieving his goals. While he did not actively discourage trade, his wars interfered with trade and taxes, and later on inflation put a burden on his people.

Assess the Validity of This View

a **Parliamentary legislation:**

Acts of Parliament which determined the succession: Succession Acts of 1534, 1536 and 1543 described what should be the order of succession on Henry's death, eventually re-legitimising Mary and Elizabeth.

Other Acts which prevented challenges to the succession: Such as the Treason Act of 1534.

Acts relating to religion which would make a Catholic succession difficult: 1532 Act of Supremacy.

Other factors:

Actions of individuals: Henry's decision to annul his marriage to Catherine. The securing of control of the regency by reformers under Edward's maternal uncle, Edward Seymour, ensured there was no possibility of Edward being usurped.

Henry VIII's will: The will of Henry specified the line of succession. However, wills lacked the legal force of Acts of Parliament, as was illustrated in 1553 when Edward VI's will was ignored and the existing Acts of Succession were followed.

Securing peace at the end of the reign: Making peace with France in 1546 on relatively favourable terms meant that there was not the prospect of a regency government facing foreign warfare.

Gaining noble support for the Tudors: The French war had been seen as a way of gaining noble support as they wanted to be involved in a war as part of their military role.

b You should choose your own judgement for this activity.

c Your introduction might:
- Show (briefly) you understand why there was an issue with Edward VI's succession in 1547 – and how this manifested itself.
- Show you understand both why parliamentary legislation and other factors might play a role in ensuring his succession.
- Give your judgement in relation to the question.

Extract Analysis

a By the end of the 1520s, domestic politics replaced foreign policy as Henry VIII's top priority. It is not known when precisely he determined that he must sacrifice Catherine of Aragon to the cause of acquiring a male heir but, by 1529, Henry was devoting the bulk of his energies and those of his ministers towards obtaining a papal annulment of his marriage. The 'King's Great Matter' became the pivot around which foreign policy turned. Clement was still paralysed by the sack of Rome. Wolsey suggested war with Spain in 1528 but the nation lacked the means to wage it. Having failed utterly to secure the annulment by diplomatic means, Wolsey was dismissed as chancellor by Henry in October 1529 and replaced by Sir Thomas More. However, when Charles made peace with France and England in 1529, England was reduced to its previous and futile policy of trying to promote French hostility toward the Emperor as a means of pressuring Charles on the divorce issue.

b From 1529 at the latest, Henry's foreign policy was dominated by his domestic policies and in particular the need to obtain a male heir by divorcing Catherine of Aragon. However despite replacing his chief minister, events abroad outside his control meant Henry could only continue to try to rouse the French against Charles V as an unlikely way of trying to get the divorce.

c
- The statement that 'domestic politics replaced foreign policy as Henry VIII's top priority' can be challenged because, as the extract admits, 'the bulk of his energies and those of his ministers' were devoted to a foreign policy objective – obtaining a papal annulment.
- The implication that the Pope would not act because he 'was still paralysed by the sack of Rome' can be challenged as not being the whole explanation. The Pope also would not act because to allow the annulment would question the actions of his predecessor. This would undermine a core Catholic belief in the Pope's authority in the Church.
- The view that England's foreign policy was reduced to simply promoting French hostility towards the Emperor can be questioned, 'as other strategies were adopted', such as promoting good relations with France in order to gain support and seeking academic support in Europe in favour of the king's case.

Plan Your Essay

a **Strengths of Henry's international position 1534–47:**
- There was no immediate prospect of a crusade except briefly in 1538–40 due to the enmity of France and the Holy Roman Empire.
- Henry had spent largely on the military, mustering a large army of 42,000 soldiers to invade France in 1544.
- Scotland was ruled by his nephew to 1542; when relations deteriorated, the Scots were defeated in 1542; Scotland was ruled by Mary, Queen of Scots, an infant.

Weaknesses of Henry's international position 1534–47:
- England was a much weaker state than either France or the Empire.
- The Scots were still at war with England after 1543. The chance of a marriage between Edward and Mary, Queen of Scots which would have strengthened England enormously had been lost.
- Henry's strategy of developing an alliance with Charles V against the French backfired in 1544 when Charles made a separate peace with France. England failed to pursue Protestant allies and was diplomatically isolated.

Other factors, e.g. the failures of domestic opposition:
- The leading Catholics had either made their stands alone – like More – or stayed relatively loyal to Henry until late in his reign – like the Duke of Norfolk's family. The Pilgrimage of Grace had 40,000 supporters but was not a rebellion to remove the king, only to make him change policies.
- Henry's use of factionalism after 1540 and ultimate support for the Protestant reformists who would favour his son who was brought up a Protestant and was the nephew of their leader Edward Seymour.
- The removal of potential claimants to the throne from outside the Tudor family.
- Henry's popularity as a chivalric monarch who generally enjoyed the support of the nobility whom he treated well at court.

b and c You should consider how you would approach your own argument for this activity.

Chapter 10

Apply Your Knowledge

a) **Social change**

Nobles and gentry: Gentry class grew enormously, often buying Church land

Urban elite: Growing numbers in commercial and professional activities

Town workers: Increasing numbers due to migration from the country

Peasants: Prosperous peasants became copyholders or yeomen

Social structure

Nobles and gentry: Henry still relied on these 2 groups

Urban elite: Still considered below the landed interests even if they could become MPs

Town workers: Still largely below the urban elite in terms of income and status

Peasants: Most stayed as self-sufficient farmers in rural communities

b This is your choice, but many historians think that the gentry experienced the greatest change.

Assess the Validity of This View

a You might choose to prioritise the statements like this:

1 **Monastic estates of 2 million acres (16% of England and Wales) were sold.** This allowed the growth of the gentry class and of some of the peasant class.

2 **The gentry families of England and Wales rose to 5000 by 1540.** This meant that the position of the nobility was under threat which would later challenge the social system.

3 **The population of England and Wales rose from 2.1 million to 2.9 million.** This showed that despite inflation and bad harvests, England was probably still prosperous. This suggests that the economic growth of the gentry was part of a wider growth.

131

4 **Enclosure and engrossment turned many peasants into labourers or migrants.** This contributed to the growth of the wealth and estates of the gentry at the expense of peasants.

5 **The closure of 900 monasteries ended their charitable functions.** The impact of this was severe but tended to be localised to the vicinity of the monastery itself. This affected only parts of the country; the growth of the gentry was universal.

6 **Some peasants became yeomen or copyholders and capitalist farmers.** However, the vast majority of peasants remained subsistence farmers. This suggests only a minor change, unlike the growth of the gentry which had impacts on other groups.

b Based on the prioritisation above, you might conclude that the key social change was in fact the closure of the monasteries, because it facilitated the rise of the gentry and of some peasants as well as harming the poor due to the loss of its charitable functions. This would lead many poor people to migrate to towns to look for work and equally may have contributed to the rise of secular education because monasteries no longer served this purpose.

c One way of structuring your essay might be:
- to begin with the rise of the gentry, as this is in the question, and show its political and economic influence in a paragraph
- to explain how the rise of the gentry was in large part due to the closure of the monasteries and to develop the other 'lesser' consequences of the closure; these might be combined into 2–3 paragraphs and explained
- a 'balancing' paragraph looking at the more minor unrelated changes and justifying their lesser priority – for example that they affected fewer people
- a summary of the argument in a judgement supported by a key piece of evidence

Extract Analysis

While the accumulation of capital by the wealthy merchants and gentry through the seizure of land by enclosure and engrossment continued, capitalism was secured by legal changes and the peaceful exploitation of the class who did not own land. However, there was opposition, such as the Pilgrimage of Grace. This appears to have been a reactionary, Catholic movement of the north, led by the still half-feudal local nobility and aimed against the Reformation and the dissolution of the monasteries. But if the leaders were nobles, the mass support for the rising indicated a deep discontent and the rank and file largely came from the dispossessed and from the threatened peasantry. The government had no standing army to fight the rebels and was saved only by two things. One was the support of the south and east. The other was the extreme simplicity of the rebels, who entered long negotiations with the government, during which their forces melted away and they were easily dispersed.

a Purple highlighter marks the distinctive view on social change and how feudal society was undermined: the introduction of capitalism led to land being acquired by the rich and the peasants being turned into rent-paying tenants or landless labourers. Protest against this change came from the dispossessed.

Yellow highlighter represents the sub-arguments and views: this change was brought about by engrossment and enclosure, legal changes and peaceful exploitation. The Pilgrimage of Grace was a protest against this change under the guise of a religious revolt.

b **Evidence to support the author's argument:** Detail the failure to control engrossment and enclosure and possibly the impact of the dissolution of the monasteries leading to the growth of a capitalist class; the 40,000 people involved show it was a mass movement; Captain Poverty letters and tenant grievances.

Evidence that would contradict the author's argument: The timing of the rebellion coinciding with the dissolution; economic causes may simply be fear of poverty, not the rise of capitalism; some peasants were gaining from the economic changes; most peasants remained subsistence farmers; the role of feudal nobility in leading the rebellion.

Evidence to support other views/interpretations/arguments: The timing of the rebellion with the dissolution of smaller monasteries; the Pontefract Articles suggest religious and political motives; the involvement of court members.

Evidence that would contradict other views/interpretations/arguments: Pontefract Articles were drawn up by leaders; many of the articles were economic demands. The dissolution was a catalyst but not the underlying cause.

c Your answer should show your understanding of part **a**, supported and criticised by the evidence collated in part **b** above.

Improve an Answer

a The first sentence is not giving the overall interpretation and is incorrect in detail. The answer does reach a judgement, concluding that the extract clearly shows the impact of economic factors on the Pilgrimage of Grace, but does not give the whole argument based on the growth of capitalism, nor does it explain why the extract is convincing.

b **Strengths:**
- Shows some understanding of content.
- Provides a limited judgement at the end.

Weaknesses:
- There is no own knowledge shown in the response.
- Goes through the source merely repeating in a different order what is said rather than commenting on interpretations and then supporting these views.
- There is a lack of precision in its understanding of the views.

Chapter 11

Apply Your Knowledge

Henry VII: Trade:
- Navigation Acts support for merchants
- Trade treaties

Henry VII: Exploration:
- Support for Cabot and Weston

Henry VIII: Trade:
- Continued support for wool trade and merchant adventurers
- No trade treaties

Henry VIII: Exploration:
- Little encouragement except to Thorne

a Trade mattered more than exploration for both of them.

b Henry VII encouraged trade and exploration more than Henry VIII.

Improve an Answer

a **Weaknesses:**
- Some dates and detail (length of rule) are irrelevant.
- The meaning of some sentences is unclear (e.g. 'He encouraged Cabot to discover Newfoundland ...').
- There is no direct judgement on the question.

Strengths:
- There is some awareness of the differences between Henry VII and Henry VIII.
- There is some relevant knowledge about the wool trade and the Intercursus Magna.

b A good introduction would:
- set out the argument of the essay
- clearly explain Henry VII's approach to both trade and exploration
- consider the term 'build on'

Chapter 12

Apply Your Knowledge

Erasmus: Humanist. He was the leading thinker of the humanist movement who influenced English humanists like More and Fisher when he was Professor of Greek at Cambridge University.

More: Humanist. The leading intellectual in England who became Lord Chancellor; he wanted to reform the Church from within but was executed for not being prepared to swear his support for Henry's reformation of the Church.

Cranmer: Protestant/reformist. Member of a Protestant group at Cambridge who rose to be Archbishop of Canterbury because he was willing to support the annulment and the marriage of Henry to Anne Boleyn.

Cromwell: Protestant/reformist. Cromwell organised the Reformation for Henry and managed the introduction of an English Bible and the closure of Catholic monasteries.

Gardiner: Catholic conservative. Along with the Duke of Norfolk, he led the conservative faction which led the reaction against Protestant changes after 1539 with the Six Articles.

How important?

You should produce your own diagram for this activity, using your own judgement to show as many factors as you can.

Key Question

a and b **Key developments 1509–29**

Political: Accession of Henry VIII; Wolsey as chief minister and a cardinal.

Economic and social: Some population growth and urban migration; resistance to paying Amicable Grant. Growing impact of humanist educational institutions.

Intellectual ideas: Humanists called for a reform of the Church from within; Lollards and Protestants demanded changes to an English Protestant faith.

Opposing religious groups: Lollards still in existence; in a Cambridge-based group of Protestants in the 1520s.

Key developments 1529–40

Political: Dismissal of Wolsey, ultimately replaced by Cromwell until his execution in 1540. Changes increasing power of Parliament (the 'Tudor revolution in government').

Economic and social: Continued population growth and migration; enclosure and engrossment proceeded; closure of the monasteries.

Intellectual ideas: Conflict between Catholics and humanists who believed in papal authority. Rise of education and printing.

Opposing religious groups: Protestants grew in number partly in combination with the Lollard movement, and became influential in what was still essentially a Catholic Church. Some persecution of Protestants after 1538.

ACTIVITIES: SUGGESTED ANSWERS

Key developments 1540–47

Political: 1540–47 government dominated by factionalism between reformists and conservatives. Eventually reformists dominated in 1547 and 2 leading conservatives – Duke of Norfolk and the Earl of Surrey – arrested for treason. Henry died.

Economic and social: Inflation and rise of the gentry and yeomen due to sales of ecclesiastical land.

Intellectual ideas: Henry's supremacy over the Church not publicly questioned. Protestants control the future king's education. Rise of non-monastic education.

Opposing religious groups: Reformist faction under pressure and several prominent Protestants arrested.

c Your answer might refer to the following:

1509–1529: The economic and demographic growth of towns and the rise of education led to a more literate population able to read the ideas of the humanists and even the Protestants. Increasing frustration over the 'King's Great Matter' led to some hope of progress among Protestants in reforming the Church.

1529–40: The 'King's Great Matter' gave the opportunity for Protestants – especially Cromwell who replaced Wolsey – to shape the new Church which Henry decided to develop. Parliament's increased role (the 'Tudor revolution in government') allowed greater scope for middle-class Protestants in the Commons to be heard. The closure of the monasteries increased the secularisation of education and the publication of a printed English Bible allowed the spread of new ideas.

1540–47: The education of the future king as a Protestant gave Protestants great hope for the future, despite Henry playing the 2 factions off against each other. The sale of ecclesiastical land reinforced the opposing religious groups because it made it very difficult to restore one of the bastions of traditional Catholicism – the monasteries.

Plan Your Essay

a You should produce a mind-map for this activity. For an example of a good mind-map see pages 12 and 64.

b, c and d Using your mind-map, plan your essay:
- Address the factor in the question – lack of leadership – first, giving examples in support e.g. the unwillingness of leading Catholics to oppose the king directly and also refer to individuals like More.
- Evaluate the other types of factors and comment on their importance.
- Ensure you make your overall view clear in the introduction, substantiate it in the essay and repeat it in the conclusion. In this way you should show sustained judgement.

Chapter 13

Apply Your Knowledge

Henry VIII died (1547)
- Hertford had control of the dominant faction and so was able to control the Regency Council.

Earl of Hertford (later Duke of Somerset) became Lord Protector (1547)
- Hertford as Duke of Somerset created enemies; this was exploited by Dudley.

Dudley (later Duke of Northumberland) became Lord President of the Council (1550)
- Edward's terminal illness; he wanted to be succeeded by a Protestant.

Edward wrote the *Devyse*, naming Lady Jane Grey as his successor (1553)
- When Edward died, Northumberland proclaimed Jane as queen but the public rose up against him.

Mary became queen (July 1553)

To What Extent?

a **Continued:** None of his key aims was completely continued.

Partially continued: Somerset carried on war against Scotland (military glory/conquest of Scotland/succession); Northumberland abandoned the war.

Failed or ignored: Boulogne [land in France] was given up; annulment was not relevant now; crusade became unlikely.

b A good answer would:
- Consider Somerset's need to maintain his position and thus to gain victories in foreign wars to sustain his position.
- Consider Northumberland's need to distance himself from Somerset's actions and restore the economy by ending the war.
- Consider that times had changed, so key aims like gaining the annulment and avoiding a crusade no longer really applied; also Mary, Queen of Scots' escape and marriage made union with Scotland impossible, especially with French troops now present there.

Key Question

Your spider diagram may contain the following points, for example:

Effective
- There was no challenge to Edward's rule during his lifetime
- All rebellions during Edward's rule were ultimately defeated
- Northumberland did improve the royal finances and reorganised the Poor Law in 1552

Not effective
- Edward's age – he ruled from the ages of 9 to 15 and so needed regents to rule for him
- The differences over religion – he was a Protestant when most of his subjects were Catholic
- Conflict – England was at war with Scotland

Improve an Answer

a The paragraph considers the legacy of Henry VIII to the governments of Somerset and Northumberland. It looks at the main things that Henry actually did as ruler but it does not show how significant these would be to the governments which followed. Instead it should have evaluated how his legacy affected the governments of Somerset and Northumberland.

b One of the most significant legacies Henry VIII left was the problem of the relationship between the government and religion. While the Church was run by the king and monasteries had been closed, many Catholic practices remained, such as services largely in English and priests not being allowed to marry. This satisfied neither Catholics nor Protestants. Moreover, not ruling with a chief minister after Cromwell's execution had allowed the two religious groups to develop factions which struggled for power both during and after Henry's death. Although Henry wanted to leave the legacy of a balanced Regency Council, his destruction of the Norfolk family and his favouring of the reformists in his dying months left a legacy to be exploited – by both Somerset and Northumberland – in creating a reformist government with increasingly Protestant prayer books. However this also meant that the conservatives in Henry's carefully crafted and balanced Regency Council needed careful management, as in the case of the Earl of Southampton, who was courted and then rejected by both Somerset and Northumberland.

Chapter 14

Apply Your Knowledge

You should produce a mind-map for this activity. For an example of a good mind-map see pages 12 and 64.

Extract Analysis

a **Extract A key statement:** 'But when all that is said, in the majority of English villages, men breathed easier for the accession of a Catholic queen.'

Extract A main argument: Despite the clear influence of Protestantism on the people, most people were still Catholic in belief in 1553.

Extract B key statement: 'It is probably true that most people were not committed to either Protestantism or Catholicism, or even thought in such hard and fast terms.'

Extract B main argument: The reformists had some impact but it is unlikely that a real divide between 2 differing religious groups existed.

Extract C key statement: 'The machinery of coercion and supervision deployed by Edwardian governments was so effective that for most parishes passive resistance to reformist changes was simply not an option for a largely Catholic population.'

Extract C main argument: The population was still largely Catholic in 1553 but was forced to adopt Protestant practices.

b **Extract A – support:** The rapidity with which most churches adopted Catholic practices and decorations; the support for Mary Tudor to replace Lady Jane Grey, a Protestant.

Extract A – criticise: It is virtually impossible to establish evidence of people's opinions.

Extract B – support: Absence of widespread popular protest.

Extract B – criticise: Survival of Catholic beliefs and practices and Catholics welcomed the return of their Church under Mary.

Extract C – support: The loss of chantries shows the determination to attack Catholicism and force them to adopt Protestant practices.

Extract C – criticise: John Hooper's comment about the resistance of the people to change does not fit with the picture of coercion.

c You should produce your own conclusions for this activity. Extract A has some evidence but one major assertion at the end. Extract B points out that it is hard to gauge the impact but supplies virtually no evidence. Extract C may be more convincing since it is based on a detailed study of churchwardens' accounts.

Key Question

Method of governing: Somerset ruled dictatorially but Northumberland at the start ruled through the Privy Council. Somerset called himself Lord Protector but Northumberland called himself Lord President of the (Privy) Council.

Attitude to Scotland: Somerset wanted to continue the war but Northumberland made peace. He abandoned English garrisons in Scotland.

Attitude to France: Somerset wanted to retain Boulogne but Northumberland returned Boulogne to the French.

Religious policy: Somerset was a more moderate reformer than Northumberland. Comparison of the 2 prayer books shows this.

Economic policy: Somerset spent highly on war but Northumberland reduced expenditure. Somerset debased the coinage but Northumberland improved the administration of royal finances and ended the wars.

Social policy: Somerset's policies on enclosure and taxes provoked rebellions but Northumberland did not encounter rebellions. Northumberland's poor law regulated assistance for the poor.

133

Chapter 15

✏️ Ⓐ Plan Your Essay

a Key elements of Henry's treatment of Catherine could include the following:
- Henry had his marriage with Catherine dissolved against her will by Protestants; impact – Mary would want a successful marriage to a Catholic as a reaction to her mother's treatment by Protestants.
- Henry blamed Catherine for his failure to have a male heir and had Mary – his daughter with Catherine – excluded from the succession; impact – Mary would realise the importance of a male heir to ensure a Catholic succession and so the marriage was based on the need for a child rather than anything else.
- Henry's action against a Spanish princess soured Anglo-Spanish relations which was not favourable for Mary's marriage.

b and **c** Other points which might appear on your spider diagram could include:
- Philip was not treated well personally by the English – they prevented his coronation as king and Mary was protected under a Treason Act while he was not. Significance: 4
- This was not a love match. Mary was only concerned about a male heir; Philip with aggrandisement. Significance: 1
- The marriage was opposed by many English people due to foreign influence – Wyatt's Rebellion was an example of this. Significance: 3
- Mary was 37 when they married and so the chances of having a male heir – one of the main goals of the marriage which would make it successful – were small. Significance: 2

Your judgement could be that the marriage failed ultimately because of Philip's lack of interest in Mary and the length of time they were separate. Mary's age was also important while other factors were less so because while it put pressure on the marriage it did not lead to its ending.

d You should produce your own essay plan for this activity. You may well decide that the treatment of her mother had only an indirect effect on the failure of Mary's marriage and that other factors were more important.

⬆️ Ⓐ Improve an Answer

The reigns of Edward VI and Mary provide a vivid contrast between the two forms of government. Edward as an infant had to rely on two regents, the Dukes of Somerset and Northumberland, whose periods of government almost led to disaster. They tried to exploit their position for their own advantage one way or another and they showed the problem of ruling by ministers when the ministers were self-seeking and plainly incompetent. On the other hand, Mary was a much more effective ruler of the country. She never employed a chief minister and so, despite qualms about her capacity to govern as a woman, she ultimately made all the key decisions herself. Her decisions, taken on the whole, were far better than those of Somerset and Northumberland and had she been spared beyond her 42 years, her decisions would probably have had time to become far more effective and permanent. This clearly shows that in the latter part of the period at least, monarchs were far more effective rulers than ministers.

a Yellow highlighter marks the opinions.

b Purple highlighter represents the supporting evidence.

c 'periods of government almost led to disaster' – Somerset's disastrous war; Northumberland's attempt to change the succession.

'They tried to exploit their position' – Somerset and Northumberland both made themselves dukes.

'self-seeking and plainly incompetent' – Somerset and Northumberland both made themselves the leading regents in turn; Somerset failed to deal with rebellions and Northumberland misjudged popular opinion in 1553.

'made all the key decisions herself' – the decision to marry Philip of Spain, to go to war with France, and to restore the Catholic faith.

'had she been spared' – her attempts to re-establish the Catholic Church and deal with heresy did not have a real chance to be consolidated in less than 5 years.

💡 Key Question

Foreign policy only:
- Restored papal supremacy
- Paget and others hoped to gain credit from a military expedition to France

Succession only:
- Executed Lady Jane Grey and imprisoned Elizabeth
- Refused to marry English suitors

Overlap:
- Married Philip II of Spain in 1554
- Followed him into war against France to retain his alliance despite the harm to papal relations

⚙️ Apply Your Knowledge

a One possible opening sentence providing a judgement could be: Mary's foreign policy between 1553 and 1558 was intended to help her gain and retain her husband and so help the succession; this would seem to have been more important than her other main objective: to restore Catholicism in England.

b Your answer could include 4 pieces of information from the following:
- The decision to marry Philip II shows the importance of both the roles of succession and foreign policy, as he was the leading Catholic monarch in Europe.
- The importance of both is also shown by her willingness to face the opposition of both Parliament and the people in Wyatt's Rebellion.
- However, the decision to go to war against France jeopardised her religious objectives as the Pope supported France, but she was desperate to retain Philip's interest in her so that she could get pregnant.
- The importance of the succession over religion in her mind is shown further by the decision to continue the war despite the Pope's subsequent decision to remove Pole as a legate.
- The war was still continued despite the loss of England's last possession in France, Calais.

c Your should write your own paragraph using the earlier parts of this activity to help you.

Chapter 16

⚙️ Apply Your Knowledge

a Possible order of importance:
1. Shortness of the reign
2. Protestant opposition
3. Ownership of former Church lands
4. Lack of papal support
5. Reaction to persecution
6. Influence of Church reformers
7. Succession problems
8. Need to repeal reformist legislation
9. Married priests

b **Shortness of the reign:** Why? Mary's key difficulty proved to be the brevity of her reign. In only 5 years, she had little chance to reverse the impact of 20 years of movement towards Protestantism. Protestant opposition in Parliament and Wyatt's Rebellion were serious but they were overcome.

c **Married priests:** Why? The issue of married priests was a relatively minor one. (Many priests seemed to have been prepared to give up their wives!)

💡 Key Question

Advisers

Role: Gave personal advice to Queen Mary.

Influence: Renard influenced her towards the Spanish marriage. Pole strongly advised on religious issues.

Helped to govern England effectively? Gave rise to opposition because it seemed that foreign influences were dominating and the Spanish marriage was a failure in terms of succession and retention of Calais. Paul IV's personal animosity to Pole after 1555 hampered good government; although his policies did try to improve the Church, he supervised the campaign of burning heretics which caused problems.

Privy Council

Role: To give official advice to Queen Mary and administer the system of local government.

Influence: Mary had a large Privy Council including many Catholic supporters to assist moderates like Paget – but Mary largely ignored her Privy Council, for example in her unalterable decision to marry Philip II.

Helped to govern England effectively? They were not given much chance to do this. However, despite some factionalism and self-seeking like that of Paget, they were experienced and helped draft important legislation about the Church and society.

Parliament

Role: To advise the monarch of the views of the leading landowners and merchants of the country and to make binding laws.

Influence: Some opposition to the restoration of Catholicism and would not agree to the surrender of monastic lands. Blocked Philip's coronation.

Helped to govern England effectively? Depends on your viewpoint; they delayed and limited Mary's policies to restore the Church. Many useful Acts passed on social and economic matters and had good relations with the monarch.

Philip II

Role: As husband of the queen, would enjoy personal influence but had no legal role.

Influence: Led her into the wars against France and hostility to the Pope.

Helped to govern England effectively? Although his powers were limited, his influence helped to create a rebellion, limited the restoration of Catholicism and led to heavy expenditure on war and the loss of Calais.

Mary

Role: The ultimate decision maker.

Influence: Despite her gender and lack of experience and training, she played an important role in government. All the key decisions were hers.

Helped to govern England effectively? Unlike the views of earlier generations, many historians see her as an able ruler constrained by problems like the papacy which were out of her control. She did allow others to influence her due to her desire for a successor.

⚙️ Apply Your Knowledge

You should produce a mind-map for this activity. For an example of a good mind-map see pages 12 and 64.

✅ Revision Skills

You should produce a timeline using your own judgement to select the most important key events. For an example of a good timeline, see page 9.

ACTIVITIES: SUGGESTED ANSWERS

Chapter 17

Apply Your Knowledge

a You should copy the diagram 3 times.

b **Consolidate her position**
  Yes: Accepted by Privy Council; accepted by people
  Settle religious issues
  Yes: Compromise accepted by many
  No: Compromise disliked by many
  End war with France
  Yes: Peace treaty 1559 at Câteau-Cambrésis
  No: Tempted back into war in 1562 and lost Calais permanently

c You will probably rank 'consolidating her position' as the most feasible aim and 'settle religious issues' as the least feasible due to the depth of differences over religion.

Apply Your Knowledge

You should produce a timeline using your own judgement to select the most important key developments. For an example of a good timeline, see page 9.

Assess the Validity of This View

a You should select or formulate your own first sentence for this activity.

b Your introduction should start with the opening sentence that you chose in part **a**. It might show an awareness of the nature of the religious divisions and the impact that they had made over 20 years. The nature of the religious divisions might include:
  - A basic understanding of the two groups – reformists and Catholics.
  - The supremacy of the monarch or the Pope over the Church.
  - The use of English in the Bible and services.
  - The teachings of the Church over such issues as transubstantiation and purgatory.
  - The existence of institutions like monasteries and chantries.

The impact that they had had might include: rebellions such as the Pilgrimage of Grace, the Western Rebellion and the Wyatt Rebellion which all had some religious overtones; the execution of heretics, most notably under Mary; the removal of politicians from power like Thomas Cromwell or the Duke of Northumberland; arguments over the succession.

Key Question

Radical clergymen and MPs
- **View:** Viewed the settlement as too Catholic but favoured more Protestantism.
- **Importance:** Many radicals entered the Church and pushed for change from within after 1559 although they were not an organised party. Helped to influence the Protestant prayer book.

Catholic bishops and Conservative peers
- **View:** Viewed the settlement as too Protestant and opposed the Uniformity bill.
- **Importance:** Catholic bishops helped to block the first proposals for a settlement in the House of Lords but they were removed and unable to block changes like the Thirty-Nine Articles and the new Book of Common Prayer. Conservative peers also played a major role in making the settlement more favourable to Catholics.

William Cecil and the mainly Protestant Privy Council
- **View:** William Cecil and the Privy Council wanted a more Protestant settlement.

- **Importance:** They drafted the legislation and also they managed the Puritan opposition in Parliament to push for more Protestant changes.

Elizabeth herself
- **View:** Elizabeth may have wanted a Protestant settlement and was pushed into a more Catholic settlement by the opposition.
- **Importance:** It is doubtful whether the settlement was exactly what Elizabeth wanted (she did not like married priests for example). However, once in place in 1563 she enforced it.

Chapter 18

Apply Your Knowledge

Events in red are start points, events in green are end points.

1534: Acts of Supremacy and Succession – start of break with Rome and subsequent religious discord.

1540: Execution of Thomas Cromwell for heresy – start of rise of factionalism and Henry VIII's weak government.

1547: Accession of Edward VI – start of the reigns of an infant and then a woman (the first since Matilda).

1558: Accession of Elizabeth I – end of the short reigns of Edward and Mary.

1559: Acts of Supremacy and Uniformity – end of the religious dispute to an extent.

1563: Thirty-Nine Articles – end of the religious dispute as it gave clarity and permanence to the Church settlement in terms of belief.

Apply Your Knowledge

a 1558 should be on the extreme left; 1547 halfway between the pendulum and the left-hand side; 1549 and 1564 halfway between the pendulum and the right-hand side; 1553 on the extreme right.

b The biggest change is between Northumberland and Mary because he was very reformist and she was a traditional Catholic.

c Elizabeth's religious settlement is moderately Protestant. It is called the middle way because it is roughly half way between a Catholic and a Protestant Church.

Key Question

Henry VIII from 1540
Social:
- Rise of the gentry
- End of charitable role of monasteries

Economic:
- Rising land market
- Inflation and debasement

Effects:
- Undermined role of nobility
- Increased social distress for the poor

Edward VI
Social:
- End of charitable function of chantries
- Growing numbers of vagrants

Economic:
- Royal financial administration improved
- Enclosure continued

Effects:
- Poor Law 1552 to address poverty
- Rebellions due to enclosure

Mary
Social:
- Bad harvests and disease
- Growing numbers of vagrants

Economic:
- High taxes
- Inflation due to war and earlier debasement

Effects:
- Poor Law 1555 to address poverty
- Encouragement of arable farming
- Recoinage planned

Elizabeth I to 1563
Social:
- Continued problems of vagrancy and lack of help for the poor

Economic:
- Inflation
- Demands for higher wages

Effects:
- Recoinage
- Legislation – Poor Law 1563

Overview
Social:
- Growing vagrancy and poverty
- Rise of gentry

Economic:
- Inflation
- Rising taxes

Effects:
- Discontent
- Beginnings of social legislation
- Recoinage
- Peace policies to reduce costs and so improve economy

Assess the Validity of This View

a You will notice that the benchmark for a crisis varies between the very serious and the less serious. The definition you choose will influence the answer. If the benchmark is low, e.g. arguments in the government about policy, then there is a greater likelihood that you can demonstrate there was a crisis.

b 1540 was the end of Thomas Cromwell and the rise of factional government – this hints at weak government as a criterion; 1563 marks the consolidation of Elizabeth's religious settlement, suggesting a reduction of the profound religious differences.

c This will be based on your own view of what constitutes of a crisis.

d The judgement is your own choice. Most historians reject the idea of a mid-Tudor crisis and point to the positives in government during this time, using a high benchmark to define crisis.

Chapter 19

Apply Your Knowledge

a One key point to notice is that your mind-map has links between problems. For example, in 1587 and 1593 Wentworth was imprisoned for raising issues in Parliament about both religion and succession.

b **'royal prerogative'** – refers to rights or powers which the monarch could exercise without requiring the consent of Parliament (such as marriage and succession)

Apply Your Knowledge

a Suggested methods:
  - Used royal Secretary (Cecil) and privy councillors to manage the House of Commons (you may have subdivided this into several points)
  - Only called Parliament when monarch wished

135

- Refused assent to bills monarch did not like
- Used the Speaker to control debate
- Punished MPs and Lords
- Banned areas of debate

b The most effective methods were the first 3 on the list above and arguments could be advanced for each of them. The 2nd might have been considered the most effective although the queen had to call parliaments when she needed laws or taxes.

c The first reason in the list above (using the royal Secretary and privy councillors to manage the House of Commons) should be considered a continued problem, since it depended on the personality of the Secretary and management of the Privy Council.

Key Question

Maintaining a working relationship

Issues well managed:
- Generally positive, with agreement over most issues e.g. overseeing local government

Problems:
- Some disagreements e.g. over religion and execution of Mary, Queen of Scots

Working together to provide constructive advice

Issues well managed:
- Well managed e.g. with a balance between Dudley and Cecil – the factions agreed over religion

Problems:
- Damaging competition between factions remained. Leicester and Cecil were rivals and fell out over the queen's potential marriage

Management of Parliament

Issues well managed:
- The business of the house was managed well by the Privy Council e.g. preparing bills. Debate in the house was usually well controlled by the Speaker

Problems:
- Parliament was still able to develop legislation which the queen opposed e.g. 60 bills were refused royal assent
- The Privy Council often managed Parliament in their own interests e.g. to press Elizabeth to marry in 1566

Loyalty about religion

Issues well managed:
- The issue of Catholics was well managed after 1570 by agreed policies on repression e.g. the 1581 Obedience Act

Problems:
- The Northern Rebellion was supported by the leading conservative on the Privy Council, the Duke of Norfolk

Protection of queen

Issues well managed:
- Plots against Elizabeth were dealt with effectively by spies e.g. the Ridolfi Plot

Problems:
- The Privy Council sought to protect the queen and her religion by leading her into dangerous foreign conflicts e.g. war with Spain after 1584

Foreign policy

Issues well managed:
- The problem of a war against Catholic Spain was avoided until 1584 but largely due to Elizabeth

Problems:
- Dangerous interventions in foreign policy due to the Privy Council's support for Protestantism e.g. in France in 1562–63 and in the Netherlands from 1584

 Improve an Answer

a Parts are irrelevant (for an essay on the success of Elizabeth's management of the Privy Council): 'although he was not a leading civil servant … and rumours abounded about their relationship. She had a portrait of him in her bedroom bearing the words "My love".'

b For the most part, Elizabeth managed the Privy Council effectively from 1558 to the mid 1580s, both in managing Parliament and in controlling factionalism, although the Privy Council did not always do as she wished.

c You should use the points you have identified in the earlier parts of this activity to help you write your paragraph.

Chapter 20

Apply Your Knowledge

Erik of Sweden

For: Same religion as Elizabeth

Against: Sweden is distant from England and would not have been a very helpful ally

Robert Dudley

For: Same religion as Elizabeth

Against: Cause faction fighting; bad reputation due to first wife's death

Philip II of Spain

For: Ruler of a powerful state – a useful ally

Against: Different religion from Elizabeth; like Mary, could lead Elizabeth into war

Archdukes Ferdinand and Charles

For: Members of a powerful ruling family in Europe

Against: Different religion from Elizabeth

Duke of Anjou

For: Supported by her chief minister

Against: Different religion from Elizabeth; could lead Elizabeth into conflict in Europe

Key Question

a Possible order: **D, A, E, F, G, B, C**.

b A possible answer is that reasons revolving around a loss of power seem to have been the most important.

c Among the points you could mention are:
- She could govern more effectively because she could not be influenced by her husband into decisions which did not fit her policies.
- She could also govern more effectively because she could stay above the Privy Council, and Parliament and factionalism.
- She would not govern as effectively as she would face regular confrontation with the Privy Council and Parliament on the issue.
- She would not govern as effectively as the issue of succession would be left open, which led to Mary, Queen of Scots being her heir for a long time and creating many problems.

 To What Extent?

a **1569: Northern Rebellion**

Case for: Philip for the first time acted against Elizabeth; because of this, the Pope excommunicated Elizabeth in 1570, confident of Spanish support. Plots followed.

Case against: There was no active war between the 2 nations, alternatively, Elizabeth had already soured relations by seizing some Spanish bullion ships in 1568.

1584: Anglo-Spanish War

Case for: English and Spanish forces were left in direct confrontation.

Case against: English pirates had long been committing acts of aggression against Spain; a kind of surrogate war, not fought in Spain or England.

1587: Execution of Mary, Queen of Scots

Case for: Gave Philip the excuse for the Armada; ended chance of a Catholic succession in England.

Case against: Execution a pretext – the critical change was the need to deal with the nuisance England presented to trade and to the counter-reformation (see Chapter 23 for more on the latter).

1588: Spanish Armada

Case for: First direct attempt to conquer England by Spain.

Case against: Armada was the end result of crucial changes beforehand; it was more of a consequence than a watershed.

b Based on the evidence above, you might conclude that the statement is broadly valid – i.e. that as this marked the start of actual armed conflict between the 2 states, it is the key watershed as it committed first Elizabeth and then Philip to intervention. However, the other dates do mark changes in the relationship and indeed the whole relationship is one of steady deterioration, and it is hard to see any specific point which stands out as a watershed.

Key Question

Improvement or deterioration in relations with France, Spain and Scotland:
- relations with France improved
- relations with Spain got worse
- relations with Scotland improved

How the succession was secured:
- the Catholic heir was imprisoned and executed
- Elizabeth named James VI of Scotland as her heir (but only on her deathbed)
- Cecil made arrangements for a smooth transition for James when Elizabeth died in 1603

Comparison – the better relations with Scotland and the inheritance of James seem to overlap.

Revision Skills

You should create your own timeline for this activity. For an example of a good timeline, see page 9.

Chapter 21

Apply Your Knowledge

vagrancy – the crime of being an able-bodied person who took to the road and did not work

undeserving/impotent poor – these were poor people who could not help their poverty, like the old, the young and the disabled

martial law – under martial law, the country is under the control of the army

almshouses – these are dwellings built out of charity for the deserving poor, usually the old or the disabled

house of correction – this is the Tudor word for a prison

poor relief – money collected from local ratepayers to pay for the care of the poor

parish – an area served by a church; it is usually the same as a village or a town

Assess the Validity of This View

a Rebellion sparked by religious belief was more dangerous to rulers than courtly conspiracies in the years 1536 to 1569.' Assess the validity of this view.

The terms 'courtly conspiracies', which means plots based on noblemen at court, and 'dangerous' will require clarification.

b **1536–47: Henry VIII (later years)**

Rebellion sparked by religious belief:
- 1536 Pilgrimage of Grace – due to dissolution of the monasteries and issues of supremacy
- Local disputes with other economic and social causes. Never a real threat to Henry, although 40,000 rebels were involved

Courtly conspiracies:
- 1536 Pilgrimage of Grace may have been the outcome of a courtly conspiracy by supporters of Catherine of Aragon, but was not a serious threat to overthrow Henry
- 1547 Somerset's plan to overturn Henry's will – succeeded but did not overthrow Edward VI

1547–53: Edward VI

Rebellion sparked by religious belief:
- 1549: Western Rebellion – due partly to Somerset's prayer book
- Localised and other economic causes important
- Easily repressed, so no real threat

Courtly conspiracies:
- 1549: Dudley's plot to replace Somerset. This succeded but was not a threat to Edward
- 1553: Lady Jane Grey plot; a real threat but Mary was able to overcome it with popular support

1553–58: Mary I

Rebellion sparked by religious belief:
- 1554: Wyatt's Rebellion due to Catholicism
- Localised with other economic causes
- Reached gates of London but small in size, so not a serious threat

1558–69: Elizabeth I (early years)

Rebellion sparked by religious belief:
- 1569: Northern Rebellion due to Catholics wanting Mary, Queen of Scots and restoration of Catholicism; localised and easily dealt with

Courtly conspiracies:
- 1569: Duke of Norfolk's involvement in Northern Rebellion and plans to marry Mary, Queen of Scots
- Potentially dangerous but the duke lost his nerve

Evidence would suggest a greater threat from courtly conspiracies than from rebellions.

You might include in your introduction:
- The danger to the leader came primarily from potential loss of authority – only the courtly conspiracies had any real impact on the ruler's authority; when coupled with rebellions as in 1536 and 1569 the threat was much less. Courtly conspiracy did lead to the proclamation of a temporary queen and the adjustment of the leadership and style of government under Edward VI.
- The 'danger' to political authority from rebellions caused by religious belief was minimal; there was in any case other causes of rebellions; also the rebellions were localised, badly organised and often did not have as aims the overthrow of the monarch.

Asses the Validity of This View

a **Rebellions were ineffective:**
- No change of ruler occurred due to rebellions.
- No change in the religious policy of the state resulted from rebellions.
- Rebellions were always localised and only once posed any sort of direct threat to the ruler.

Rebellions had some effect:
- After the Pilgrimage of Grace, Henry recognised Mary as an heir to the throne and changed some of his plans for tax and political changes for the Council of the North.

- Rebellions helped to remove Somerset.
- Failure to deal effectively with rebellions led to the fall of Somerset.
- If they had any effect it was often the opposite of what was intended – accelerated closure of monasteries in 1536 and persecution of Catholics in 1569.

b You should use the points you have identified in the earlier part of this activity to help you write your paragraph.

Plan Your Essay

a **There was a 'transformation of society' under Elizabeth:**
- Growing numbers of gentry
- Widening gap between rich and poor
- Growing mercantile and profession class in towns forming a consumer class

There was not a 'transformation of society' under Elizabeth:
- Population growth continued
- Most people lived in the countryside

There was no social disorder:
- Only sporadic food riots
- 'Oxfordshire rising' was very small
- A good deal of poor law legislation addressed social problems before they got out of hand

There was social disorder:
- 'Oxfordshire rising' and Northern Rebellion involved discontent from poverty
- Irish rebellion showed discontent with growing English influence
- Increasing vagrancy certainly led to claims of rising crime and disorder and produced the Poor Law legislation

b You should use the points you have identified in the earlier part of this activity to help you write your conclusion.

Chapter 22

Apply Your Knowledge

Trade

Successes and achievements: External trade flourished to both the Netherlands and new overseas markets; slave trade began; new trading companies formed and tended to become joint-stock companies with shareholders

Failures and limitations: Trade to the Netherlands limited to the north; expeditions were not always successful; trading was relatively small

Exploration and colonisation

Successes and achievements: Successful voyages of exploration including a circumnavigation of the world; first colonial ventures were started and set a precedent for future development

Failures and limitations: Many voyages of exploration failed; no permanent settlements established

Industry

Successes and achievements: Many towns grew in size and prosperity; key industries prospered, such as cloth, coal and shipbuilding; taxes on trade suggests its prosperity; government legislation to promote industry

Failures and limitations: Some towns declined; taxes and to a lesser extent regulations might have limited trade

Agriculture

Successes and achievements: Output increased overall

Failures and limitations: Four bad harvests 1594–97 led to riots, disease and starvation, vagrancy and growing divide between rich and undeserving poor

Apply Your Knowledge

a The main social changes could include the growing gap between rich and poor, increased vagrancy and poverty, the rise of towns and the middle classes, and the continued rise of the gentry.

b The main economic links are: the growing gap between rich and poor and the increase in vagrancy and poverty both link to the various failures in agriculture and the decline in some towns; the rise of towns and the middle class links to the prosperity of key trades, growing international trade and the impact of government economic legislation.

Extract Analysis

a *Poverty was prevalent in Tudor towns.* Supports.

The government always accepted the need to take responsibility to help the unemployed. Opposes.

Merchants acted purely out of fear of threats to their social position. Opposes.

Charity kept many people out of destitution. Supports.

The poor were out of control in the Tudor period. Opposes.

Poverty was addressed both at the local and the national level. Supports.

The poor behaved with a surprising lack of violence. Supports.

b **Overall argument:** Poverty was only rife in towns and was contained effectively through charity and legislation; the government was always in control of the situation.

Contextual evidence supporting: The accelerating range of social legislation of the government leading to the Poor Law of 1597. The measures taken by parish authorities in Norwich for example shows that local initiative was also important.

Contextual evidence opposing: Poverty played a role in rebellions and risings and there was certainly a great fear of a Tudor crime wave which often led to actual legislation. The existence of starvation and a growing gap between rich and poor may seem to undermine the idea that the situation was 'fairly well contained'.

Key Question

You should produce a mind-map for this activity. For an example of a good mind-map see pages 12 and 64. Use your mind-map to assess the question for this activity.

Chapter 23

Apply Your Knowledge

The Church should have bishops: Catholics and Anglicans

There should be a state Church: Anglicans and Presbyterian Puritans

Brightly coloured vestments should not be worn by clerics: Puritans (including Presbyterians and Separatists)

The Pope is not the spiritual head of the Church: Anglicans and Puritans (including Presbyterians and Separatists)

The Bible and services should only be in Latin: Catholics

The Church should be governed by ministers and lay elders: Presbyterians

Key Question

Religious settlement: Protestant ideas lay behind the original intention of the settlement. Catholic ideas had to be accepted or allowed to a certain extent so that the Act of Settlement would be approved by the House of Lords and be accepted by the mass of the people.

Foreign policy: Belief in Protestantism led to support for Scottish Presbyterians against Mary, Queen of Scots, Dutch Protestants against Spain, and French Huguenots against the Catholic League.

Popular culture: Popularity of Foxe's Book of Martyrs and English Bibles due to Protestantism. Religious music supported by Catholics and Anglicans despite criticism of Puritans. Rise of madrigals and part songs reflected Renaissance ideas as did the development of drama and poetry.

Key Question

a **The context of Elizabethan peace and stability:** Elizabeth's avoidance of war and resolution of religious issues provided the stability where the economy could prosper and so the arts could be supported financially.

Patronage: Elizabeth was a major patron of the arts, including leading artists who produced many copies of her image, and Shakespearean plays were performed at court and to the public.

Propaganda: Elizabeth employed artists, musicians and writers to produce propaganda to support her image as 'Gloriana'.

b **Growing numbers of schools and increased literacy:** 30 more grammar schools were established in Elizabeth's reign so more people were literate and aware of artistic values. The rise of towns and prosperity among the middle class and skilled workers meant that there were large enough settlements to support the arts in towns – especially London – and a large enough number of people able to support it.

Demand from all classes: Workers and nobles alike were drawn to differing art forms, particularly plays.

c This is your own choice. Her patronage and the stability of her rule were important but economic, technological and social change was essential for an educated society interested in the arts to emerge. However it was only in her reign that a highly literate public emerged, leading to the flourishing of English plays and poetry.

Plan Your Essay

a Other factors might include: the decline in appeal of Catholicism as a result of passing time and a new generation educated in reformed ways; action in the reign of Edward VI; general prosperity and sense of well-being and loyalty under Elizabeth; the treasonable activities surrounding Mary, Queen of Scots making Catholicism unpatriotic.

b **Government action and policies**

Important: Elizabethan settlement provided for a 'via media' embracing many former Catholics; there were harsh penal laws against those who failed to conform – 1559 Oath of Supremacy; 1571 publishing papal bulls became treasonable; 1581 Due Obedience Act. 1585 – being a Catholic priest became treasonable; Catholicism was only found in country houses.

Not important: In the 1560s many only conformed outwardly. Some evaded laws and we cannot be certain how forcefully they were maintained in all parts of the country.

Weaknesses of Catholic Church

Important: The Pope failed to show leadership and only excommunicated Elizabeth in 1570; the Catholics were divided – there were two separate groups of missionary priests.

Not important: Catholicism remained a strong international religion.

Tolerance of 'via media'

Important: The compromise was supported by the majority of the population including many Catholics – queen was only 'governor' of the Church; vestments allowed; moderate prayer book. Most people knew only the Protestant form of service; by Elizabeth's death, very few people would remember Catholic services.

Not important: Many Catholics conformed only temporarily hoping for a Catholic succession – Queen Elizabeth never married and might die e.g. 1562 smallpox; the Catholic Mary, Queen of Scots was the heir until 1587.

You should complete the rest of your chart based on any other alternative factor you have chosen.

c Your judgement might be that it was the success of the 'via media' which was most important for the decline of Catholicism. The compromise which could be looked at as a government policy but was also a factor in its own right had a chance to establish itself and lessen the attractions of Catholicism.

d You should use your answers to parts **a**, **b** and **c** to write your essay.

Chapter 24

Apply Your Knowledge

You should produce your own revision cards, diamond 9, and chronological order for this activity.

Assess the Validity of This View

a You should produce your own chart for this activity.

b and c You might decide that the economy of England was in a much stronger position in 1603 than it had been in 1558 (although it is perfectly possible to argue the other way round). If so, you could substantiate your argument with points such as:

1558: England emerging from a time of warfare and heavy debts

- **Trade and commerce:** High levels of unemployment in towns; inflation leading to high wage demands; warfare interfering with trade; limited growth of trading markets abroad.
- **Agriculture:** Series of bad harvests 1555–56 and prevalence of sweating sickness 1557–58 indicates economic problems; lack of arable land indicated by encouragement to convert land from pasture.

1603: Despite 15 years of warfare and problems with royal finances and bad harvests, the growth of trade, town and industry over the period left England wealthy enough to survive these major problems

- **Trade and commerce:** Growing cloth-making domestic industry in rural areas; coal industry growing to supply London especially; shipbuilding growing to satisfy demands of defence and trade. Flourishing international cloth trade, especially with the northern Netherlands; broadening of overseas markets; formation of trading companies; successful trading expeditions with the New World by Drake and Hawkins.
- **Agriculture:** Agricultural production increased overall (despite interruptions from bad harvests), rising demand from abroad for wool; rising demand in towns for wool and foodstuffs and shipbuilding yards for timber.

Extract Analysis

a **Turning points:** English force dispatched to the Netherlands; trial and execution of Mary, Queen of Scots in 1587; deaths of 4 privy councillors 1588-90.

Factually correct: War with Spain and French Catholic League; costs and casualties of the war; England was often threatened with conquest; Essex's attempted coup.

Overall view: Elizabeth's reign can be split into 2 'reigns' with very distinctive features, with the 2nd one being interventionist and characterised by crises faced largely with new privy councillors.

b The argument is convincing in that it makes points which can be supported by contextual evidence, e.g.:

- The attempted invasions of England by Spain in 1588, 1596 and 1597.
- The disputes with Parliament over monopolies and the queen having to give way over legal challenges to monopolies.
- 88 Catholics were executed between 1590 and 1603.

It can be argued to be not convincing as it overlooks evidence which undermines or qualifies it e.g.:

- Elizabeth had been interventionist on occasion before 1585, sending troops to Scotland and France, and the actions of privateers does not seem like non-intervention. The scale of intervention may have increased but not the interventions.
- Essex's attempted coup had other causes than factionalism, such as his failure in Ireland and his loss of the sweet wines monopoly, which seem to have been the sparks.
- The deaths of 4 privy councillors would not necessarily mean a change in policy; the most important privy councillor, Burghley, only died in 1598.

Revision Skills

You should produce your own cards, charts or timeline for this activity. For an example of a good timeline see page 9.

Glossary

A

Act of Attainder: declared a landowner guilty of rebelling against a monarch

Amicable Grant: ordered by Wolsey in 1525 to raise more money for war

annates: revenue paid to the Pope by a bishop or other cleric on his appointment, collected in England and sent to Rome; also known as the 'First Fruits' (*primitiae* in Latin)

anticlericalism: opposition to the Church's role in political and other non-religious matters

B

bond: a legal document which bound an individual to another to perform an action or forfeit a specified sum of money if they failed to do so

C

Calvinism: ideas on Church doctrine and organisation put forward in Geneva by the French reformer John Calvin

Chamber: the private areas of the Court; also a key department for the efficient collection of royal revenues

chancery: the main court of equity in the kingdom

chantries: chapels where Masses for the souls of the dead took place

common rights: denotes the legal right of tenants to use common land, for example for keeping animals; the exact nature of these rights varied from place to place

E

Erasmianism: the body of ideas associated with Erasmus and his followers

extraordinary revenue: money raised by the king from additional sources as one-off payments when he faced an emergency or an unforeseeable expense of government; this could be made up of parliamentary grants, loans, clerical taxes, for example

F

feudal: the medieval system by which society was structured depending on relationships in which land was held in return for some form of service

G

Gothic: the style of architecture prevalent in Western Europe in the 12th to 16th centuries, characterised by pointed arches and large windows

grace: the pure state a soul needed to be in to enter heaven

H

heresy: the denial of the validity of the key doctrines of the Church

I

iconoclasm: the rejection or destruction of images associated with established values and practices

Intercursus Magnus: the major commercial treaty between England and the Duchy of Burgundy which restored normal trading links between the two

M

magnate: a member of the higher ranks of the nobility

martial law: legal authority and political control exercised by military authority

P

parliamentary sanction: an official confirmation or ratification of a law given by Parliament as the acclaimed body of the state

perpendicular style: the dominant form of church architecture in England from the later 14th to the early 16th century, so-called because of its emphasis on vertical lines

praemunire: a parliamentary statute enacted in 1393 to prevent papal interference in the rights of the Crown to make appointments to Church office

prerogative rights: describes those rights or powers which the monarch could exercise without requiring the consent of Parliament

purgatory: the state in which the souls of the dead were purged of their sins before they could enter the kingdom of heaven

R

recognisance: a formal acknowledgement of a debt or other obligation which could be enforced by means of financial penalty

Renaissance: a cultural and intellectual movement which, beginning in Italy, emphasised a revival of interest in classical learning and the arts

S

Submission of the Clergy: the formal surrender of the Church's independent law-making function

subsidy: historically, a grant issued by Parliament to the sovereign for state needs

Supplication against the Ordinaries: a form of petition directed against alleged abuses of ordinary jurisdiction

T

tonnage and poundage: the right to raise revenue for the whole reign from imports and exports

transubstantiation: the Christian belief that the substance of bread and wine was completely changed into the substance of Christ's body and blood by a validly ordained priest during the consecration at Mass

Top revision tips for A Level History

The Tudors: England 1485–1603

The History revision tips on this page are based on research reports on History revision and on the latest AQA examiners' reports.

General advice

- [ ] Make a realistic revision timetable for the months leading up to your exams and plan regular, short sessions for your History revision. Research shows that students who break down their revision into 30- to 60-minute sessions (and take short breaks in between subjects) are more likely to succeed in exams.

- [ ] Use the **progress checklists** (pages 3–4) to help you track your revision. It will enable you to stick to your revision plan.

- [ ] Eat healthily and make sure you have regular amounts of sleep in the lead-up to your exams. This is obvious, but research shows this can help students perform better in exams.

- [ ] Make sure your phone and laptop are put away at least an hour before you go to bed. You will experience better quality sleep if you have had time away from the screen before sleeping.

Revising your History knowledge and understanding

- [ ] Using a variety of revision techniques can help to embed knowledge successfully, so don't just stick to one style. Try different revision methods, such as: flashcards, making charts, diagrams and mind-maps, highlighting your notebooks, colour-coding, re-reading your textbook or summarising your notes, group study, revision podcasts, and working through the activities in this Revision Guide.

- [ ] Create a timeline with colour-coded sticky notes to make sure you remember important dates relating to the six Tudors Breadth Study key questions (use the **timeline** on page 9 as a starting point).

- [ ] Make sure you understand key concepts for this topic, such as royal authority, humanism and Renaissance. If you're unsure, attend your school revision sessions and ask your teacher to go through important concepts again.

- [ ] Identify your weaknesses. Which topics are easy and which are more challenging for you? Give yourself more time to revise the challenging topics.

- [ ] Answer past paper questions and check the answers (using the AQA mark schemes) to practise applying your knowledge correctly and accurately to exam questions.

Revising your History exam technique

- [ ] Review the **AQA mark scheme** (page 8) for each exam question, and make sure you understand how you will be marked.

- [ ] Make sure you revise your skills as well as your knowledge. In particular, ensure you know how to approach the extracts question. Practise identifying the overall interpretation in extracts.

- [ ] Find a memorable way to recall the **How to master your exam skills** steps (pages 6–7) – it will help you plan your answers effectively and quickly.

- [ ] Ask your teacher for the examiners' reports – you can find out from the reports what the examiners want to see in the papers, and their advice on what not to do.

- [ ] Time yourself and practise answering past paper questions.

- [ ] Take mock exams seriously. You can learn from them how to manage your time better under strict exam conditions.

Notes:

Notes:

Notes:

Topics available from Oxford AQA History for A Level

Tsarist and Communist Russia 1855–1964
978 019 835467 3

Challenge and Transformation: Britain c1851–1964
978 019 835466 6

The Tudors: England 1485–1603
978 019 835460 4

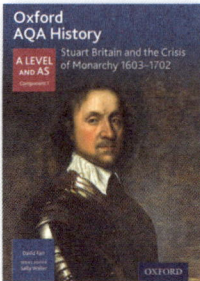
Stuart Britain and the Crisis of Monarchy 1603–1702
978 019 835462 8

The Making of a Superpower: USA 1865–1975
978 019 835469 7

The Quest for Political Stability: Germany 1871–1991
978 019 835468 0

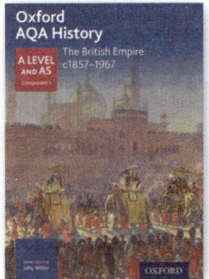
The British Empire c1857–1967
978 019 835463 5

Industrialisation and the People: Britain c1783–1885
978 019 835453 6

Wars and Welfare: Britain in Transition 1906–1957
978 019 835459 8

The Cold War c1945–1991
978 019 835461 1

Democracy and Nazism: Germany 1918–1945
978 019 835457 4

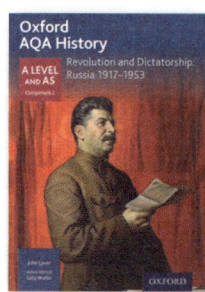
Revolution and Dictatorship: Russia 1917–1953
978 019 835458 1

Religious Conflict and the Church in England c1529–c1570
978 019 835471 0

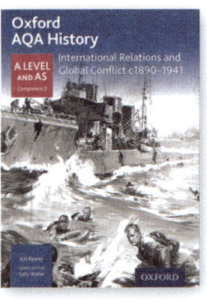
International Relations and Global Conflict c1890–1941
978 019 835454 3

The American Dream: Reality and Illusion 1945–1980
978 019 835455 0

The Making of Modern Britain 1951–2007
978 019 835464 2

The Crisis of Communism: the USSR and the Soviet Empire 1953–2000
978 019 835465 9

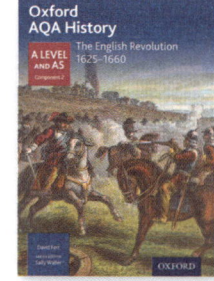
The English Revolution 1625–1660
978 019 835472 7

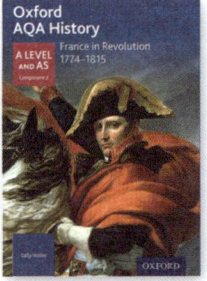
France in Revolution 1774–1815
978 019 835473 4

The Transformation of China 1936–1997
978 019 835456 7

RECAP · APPLY · REVIEW · SUCCEED

The Tudors: England 1485–1603 Revision Guide
978 019 842140 5

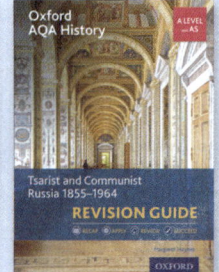
Democracy & Nazism: Germany 1918–1945 Revision Guide
978 019 842142 9

Tsarist & Communist Russia 1855–1964 Revision Guide
978 019 842144 3

The Making of Modern Britain 1951–2007 Revision Guide
978 019 842146 7

Oxford AQA History for A Level Revision Guides offer step-by-step strategies and the structured revision approach of Recap, Apply and Review to help students achieve exam success.

Also available in eBook format

Order online at www.oxfordsecondary.co.uk/aqahistory

OXFORD